THE SOCIAL & POLITICAL IDEAS OF SOME REPRESENTATIVE THINKERS OF THE VICTORIAN AGE

Uniform with this Volume

MEDIÆVAL CONTRIBUTIONS TO MODERN CIVILISATION

THE SOCIAL AND POLITICAL IDEAS OF SOME GREAT MEDIÆVAL THINKERS

THE SOCIAL AND POLITICAL IDEAS OF SOME GREAT THINKERS OF THE RENAISSANCE AND THE REFORMATION [*Out of print*

THE SOCIAL AND POLITICAL IDEAS OF SOME GREAT THINKERS OF THE SIXTEENTH AND SEVENTEENTH CENTURIES

THE SOCIAL AND POLITICAL IDEAS OF SOME ENGLISH THINKERS OF THE AUGUSTAN AGE

THE SOCIAL AND POLITICAL IDEAS OF SOME GREAT FRENCH THINKERS OF THE AGE OF REASON

THE SOCIAL AND POLITICAL IDEAS OF SOME REPRESENTATIVE THINKERS OF THE REVOLUTIONARY ERA

THE SOCIAL AND POLITICAL IDEAS OF SOME REPRESENTATIVE THINKERS OF THE AGE OF REACTION AND RECONSTRUCTION

THE SOCIAL & POLITICAL IDEAS OF SOME REPRESENTATIVE THINKERS OF THE VICTORIAN AGE

A SERIES OF LECTURES DELIVERED AT KING'S COLLEGE UNIVERSITY OF LONDON DURING THE SESSION 1931-32

EDITED BY

F. J. C. HEARNSHAW M.A. LL.D.

FELLOW OF KING'S COLLEGE AND PROFESSOR OF MEDIÆVAL HISTORY IN THE UNIVERSITY OF LONDON

BARNES & NOBLE, INC., NEW YORK

PUBLISHERS • BOOKSELLERS • SINCE 1873

First published 1933
by George G. Harrap & Co. Ltd.
Facsimile reprint 1967
Barnes & Noble, inc.
New York, N.Y., 10003

PRINTED IN GREAT BRITAIN
BY PHOTOLITHOGRAPHY
UNWIN BROTHERS LIMITED
WOKING AND LONDON

PREFACE

THE present course of lectures completes the King's College series of studies of social and political idealists. Eight volumes are now in the hands of the public, covering the whole process of European thought from St Augustine to Matthew Arnold. I sincerely hope that the careful examination by experts of the ideas of some six dozen of the leading thinkers of the Christian era may prove to be permanently valuable to students who are concerned to penetrate beneath the surface of historical events and to discover the hidden movements of the mind, of which many outstanding events are the mere external manifestations.

It only remains to me now to thank most heartily, first, the lecturers who have gracefully and gratuitously placed their skill and knowledge at the service of King's College and of the large public audiences that have, year after year, assembled in the College to hear them; and, secondly, the publishers who—without, I fear, so much encouragement as I could have wished—have continued to issue these volumes in their present attractive form; and, finally, to Mr C. C. Wood, Messrs Harrap's editor, and his staff, whose careful reading of the proofs of these volumes has resulted in the elimination of many minor mistakes which otherwise would have marred their symmetry.

F. J. C. HEARNSHAW

KING'S COLLEGE
UNIVERSITY OF LONDON
April 1933

CONTENTS

THE SOCIAL AND POLITICAL IDEAS OF SOME REPRESENTATIVE THINKERS OF THE VICTORIAN AGE

I

INTRODUCTORY

THE VICTORIAN AGE, 1837–1901

A SURVEY of the Victorian age must begin with the Queen whose name it bears. Lytton Strachey, in the best of his books, has painted the portrait of a woman of unwearying industry, of unfailing patriotism, of violent prejudices, personal and political. The biographies of her advisers and her own correspondence show her working at top speed for sixty years, while statesmen and parties came and went, while generations of men and women grew up who had known no other sovereign. Victoria possessed her fair share of the minor human infirmities, but she emerges unscathed from the ordeal of publicity as the embodiment of the maxim of Frederick the Great that the ruler should be the first servant of the State.

The official biography of the Prince Consort, nowadays too little read, records her debt to the only human being whom she ever loved with entire devotion. But the widow of forty-two had learned her lesson in the school of experience, and there is no lack of sturdy self-confidence in the discussions and decisions of the later portion of her reign. Politics were her passion as well as her trade. Her intellectual range was limited, and her mind was inhospitable to new ideas; but within her chosen field she was a formidable controversialist, and she could hold her own against all comers. "She knows what she is talking about," Salisbury used to remark; and he added that no Minister disregarded her advice without feeling that he had incurred a dangerous responsibility.

Though the personal prestige of the Queen increased by leaps and bounds with advancing years, with the extension of her realm, and with the assumption of the title "Empress of India," her reign witnessed a gradual decline in the political power of the sovereign. The reaction which followed the downfall of Napoleon was nearly over at her accession, and the forces released or set in motion by the French Revolution regained their sway. The revolutions of 1830 and 1848 were milestones on the road to European democracy. The growth of wealth and education made the claims of the middle classes irresistible, and industrialisation enabled the Fourth Estate to organise its strength. Victoria believed that it was her right and her duty to govern the country with the assistance of her Ministers; but she was the last British monarch to hold the theory of *condominium*, and to attempt to apply it in a rapidly changing world.

The two main political features of the Victorian era were the growth of democracy and the expansion of the Empire. The French Revolution had interrupted the Reform movement for a generation and scared the possessing classes into a stagnant Toryism; but after the return of peace in 1815 the fear of Jacobinism began to evaporate, and the Whigs raised their heads once more. No one could say of Grey what Gibbon said of Fox, that "his inmost soul was deeply tinged with democracy"; but the Whig nobleman stood, at any rate, for Parliamentary reform, which was the indispensable preliminary to further advance. The passing of the Reform Bill in 1832 was a landmark not only in British but in world history. Great Britain became, and has remained, the home of ordered liberty, and our success in self-government encouraged reformers in every country to battle with the powers of darkness. Synchronising with the expulsion of the Bourbons from France, it announced that the era of the counter-revolution in Western Europe had reached its end. Foreign Liberals like Dahlmann and Cavour turned longing eyes towards the island kingdom where freedom and peace, prosperity and power, appeared to reign. That England passed virtually unscathed through 1848, the year of revolutions, seemed to confirm the prescience of her statesmen.

We are sometimes told that we must emancipate ourselves

from the seductive spell of the great Whig historians. In redressing the balance let us not minimise the priceless services of the Whigs and Liberals of the nineteenth century, to whom we owe the peaceful transformation of the aristocratic system of the eighteenth century into the full-blooded self-determination of to-day. From the first Reform Bill to the World War the domestic political history of Great Britain was above all the realisation of Liberal principles; for in the two cases where a great measure of reform was carried by Conservative Premiers—the abolition of the Corn Laws and the passing of the Reform Bill of 1867—it was only the final stage of a movement which had been initiated by their political opponents and to which they were reluctant converts. That the monopoly of power by the great landowners gave way to the rule of the *bourgeoisie*, that the dominion of the *bourgeoisie* was gradually limited by the enfranchisement of the manual worker, and that these two momentous changes took place without bloodshed was mainly due to the courage and foresight of Grey, Russell, and Durham, Cobden, Gladstone, and Bright, who realised that, to quote Lord John Russell, "there is nothing so conservative as progress." The House of Commons has shown that it deserved to enjoy the authority that it has won; the House of Lords is to-day little more than a debating society; and the monarch, the grandson of Victoria, is wisely content to be the symbol of the unity of the Empire and the continuity of our race. In the Victorian era the British people, accepting democracy with its implications and its risks, learned to govern itself, and timid reactionaries discovered, to their amazement, that reform was the preventive, not the cause, of revolution.

The second outstanding political event of the Victorian era was the expansion and consolidation of the British Empire. The bitter experience of the loss of the American colonies had taught its lesson, and the principle of government by consent, on which our domestic liberties are based, was applied in an ever-increasing degree throughout the illimitable territories of the Crown. The Liberal tradition postulates a certain confidence in the ultimate sanity of human nature, at which cynics and pessimists may mock, but which has justified itself on the whole, at any rate among Anglo-Saxon communities. The Durham Report forms a landmark in the history of Colonial administration, and the affectionate loyalty of the Dominions to the Mother Country in times of danger is a tribute to the far-sighted wisdom of its philosophy. In Canada the tide of colonisation flowed up to and beyond the Rockies; the provinces were unified by the federation of 1867 and the construction of transcontinental lines; while the French in Quebec were won and held by the provision of cultural autonomy. The development of the Australian continent was equally peaceful, and the Queen lived just long enough to witness the federation of its component parts. Far less tranquil, on the other hand, were the fortunes of South Africa, where the normal difficulties of colonisation were complicated by the presence of a large and formidable native population. Most of the Boer settlers had retired northward from Cape Colony with the establishment of British rule, but the discovery of gold and diamonds attracted a swarm of fresh immigrants, whose claims led to the last and greatest Colonial struggle of the nineteenth century. The two smaller colonies of Newfoundland and New Zealand, like their larger sisters, also received the blessings of constitutional self-government.

A lively interest in our white Empire arose in the last two decades of the Queen's reign, and the Colonial Conference of 1887 inaugurated the practice of co-operation, which was to reach its goal forty years later in the declaration of equality of status. The Victorian era opened with backward and more or less empty territories governed from Downing Street. It closed with vigorous, prosperous, and virtually independent communities. We had lived down the humiliations and the discouragement of the American War of Independence. Bonds of sentiment had been substituted for military occupation, commercial dictation, and political control. "*Imperium et libertas!*" exclaimed Beaconsfield at the Guildhall, and Kipling embodied the new relationship in his famous lines:

> Daughter am I in my mother's house,
> But mistress in my own.

With our usual inspired empiricism we allowed the situation to develop in its own way, without attempting to formulate the constitutional relations between the Mother Country and her children overseas.

The portion of the Empire inhabited by coloured races, like our white settlements, grew in size and advanced cautiously along the path towards self-determination during the Victorian era. It was not till after the Mutiny and the transfer of all authority to the Crown that the problem of Indian self-government began to be faced, and a clear note was struck in the Queen's Proclamation of 1858, which announced that no disabilities on the ground of race or religion would be recognised. From that time onward almost every decade witnessed an advance towards associating the Indian peoples with the control of their destinies. The introduction of British culture and British political ideas, the spread of education in the towns, the unification of the *intelligentsia* by the use of a common tongue, and the establishment of the Congress in 1885 prepared the soil and created the demand for provincial autonomy, and ultimately for Dominion status. Many of the strongest brains of the time, from Dalhousie to Curzon, were employed in the administration of our greatest dependency, and, though India remained a poor country, we gave her what she had never hitherto possessed—internal peace, impartial justice, and capital for the development of her resources. In India, as throughout the vast African territories added to the Empire during the closing decades of the reign, the principle of commercial exploitation gradually yielded to the uplifting conception of trusteeship. Some rough-handed pioneering work in the backward places of the Dark Continent was carried out by chartered companies ; but they were a passing phase. The home Government, coached by the Anti-Slavery and Aborigines Protection Societies, and responsive to the growing humanitarianism of the age, gradually raised the moral standard of the adventurous spirits who took up the white man's burden.

While the Victorians devoted their political energies in the main to the establishment of democracy and the extension of the Empire, they never lost sight of the European situation, and from time to time took a hand in the ever-changing diplomatic game. The long struggle with France had sickened the British people of Continental wars, and the responsibilities of an ever-growing realm diminished their inclination to interfere in the rivalries of Europe. There were, however, two governing principles or tendencies at work throughout the reign, one centuries old, the other comparatively new. The first of them, the principle of the Balance of Power, which had moulded our policy since the Tudors, carried us into the Crimean War, and brought us within sight of a second conflict with Russia in 1878.

England, like other states, has blots on her 'scutcheon; but we shall never understand the course of our foreign policy during the nineteenth century if we seek the key in the Balance of Power alone. Lord Newton once observed that Great Britain was the only sentimental country in the world, and, with the possible exception of the United States, the statement is historically true. Fox was the founder not only of the Liberal Party, but of the Liberal tradition in foreign affairs, which approaches problems not solely from the angle of British interests, but also from that of a large-hearted humanitarianism. From the time that he hailed the fall of the Bastille with rapturous applause a vein of idealism has run through our policy. Enjoying as we did the twin blessings of national independence and political self-government, leading statesmen of both parties again and again employed the moral influence of a Great Power to foster the cause of liberty and humanity abroad. Canning's veto on the reconquest of the Spanish colonies and his share in the liberation of Greece from the Turkish yoke; Palmerston's creation of an independent Belgium and his encouragement to Turkey to resist the demand for the surrender of the Hungarian refugees; Russell's resounding approval of the efforts of Garibaldi and Cavour to unify Italy; the cession of the Ionian Islands to Greece; Gladstone's oratorical campaigns for the Bulgarians and the Armenians; Salisbury's approval of the union of Eastern Roumelia with Bulgaria—such incidents are not to be explained on the principle that our pilots steered exclusively by a cold-blooded calculation of national advantage.

The unity of Christendom and the moral obligations of civilised communities were proclaimed with eloquent conviction by Gladstone in the Don Pacifico debate, and in an age of rampant nationalism we paid more homage to a noble ideal than any of the Great Powers of the world. The reference of the *Alabama* dispute to a tribunal of jurists sitting at Geneva was one of the loftiest achievements of Gladstone's life. While short-sighted critics grumbled at the heavy damages, as they then seemed, of three million pounds which we were called upon to pay, men of keener vision realised that the healing of a running sore was cheap at the price. The precedent was copied in the Venezuela controversy and the Bering Sea Fisheries dispute, and the first Hague Conference was saved from ignominious failure by the creation of the Hague Tribunal, of which Lord Pauncefote, the chief British delegate, was the principal architect. In another direction we set an excellent example to the world. The Victorian Empire differed from its predecessors and rivals not only in its liberal institutions, but by its practice of Free Trade. Beginning, like other Empires, by tying our colonies to the commercial apron-strings of the Mother Country, we gradually learned the wisdom of allowing them to make their own fiscal arrangements not only with the rest of the world, but with the Mother Country herself. A good deal of jealousy and resentment was inevitably aroused by the spectacle of the British flag waving over so large a portion of the globe, but it was limited by the knowledge that other countries could buy and sell in our markets on equal terms.

Turning from politics to economics, we watch the Victorians reaping both the wheat and the tares sown in the eighteenth century. The lead that was gained by Watt and the inventors of textile machinery was maintained for over a century, until the United States and Germany, with their larger population, caught us up in the race. As we were first in the field with machine industry, so we were first in the race with railways. George Stephenson inaugurated a second revolution, which brought with it a period of feverish enterprise. The first steamship crossed the Atlantic in 1838, and our geographical position enabled us to take full advantage of the new markets beyond the seas. In the opening decades of the reign our wealth, obtained by exploiting our coal and iron, by working up imports of raw cotton and wool, by exporting the finished article in a mercantile marine which secured the larger part of the carrying trade of the world, and by the investment of our surplus capital in profitable enterprises abroad, accumulated with a rapidity hitherto unknown. The repeal of the Corn Laws and the Navigation Act, the abolition of fettering duties on trade, and the skilful finance of Peel and Gladstone accelerated the production of wealth. London became the nerve centre of the financial world. Macaulay sang full-throated pæans to our material progress, and the Great Exhibition of 1851 appeared to set the seal on our triumphs. All eyes turned to the freest and richest country in the world, the home of unfettered trade, untaxed food, and vigorous private initiative.

Behind this glittering fabric of power and wealth there lay in the earlier part of the reign an abyss of suffering and despair. The creation of riches proved an easier task than their equitable distribution. The countryside still shudders at the memory of the hungry forties; but the plight of many of the workers in the industrial towns which sprang up like mushrooms was no better. Professor Clapham assures us that their condition was not quite so bad as it has been painted by the Hammonds and other investigators, but there is plenty of evidence that masses of the population, of both sexes and of all ages, were hideously overworked and underfed. The birth-rate rose by leaps and bounds during the first half of the century, and the death-rate was increased by the herding of the industrial armies in the slums. Foresight is among the rarest of human qualities, and the country, absorbed in the production of wealth, allowed a condition of affairs to arise which disgraced the richest nation in Europe. Byron had declared in the House of Lords that even in Turkey he had never witnessed such scenes of squalid degradation as in the land of his birth. Engels' grim survey of the working classes in 1844 suggested that the situation was as bad as ever, and Karl Marx based his *Capital* mainly on the experience of England. The Chartists clamoured for the extension of political democracy as an instrument of amelioration; but the Charter is significant as an expression of smouldering discontent rather than as an indication of the way out.

The corroding evils of unchecked industrialism were recognised by a few enlightened employers, working men, statesmen, and writers. The father of British socialism was not Karl Marx, but Robert Owen, who, beginning with an experiment in 'patriarchal' management, advanced towards a system of co-operative control. The Rochdale pioneers inaugurated a scheme of distribution which eliminated private profit, and which has grown into one of the most beneficent enterprises of the industrial age. Shaftesbury, the greatest of social reformers, devoted his public life to legislative reform and his private life to philanthropy. In the forties and fifties the literature of protest—Carlyle and Disraeli, Kingsley and Mrs Gaskell, Dickens and Charles Reade—tore aside the veil of complacency and revealed the 'two nations' dwelling side by side and knowing little of each other's life. Ruskin proclaimed with burning eloquence that welfare, not wealth, was the test of civilisation, and Mill began to move away from the hard-shelled individualism of his youth. A new conception of citizenship, postulating a minimum standard of life, gradually took shape. The partition between politics and economics crumbled away, and the idea of equality began to invade the economic sphere. The extension of the franchise to the manual workers in 1867 and 1884 synchronised with the growing conviction of the insufficiency of political rights. Democracy, it was argued with increasing response, involved the rule of the people, and the people could not be said to rule so long as the sources of wealth were in the hands of a privileged minority. With the disappearance of the anti-combination laws the vote was supplemented by the practice of collective bargaining, which made the Trade Unions first an industrial and later a political power in the land.

The dream of a minimum standard of life postulated a series of changes extending far beyond the franchise and factory reform. The origins of elementary education go back to the opening of the century, and in the twenties Birkbeck inaugurated the movement for adult education, which was fostered by Maurice's foundation of the Working Men's College, and later still by the University Settlements. It was not, however, till the second half of the Victorian era that the upper and middle classes woke up to the fact that education is not only the birthright of civilised communities, but an essential condition of self-government. Excellent service had been rendered for two generations by the denominational schools, but the creation of Board schools in 1870 ranks in importance in the life of our people with the Reform Bill of 1832. "We must educate our masters," cried Robert Lowe in the reform debates of 1867; and the scholarship system set up the ladder from the gutter to the university for which Huxley had pleaded. The abolition of religious tests in 1871 made Oxford and Cambridge national institutions once again; the creation of new colleges and universities met the growing need for academic teaching and research; and the University Extension movement carried the fertilising flood all over the country. There was less advance in the realm of secondary education, despite the warnings and exhortations of Matthew Arnold, but a higher standard of conduct and discipline in the public schools was set by Arnold of Rugby and Thring of Uppingham.

Only second in importance to popular education among the new civilising influences was the campaign for public health inaugurated by Chadwick, which diminished infant mortality, and created a stronger, cleaner, and more self-respecting race. Simpson's discovery of chloroform and Lister's use of antiseptics in operations deprived sickness of some of its terrors; in the closing decades of the reign the higher standard of nursing, initiated by Florence Nightingale in the Crimea, was introduced in our hospitals and infirmaries; and Francis Galton's researches in inheritance emphasised the importance of eugenics.

Though the condition of the manual worker was immensely better at the end than at the beginning of the reign, the Victorian era was above all the Golden Age of the middle class. The old governing families had been knocked off their perch in 1832, and the manual workers, even after their political enfranchisement, were at first too unorganised and uneducated to challenge the rule of the *bourgeoisie*. It has often been argued that the generation between the first and second Reform Bills, the generation of Bagehot's treatise on the Constitution, was the Golden Age of British Parliamentary government, avoiding the extremes of aristocratic monopoly on the one hand and mass rule on the other. The middle class, at any rate, displayed no lack of ability. Except for Russell and Palmerston in the earlier portion of the reign and Salisbury and Rosebery at its close, the leading performers on the political stage —Peel, Disraeli, Gladstone, Cobden, Bright, Chamberlain—

were middle-class men. The Press was at last free and cheap, and took its duties seriously. The speeches of the protagonists were fully reported and eagerly read. For forty years Delane spoke with oracular authority in *The Times*. *The Morning Post*, *The Standard*, *The Daily Telegraph*, and *The Daily News* assumed their readers to be intelligent citizens. *The Spectator*, under Hutton and Townsend the best of the weeklies, catered for thoughtful Liberalism; the *Edinburgh* and the *Quarterly* maintained their authority; and the new monthlies, the *Fortnightly*, the *Contemporary*, and the *Nineteenth Century*, facilitated responsible discussion of public affairs. The Victorian *bourgeoisie*, like any other section of society, was class-conscious, and parts of it no doubt deserved Matthew Arnold's denunciations of Philistinism, but its rule was more enlightened and more successful than any that England had ever known.

In the realm of political ideas the Victorian era has an honourable record of achievement. Burke's philosophic conservatism had struck a much-needed blow at the doctrinaire ideology of the French Revolution; but his gospel of continuity was twisted into a defence of abuses and vested interests. It was the glory of Bentham's ingenious mind to challenge the dead hand of the past, to assert the claim of living men to happiness and well-being. When the elder Utilitarians and their political disciples, such as Brougham, had helped to disperse the reactionary mist which had gathered in the wake of the French Revolution it was the task of the younger Mill to expound the philosophy of the Liberal age inaugurated by the Reform Bill. In his books on *Liberty*, *The Subjection of Women*, and *Representative Government* he presented a system more complete and more humane than any other country could boast—a high-souled individualism which aimed at spiritual self-realisation, and an educated democracy which safeguarded the conscience of its members. He was attacked by Fitzjames Stephen, the champion of a strong executive, and, indeed, he was never quite fair to the State; but his plea for recognition of the worth of the individual citizen is an imperishable portion of our heritage. His distaste for the Great Leviathan and his preference for voluntary association was shared by Herbert Spencer, who retained his doctrinaire individualism to the end. Green's *Lectures on the Principles of Political Obligation* and

Bosanquet's *Philosophical Theory of the State*, on the other hand, argued for a system which was equally far removed from Austin's conception of the State as an armed policeman and from Spencer's notion of a meddlesome nuisance. Deeply influenced by Hegel's *Philosophy of Right*, they conceived an authority which represented spiritual no less than material forces, the embodiment and agent of the moral will of the community rather than an instrument of material coercion. With the coming of democracy, indeed, the old antithesis of the State and the individual lost much of its acuteness, since the Government could be controlled and transformed in accordance with the will of the community.

If Mill offered the most important contribution to political thinking in the first half of the reign, the most striking feature of the second half was the rise of socialism. Marx on Capital was read by a few eager students, but the Marxian gospel never developed into a church. British socialism, like the Continental variety, was the work of middle-class brains, but, with the exception of Hyndman and his friends of the Social Democratic Federation, it developed on independent lines. William Morris attacked the existing industrial order on the ground that it turned men into machines and produced neither beauty nor happiness. The Fabian Society, on the other hand, which expounded its programme in the *Fabian Essays* and the *Fabian Tracts*, urged the concrete advantages of collective ownership by the State or the local authorities as the only means of eliminating wasteful competition and of raising the general standard of the weaker members of the community. The dominion of *laissez-faire* had already been modified by factory legislation and by reforming municipalities, such as Birmingham under Joseph Chamberlain, before the Fabian army marched on to the battlefield ; but it is due to the writings of Sidney Webb and his colleagues more than to any other factor that a new theory and technique of administration began to win their way at the end of the reign. The establishment of elective County Councils in 1888 provided the machinery for constructive experiment, and in the first twenty years of its existence the Progressives who dominated the London County Council began a beneficent revolution in the life of our overcrowded metropolis.

THE VICTORIAN AGE, 1837–1901

Since the rise and fall of Puritanism in the seventeenth century England has witnessed three great religious movements, associated with the names of Wesley, Wilberforce, and Newman. The first was wholly spiritual in its appeal, the second largely humanitarian, and the third mainly dogmatic. The Oxford Movement, which began with Keble's Assize Sermon in 1833, was a reaction against latitudinarianism, evangelicalism, and Liberalism. It was also the counterpart of the Catholic revival in Europe which set in with Napoleon's Concordat and culminated in the Vatican decrees. Neither Keble, Pusey, nor Newman realised, when they raised the flag of revolt, that their campaign would lead men back to Rome; but their emphasis on tradition and continuity, their love of the Fathers and the Middle Ages, their hatred of Erastianism, their exaltation of the authority of the priest, and their detestation of the critical spirit were bound to carry them and their followers far away from their Protestant moorings. Though the Oxford Movement ended in confusion and disunion, its influence was no less lasting than profound. The effect of Newman's writings on the Church which he left in 1845 gave it a new orientation. The long parenthesis between 1688 and 1833, during which the English Church was distinctly Protestant, was closed, and Anglo-Catholicism, with its emphasis on dogma, its devotion to the Sacrament, and its ornate ritual, again became the dominant school of religious thought.

While Newman and his friends were busy at Oxford a Catholic revival was in full swing in London. The return of Wiseman to England in 1835, after a long residence in Rome, is an event of scarcely less importance than Keble's discourse. The English Catholics emerged from the shadows in which they had lived since the Reformation and held up their heads. The outcry against the establishment of a hierarchy in 1851 soon died down, and under the guidance of their four great Cardinals, Wiseman, Newman, Manning, and Vaughan, they won a recognised place among the most vital factors in the religious life of Victorian England. The Byzantine Cathedral at Westminster is the impressive symbol of the Catholic renaissance.

If Newman had known German, observed Dean Stanley, there would have been no Oxford Movement. The gibe must not be taken too literally, for Pusey had studied Hebrew at Leipzig without damage to his faith. But it conveys in picturesque form the reminder that the Oxford Movement occurred before the application of critical methods to the Old and New Testaments, before the study of Comparative Religion placed Christianity in a new perspective, and before the advance in natural science undermined belief in supernatural interpretations. It was the merit of the Broad Church leaders, among them Maurice, Stanley, and Jowett, to welcome the new light streaming in through many windows, and to dissociate the Christian religion from the defence of its crumbling outworks. The Broad Churchmen were neglected by successive Prime Ministers, and were numerically insignificant ; but their activities, though less spectacular than those of the High Churchmen, were of no less importance. While the latter looked back with wistful eyes to an undivided Christendom, the Modernist looked hopefully forward to a synthesis of religion and science. The Evangelical school, on the other hand, slowly withered away under the combined assault of High Church and Broad Church.

In the Free Churches the two outstanding figures were the Baptist Spurgeon, the last doughty champion of the verbal inspiration of the Bible, and the Unitarian Martineau, the persuasive teacher of a scholarly theism. Though the sects spent an immense amount of energy in combating each other's heresies, we can now see that they were all fighting a losing battle against the current which set in with the Renaissance, and which Lecky has compendiously described as the secularisation of thought. As the reign advanced authority and tradition in religion counted for less ; old beliefs, such as the creation of the world in six days, the miracles of the Old Testament, and eternal damnation, were tacitly dropped ; and regular church-going ceased to be a criterion of *bourgeois* respectability.

If politics, economics, and religion divided the Victorians into warring groups, every citizen could share in the triumphs of literature and art. The Romantic movement was over at the Queen's accession, and the best Victorian poetry embodied the widening outlook of a reflective age. If the *Idylls of the King* have lost something of their appeal, *In Memoriam* lives on in its stately beauty. Browning, though less a master of form, preached a bracing gospel of aspiration and achievement; and Matthew Arnold, less of a poet than either, proclaimed the pieties without the dogmas of the Christian faith. A very different note was struck in the *Poems and Ballads* of Swinburne, a born singer, who preferred a sensuous paganism to the philosophic moralities of his rivals. At the end of the century Kipling also broke away from Victorian precedents, making up in some measure for his inferior artistry by his amazing vitality and the novelty of his themes.

It is a matter for argument whether the Victorians, who failed in drama, found their most perfect expression in poetry or the novel; but we shall all agree that no previous era witnessed the appearance of so many imaginative works of the first rank. If any writer can challenge the claim of Scott to be the greatest of British novelists it is Dickens. Thackeray is close behind him; for, though he created fewer masterpieces, *Vanity Fair* and *Esmond* are as imperishable as *David Copperfield*. The fascination of Charlotte Brontë has increased with the passing years, and there are critics who place *Wuthering Heights* by her sister Emily above *Jane Eyre* and *Villette*. George Eliot's star has paled in recent years, and that of Trollope has risen; but they are alike in their matchless rendering of the life of rural England in the middle of the nineteenth century. Meredith had to wait for recognition, and his stylistic contortions have limited his appeal; but *Richard Feverel* and *The Egoist* can never be wholly ignored, and *Vittoria* ranks high among historical novels. Hardy's Wessex tales, culminating in the incomparable *Tess*, round off the century with a return to the great English tradition of high seriousness which a French critic has labelled ethical realism. In *Sybil*, *Coningsby*, and *Lothair* Disraeli gave us the best political novels ever written. The salt breezes of *Westward Ho!* have lost something of their savour, and, indeed, few Victorian reputations have faded so rapidly as that of Kingsley. On the other hand, the wit and wisdom of Lewis Carroll are never out of date, Stevenson continues to delight young and old, and Pater retains his hold over fastidious readers.

In contrast to its superb achievements in literature, the artistic legacy of the Victorian era is relatively meagre. The

Pre-Raphaelites attempted to recapture the devotional spirit of a bygone age, but Millais did his best work after he left their ranks. A few of Watts' symbolic pictures found their mark, but his most enduring monument is in his gallery of portraits. Leighton sought inspiration in classical models, and Burne-Jones sailed away into a delicate world of his own. In the later decades of the reign our native artists were reinforced by Whistler and Sargent from America, the former the most subtle of Impressionists, the latter the greatest portraitist of his time. Ruskin sang the praises of Turner in his *Modern Painters*, and he shares with William Morris the honour of teaching Victorians to appreciate beauty in many forms. The chief architectural achievement of the reign was Barry's imposing Houses of Parliament; and Gilbert Scott gave us not only the Gothic St Pancras, but the Renaissance Foreign Office. Of the more ambitious public buildings of the time Street's Law Courts in the Strand are perhaps the least successful. In sculpture we can point to Alfred Stevens' Wellington Monument in St Paul's. In the musical world we are justly proud of Gilbert and Sullivan; and we gave a warm welcome to Mendelssohn at the opening of the reign and to Wagner at the close.

The Victorian contribution to natural science was no less memorable than its achievement in literature. Lyell's *Principles of Geology*, published on the eve of the Queen's accession, prepared the way for uniformitarianism in other fields; but it was the publication of the *Origin of Species* in 1859 which inaugurated a new era not only in biology, but in the outlook of the human race on the nature of life and the universe. It was followed in 1871 by the *Descent of Man*, and the closing decades of the century were spent in digesting these large mouthfuls—a painful process facilitated by the vigorous advocacy of Huxley. The traditional belief in the special creation of species and of man crumbled away, and vistas of growth and decay through infinite spaces of time opened up new perspectives in history and religion.

None of the other sciences could boast such an epoch-making achievement as the demonstration of the evolution of species; but substantial progress was made in many fields. Faraday's induction of electricity from magnetism dates from

1831; but the application of his discovery to the manifold uses of industry, transport, and domestic life filled the Victorian era. Clerk Maxwell's memorable work in the electromagnetic field prepared the way for wireless telegraphy, which was perfected by Marconi, the child of an Italian father and an Irish mother. The Cambridge school of physics maintained its supremacy with the researches of Lord Rayleigh on sound, of George Darwin on the tides, and J. J. Thomson on the atom. Lord Kelvin, perhaps the greatest of them all, combined a mastery of abstruse mathematical physics with an inventive genius which perfected the compass. In astronomy the outstanding feature was the spectroscopical work of Sir William Huggins. Adams took part in the discovery of Neptune, and our knowledge of the heavens was notably increased by the construction of Lord Rosse's giant telescope. At the end of the reign Ramsay discovered helium and Rayleigh argon. In botany Sir Joseph Hooker reformed the classification of plants and made Kew Gardens a goal of pilgrimage no less than a haunt of beauty.

The rapid progress of scientific discovery, above all the proof of the evolution of life-forms, profoundly influenced the philosophy of the Victorian age. For a time it seemed as if the riddles of the universe had at last been solved, and that man was the product and the slave of mechanical forces. Matter appeared to be the one solid reality, and Tyndall, in his celebrated Presidential Address to the British Association in 1874, found in it "the promise and potency of all terrestrial life." Huxley, it is true, coined the word 'agnosticism,' and Spencer left room for the unknowable; but it was widely assumed that science had given idealism, no less than orthodox theology, a knock-out blow. Spencer's vast system of synthetic philosophy traced the working of evolution throughout the whole field of nature and human experience, while the Associationist psychology of Mill and Bain and the empirical ethics of Sidgwick reigned almost uncontested in the schools. Buckle's *History of Civilisation* was a pæan to the triumph of physical science. The latter half of the reign, however, witnessed a remarkable transformation when the teaching of Kant and Hegel at last reached our shores. Idealism once again raised its head in the writings of T. H. Green, John and Edward Caird, Bradley, Bosanquet, Wallace, James Ward, Andrew Seth, and McTaggart—a flowering of philosophy such as England had never known. By the end of the century what may be loosely described as positivism was dead, and idealism in one or other of its varieties monopolised the university chairs. How the new fashion, after a brief reign, was itself attacked by Bergson, the anti-Intellectualist, William James, the Pragmatist, and Bertrand Russell, the neo-Realist, is a story that would carry us beyond the Victorian era.

While philosophical systems chased each other across the stage our knowledge of the fortunes of the human race was rapidly extended by patient research, in which England played an honourable part. The foundations of anthropology were laid by Tylor, and Sir James Frazer began his lifelong study of primitive societies. Maine threw a flood of light on early institutions. The civilisations of the ancient East were dug up and interpreted by archæologists like Layard and philologists like Rawlinson, while Max Müller brought the religions of Asia into our field of vision. Grote restored the Athenian democracy to life; Bryce rediscovered the Holy Roman Empire; Freeman popularised the Norman Conquest; Carlyle, Macaulay, and Froude lit up the most dramatic passages of English history; and John Richard Green related for the first time the story of the English people. The more critical methods of German scholarship came in with Stubbs and Gardiner; the genius of Maitland unlocked the secrets of medieval law; and the new province of economic history was mapped out by Thorold Rogers and Cunningham. At the Queen's accession comparatively little was known and still less was understood of the age-long life of mankind. At her death the surveyor's task had been in large measure accomplished, and it is for the twentieth century to fill in the outlines. The bulk of the labour had fallen on German scholars; but next to Germany no country made a more notable contribution to the record and interpretation of the life of humanity than our own.

In the wide field of social life changes usually begin almost imperceptibly. Though the emancipation of women is in the main a twentieth-century phenomenon, the movement towards equal rights and equal opportunities took its rise in the Victorian era. Mill's eloquent attack on male domination was followed by the establishment of women's colleges at Oxford and Cambridge, and in 1882 the Married Women's Property Act gave them control of their own money. A few courageous ladies forced their way into the ranks of the medical profession, and Mrs Fawcett voiced the growing demand for the vote. The limitations of our mothers and grandmothers are often exaggerated by their freer descendants, but it is true enough that it was their sex rather than their citizenship that counted. The Queen was as stubbornly conservative in her social as in her political views, and was convinced that woman's place was in the home. Happy marriages were doubtless as common in the nineteenth as in the twentieth century; but there was far less opportunity for young people to know one another, for the parents kept a sharp look-out on potential suitors, and the chaperon stood like a dragon in the path. It is impossible to compare the actual standard of Victorian morality with that of to-day, since it defies statistical record; but a woman's slip was visited with social ostracism, and the career of Dilke and Parnell was ruined by their breach of the seventh commandment. In a neighbouring province of social habit an immense advance in decency and refinement was achieved by the virtual disappearance of drunkenness among the educated classes.

The closing years of the long Victorian epoch found the nation in a mood of exuberant buoyancy unknown since the spacious days of Elizabeth. The defeat of the first Home Rule Bill in 1886 and the secession of the Whigs installed the Unionists in power for twenty years. The massive figure and noble brow of Salisbury seemed to symbolise strength and stability. The Jubilee of 1887—and still more the Diamond Jubilee in 1897—focused the eyes of mankind on a vast, powerful, and prosperous realm; and the pageantry of Empire filled us with the almost intoxicating self-confidence which throbs in the later speeches of Chamberlain and in Kipling's spirited verse. Rhodes was the hero of the hour, and the success of Lord Cromer in Egypt showed that we still retained the secret of empire. The high-water mark of Imperialist complacency—which some might be tempted to describe by a harsher name—was reached in 1898, when the Sudan was won back at the battle of Omdurman and the French flag was hauled down at Fashoda under the threat of war. There was a serene conviction that no task was beyond our power, that our share of the earth's surface could never be too large, and that there was something almost impious in resistance to British arms or aims. My fellow-Victorians will agree that I am not exaggerating the sentiment of national pride or the optimism which filled young and old some forty years ago. Never in all the course of his life had John Bull felt so sure of himself.

There were, nevertheless, shadows creeping up to the picture, though we can now measure their length more accurately than in the glare of that blinding noon. Home Rule had, indeed, been defeated for the time, but the Irish problem remained. The Kruger telegram and the applause it evoked surprised us by its revelation of German jealousy and dislike. The advance of Russia in the Far East and of France in Central Africa involved possibilities if not probabilities of a collision. The Jameson Raid, the failure to probe the conspiracy to the bottom, the whitewashing of Rhodes, and what Lecky described as the trail of finance over our South African policy, diminished our moral prestige; and the plucky fight of the diminutive Boer Republics against the greatest empire in the world aroused almost universal sympathy. The sufficiency of our policy of splendid isolation began to be doubted by Chamberlain and some of his ministerial colleagues; but his approaches to Germany and the United States met with no response. When the Queen lay on her deathbed we stood alone in a Continent filled with scowling faces and conscript armies. The Hague Conference of 1899, with its short-lived hopes, had come and gone, and we were still taught to believe that if you wish for peace you must prepare for war. The commercial competition of Germany gave us a cold shiver in the nineties, and the German Navy Laws of 1898 and 1900 suggested that our naval supremacy might be challenged from a new quarter. At home the revelation in General Booth's *Darkest England* and Charles Booth's London survey of an abyss of squalid misery in our great cities came as a shock to many whose eyes had been fixed rather on the outposts than on the heart of the Empire. Both foreign and domestic politics, in a word, were becoming more complicated; and when the Queen passed away in 1901, full of years and honours, it was clear that a new era as well as a new century had dawned.

After thirty years we stand far enough away from the Victorian age to begin to see it in broad perspective. Unlike the sixteenth, seventeenth, and eighteenth centuries, with their religious, political, and economic revolutions, the nineteenth century, which may be said to begin with the downfall of Napoleon, was, for Great Britain at any rate, a period of tranquil and steady growth. It is not surprising that the Victorians were for the most part optimists. Like the heirs of a great estate, they could witness its rapid development with their own eyes, and they knew that the world was watching them with envious admiration. They were justly proud of their achievements in every department of human activity, political, economic, and cultural, and they looked forward to the future without anxiety. With their minerals and their technical skill, their empire and their navy, their Constitution and their Queen, they feared nobody in the world. Solidarity was assured not only by the habits of compromise, which had grown to be part of the national character, but by a general acceptance of institutions and ideas—democracy and the two-party system, Capitalism and Free Trade, a large fleet and a small army, the Christian creeds and the marriage laws. The edifice appeared so strong and so shapely that its inhabitants may be pardoned for caressing the illusion of finality. The boldest of their prophets never dreamed of the complexity of the tasks which confront us to-day. But we have shown so little skill in their solution that we at least have no title to look down on our fathers and their performances. It is true enough that we see many things through different spectacles; but we shall be well advised to confront our difficulties with the industry and thoroughness, the courage and competence, of the Victorian age.

G. P. Gooch

THINKERS OF THE VICTORIAN AGE

BOOK LIST

Cambridge Modern History, vols. xi and xii. 1909–10.
INGE, W. R.: *The Victorian Era* (in *Outspoken Essays*, second series). 1922.
LEE, SIR SIDNEY: *King Edward VII*, vol. i. 1925.
LOW, SIDNEY, AND SANDERS, L. C.: *History of England* (*1837–1901*). 1907.
MASSINGHAM, H. J. AND HUGH (editors): *The Great Victorians*. 1932.
STRACHEY, LYTTON: *Queen Victoria*. 1921.
—— *Eminent Victorians*. 1918.
TEMPERLEY, H. W. V.: *The Victorian Age in Politics, War, and Diplomacy*. 1928.
TREVELYAN, G. M.: *British History in the Nineteenth Century*. 1922.
WARD, T. HUMPHRY (editor): *The Reign of Victoria*. 2 vols. 1887.
WINGFIELD-STRATFORD, E. C.: *The Victorian Tragedy*. 1930.
—— *The Victorian Sunset*. 1932.

II

THOMAS CARLYLE

WHEN Thomas Carlyle died in 1881 he had been for half a century one of the greatest prose-writers of the Victorian age, both in volume of production and in range of influence. He had preached his gospel of silence in forty eloquent volumes.

Since his death an immense literature has been published about him. J. A. Froude immediately issued Carlyle's *Reminiscences* in two volumes, in spite of the fact that Carlyle had written therein a solemn and explicit prohibition against the publication of the chapter on Jane Welsh Carlyle without "fit editing." His *Life of Carlyle* in four volumes quickly followed. It is a great biography, but he gives a sombre picture of his hero. It is funereal in tone. "His mood," said Professor Masson, "is too uniformly like that of a man drawing a hearse." Then he gave to the world three volumes of Mrs Carlyle's letters. These nine volumes excited great controversy, which has lasted ever since. Some who knew Carlyle protested that Froude's picture was not a true one. Professors Masson and Norton, Mr Alexander Carlyle, and Sir J. Crichton-Browne have written criticising Froude and vindicating Carlyle. The last and most voluminous of these vindicators is Mr D. A. Wilson, who has recently published a new *Life of Carlyle* in five large volumes, to be completed by a sixth. Mr Wilson is a hero-worshipper, and much of his work is scrappy and trivial. He has, however, provided much new material, supplementing and criticising Froude's portrait. As literature Froude's *Life* is easily superior, and will keep its place as the classic biography of Carlyle. It is, in fact, one of the best biographies of the century. I have neither inclination nor time to discuss the merits of the bitter controversy between Froude and his critics. I will only say that while Froude, an Englishman, lacking a sense of humour, misunderstood Carlyle, a Scot, overflowing with humour and exaggeration, yet he did not consciously misrepresent him. He honestly tried to tell the truth as he believed Carlyle would have wished him to do. In this he was a pioneer of the new truth-telling, anti-adulatory biography with which we are now familiar.

Moreover, he claimed that Carlyle had given him full authority to publish the memoir of Mrs Carlyle and her letters at his sole discretion. Whether Froude was discreet or not will always remain open to dispute. Many will always feel that some of this material ought not to have been published. The whole subject has been recently fully and ably discussed by an American, Professor W. H. Dunn, and his verdict is emphatically in favour of Froude.[1]

Innumerable volumes of letters written by Mr and Mrs Carlyle have been published, including their love-letters to each other. Every scrap of their writings has been unearthed, and their domestic life has been put under the microscope. Yet in spite of this flood of literature the interest of the twentieth century has steadily declined, and the present generation does not seem to read or admire Carlyle. Probably the reason is that his style is too violent and explosive, and his message too ethical—too much like preaching. The nineteenth century liked preaching, and his books were a powerful stimulus and inspiration to the thoughtful people of his time. He was pre-eminently a moral prophet, and he was always preaching. Goethe, with characteristic insight, said of him, as early as 1827, before he was known to the world, " Carlyle is a moral force of great importance; there is in him much for the future, and we cannot foresee what he will produce and effect." This moral force was his strength, and the secret of his great influence in the Victorian age. He was the moral prophet of that age, the " Sage of Chelsea." Yet a brilliant modern writer, Lytton Strachey, thinks that this is his greatest fault. He says:

> The stern child of Ecclefechan held artists in low repute, and no doubt would have been disgusted to learn that it was in that guise that he would win the esteem of posterity. He had higher views;

[1] *Froude and Carlyle* (1930).

> surely he would be remembered as a prophet. . . . His moral preoccupation was particularly injurious to his artistic instincts. . . . In his history, especially, it is impossible to escape from the devastating effects of his reckless moral sense. Perhaps it is the platitude of such a state of mind that is its most exasperating quality. . . . Carlyle had a true gift for history which was undone by his moralisations.[1]

This illustrates the difference between the nineteenth and twentieth centuries. The Victorian age, with all its limitations, was profoundly stirred by moral issues, and this age is comparatively indifferent to them.

II

Carlyle was born in 1795 at Ecclefechan, in Annandale, Dumfries, the eldest of the children of James Carlyle by his second wife, Margaret Aitken. The father was a stonemason, a stern Puritan Scottish peasant. From him Thomas inherited many of his characteristics. In the sketch of his father in the *Reminiscences* he describes him vividly, and it is almost a portrait of himself:

> None of us will ever forget that bold, glowing style of his, flowing free from his untutored soul, full of metaphors (though he hardly knew what a metaphor was) with all manner of potent words. . . . Emphatic beyond all men. The fault was that he exaggerated (which tendency I inherit) in description, and for the sake chiefly of humorous effect. He was a man of rigid, even scrupulous, veracity. . . .[2]
>
> We had to complain that we durst not freely love him. His heart seemed as if walled in; he had not the free means to unbosom himself.[3]

The mother was, says Thomas, "a woman of, to me, the fairest descent, that of the pious, the just, and the wise."[4]

They were an affectionate, united family, and Thomas was always a devoted son and brother. The link between mother and son was specially close to the end of her life. She was deeply religious, and hoped to see her Tom a minister, but it was not to be. James Carlyle was determined, adds Thomas, against much advice, and chiefly, if not solely, from

[1] *Portraits in Miniature*, pp. 185–188 (1931).
[2] *Reminiscences*, pp. 3–4 (Everyman's Library). [3] *Ibid.*, p. 10. [4] *Ibid.*, p. 27.

his own noble faith, that his son should have a good education. He was sent to Annan Grammar School, and in 1809 to Edinburgh University. He walked the eighty miles to Edinburgh with an older boy a month before his fourteenth birthday, and attended the sessions until 1814. He was not a brilliant student, except in mathematics. From 1814 he taught mathematics in schools, first at Annan and afterwards at Kirkcaldy, where Edward Irving was his colleague; but he did not like teaching, and in 1818 he abandoned the teaching profession. The year before, 1817, he had finally decided that he could not be a minister. He had been reading Gibbon, who not only unsettled his religious opinions, but roused his interest in history and humanity. He eagerly devoured Gibbon's *Decline and Fall*, reading the twelve volumes in twelve consecutive days. How many men have been awakened by Gibbon? It is curious to note that Mr Winston Churchill in his recent autobiography has attributed the rousing of his intellectual life to reading *The Decline and Fall.*

In 1818 Carlyle tried the study of law, but soon gave it up, and in 1819 he began his literary career. The next three years were miserable ones. He was poor, ill, lonely. Hardship, poverty, and irregular meals induced dyspepsia, which was his lifelong enemy. He passed through a spiritual crisis of darkness and despair—the "Everlasting No" of *Sartor Resartus*; but he reached his deliverance to the "Everlasting Yea" in June 1821. He did literary hack-work—wrote sixteen biographical articles for Brewster's *Edinburgh Encyclopædia*, translated a French *Geometry*, with a prefatory essay on proportion, which was highly thought of. Some years later he was candidate for a chair in astronomy, but did not get it. He turned to German literature, and became the first and principal interpreter of German thought to English readers. He translated Goethe's *Wilhelm Meister* (1824), and wrote a life of Schiller (1825). He greatly admired Goethe, and owed much to him. He found in him what he lacked in himself, serenity—" repose attained after conflict." "To you I owe," he afterwards wrote to Goethe, " the all-precious knowledge that Reverence is still possible; that instead of conjecturing and denying I can again believe and know." He was also greatly influenced by Richter, and by the philosophy of Kant and Fichte. Meanwhile, through Irving, he became in 1822 tutor to the sons of Mr Buller, Charles and Arthur. Charles was a clever pupil, and remained a close friend of the Carlyles till his untimely death in 1848, after a brilliant political career as one of the Philosophical Radicals.

In 1824 Carlyle retired from this tutorship, and spent nine months in London, where he made many friends. He met Coleridge, whom he described as "a steam-engine of a hundred horse-power with the boiler burst. He speaks incessantly, not thinking or remembering, but combining all these processes in one."[1] Long afterwards he gave a vivid portrait of Coleridge in his *Life of Sterling*, but he owed nothing to that visionary philosopher. In 1825 he retired to a small farm near his father's home, and there continued his German translations.

Meanwhile he had fallen in love with Jane Welsh, a pupil of Irving, by whom they were introduced in 1821. She lived with her mother at Haddington, and had inherited from her father the farmhouse of Craigenputtock, in Dumfriesshire. She was brilliant, witty, and original. The love-letters they wrote to each other have now been given to the world, and are remarkable, both for intellectual ability and depth of feeling—though one feels that they ought never to have been published. The courtship did not run smoothly, but they were engaged in 1825 and married in 1826.

Froude probably misrepresented their married life. They undoubtedly loved each other deeply; their letters prove that, and the testimonies of many friends confirm it; but they were too much alike. She was hard and critical; he was censorious and irritable. Both suffered greatly from dyspepsia. She was delicate, nervous, and highly strung. Both slept badly, and could not endure noise. Carlyle was always complaining of poultry, cats, and pianos. Possibly they themselves were partly responsible for their sleeplessness, for they drank copious tea in the evenings. Carlyle liked five cups, and then complained that he could not sleep! He had great emotion, but could not express it. He was like his father (and like many other Scots): "His heart seemed

[1] Dr R. Garnett, *Life of Carlyle*, p. 36.

as if walled in; he had not the free means to unbosom himself." She often failed to evoke his tenderness because she did not show her own. She had great faith in him, and great admiration for his genius. She believed in him when the world was critical, but when Society lionised him she sometimes resented it. In her own way she devoted herself to him, and adapted herself to his uncertain temper. He sacrificed everything, including her, to his work. His mother had said he was "gey ill to deal with," and Jane herself was not easy to please. She said once to Thackeray's daughter, "If you wish for a quiet life never marry a dyspeptic man of genius." Tennyson, who admired both, said he could not agree that the Carlyles ought not to have married, since if they had each married elsewhere there would have been four miserable people instead of two. Absence seemed to make their hearts more tender, for, except in one period of Mrs Carlyle's illness and nervous depression, their letters were always warm and affectionate.

They began their married life of forty years at a small house in Edinburgh. Jeffrey (a distant kinsman of Mrs Carlyle), the clever, cynical editor of *The Edinburgh Review*, was kind and helpful. He invited Carlyle to write articles for the *Review*, first on German literature, then on other subjects. In 1828 they went to live at the Welsh inheritance, Craigenputtock, a lonely house on a Scottish moor. Here, "in solitude altogether Druidical," he wrote some of his best essays. That on Burns is a masterpiece, the "very voice of Scotland." Those on Voltaire and Johnson are models of literary criticism. Two other essays of this period mark the beginning of his political philosophy—"Signs of the Times" (1829) and "Characteristics" (1831). But the greatest product of this mountain solitude was *Sartor Resartus*. In his diary on October 28, 1830, he says, "Written a strange piece on clothes. Know not what will become of it. I could make it a kind of book, but cannot afford it." He was really in poverty, and had at one time "only £5 to face the world with." He did, however, expand the sketch on clothes into *Sartor Resartus* (*The Tailor Reclothed*) in 1831, and with a loan of £50 from Jeffrey departed to London to find a publisher. Mrs Carlyle had said, when he finished the manuscript, " My dear, this is a work of genius." So it was, but he could not get a publisher, until *Fraser's Magazine* published it in instalments in 1833–34.

In London, however, he found good friends—Charles Buller, Leigh Hunt, John Austin, John Mill, and others. The friendship with Mill became very close, and their correspondence (now published) on both sides was delightful and affectionate until 1842, when it rather suddenly ended. There was no quarrel, but a cooling off, due partly to the influence of Mrs Taylor and partly to the growing divergence in their views. It was a perfect friendship while it lasted, and it was mutually valuable, for each provided what the other lacked. Mill was a philosopher, but had no sense of humour. Carlyle was a born humorist, but was not a systematic philosopher. Carlyle at first thought that Mill was a " new mystic," but found he was not. Mill modestly said, " I did not deem myself a competent judge of Carlyle. I felt that he was a poet and that I was not, that he was a man of intuition, which I was not."[1] Through Mill he found two other friends, who remained intimates for the rest of their lives—Emerson, the American philosopher, and John Sterling, whose biography Carlyle afterwards wrote. It is one of his most readable books. He met Sterling through Mill, and they argued at great length on their first meeting, " not disagreeing, except in opinion," as Carlyle delightfully says.

In 1834 the Carlyles abandoned Craigenputtock and removed to London. They took a house in Cheyne Row, Chelsea, and there they lived for the rest of their lives. Carlyle always hankered after the country when in town, and after the town when in the country. He was always restless and complaining, never happy for long anywhere, but the fault was mainly in himself. The first few years in London were a hard struggle. *Sartor* was not a success. Only two people expressed admiration—Emerson and a Roman Catholic priest in Cork. It was not published in book form until 1838, though an edition appeared in America under the auspices of Emerson in 1836. Meanwhile he began to write on the French Revolution—a task he took over from J. S. Mill, who

[1] *Autobiography*, p. 101.

lent him all his books on the subject. He had been invited to join the staff of *The Times* by John Sterling's father, but, poor as he was, he characteristically refused the offer, feeling that he could not serve any political party. He must at all costs be free to tell the truth as he saw it.

So he toiled at *The French Revolution*. The first volume was finished in March 1835, and lent to Mill. He left it with Mrs Taylor, then living apart from her husband owing to her friendship with Mill. Mrs Taylor left the manuscript lying about one night, and her maid used it to light the fire. It was totally destroyed. Mill was greatly distressed, and called on Carlyle in great agitation. Carlyle took the loss in the noblest fashion, and the letter he wrote to Mill next day is a model of magnanimity. Here is part of it:

> My dear Mill,
>
> How are you? You left me last night with a look which I shall not soon forget. Is there anything I can do or suffer or say to alleviate you? For I feel that your sorrow must be far sharper than mine; yours is bound to be a *passive* one. . . . That I can never write *that* volume again is indubitable, singularly enough the whole earth could not get it back; but only a better or a worse one. . . . That I *can* write a book on the French Revolution is (God be thanked for it) as clear to me as ever, also that if life be given me so long, I will. To it again, therefore. . . .
>
> Thanks to Mrs Taylor for her kind sympathies. May God guide and bless you both.
>
> Ever your affectionate friend,
>
> T. C.[1]

Mill offered him £200, and he accepted £100.

It was a hard task, but he wrote it again by September. Mrs Carlyle thought it better than the first version. It never seemed so good to Carlyle as the first, but he could not remember what the first was. The book was finished and published in 1837. It is not my province to describe Carlyle's merits as an historian, but I will quote two contrasting estimates by other historians. Professor G. M. Trevelyan in a recent essay says that "Carlyle's great merit as an historian is that he combines the poetry and the realism of history."

[1] *Letters of Carlyle to Mill, Sterling, and Browning*, p. 108.

He praises the "unalloyed humanity, sympathy, and impartiality of his *French Revolution*," and concludes, "I still prefer his book to any other I have read." [1]

On the other hand, Lord Acton says, "Excepting Froude, I think Carlyle the most detestable of historians. There is a flash of genius in *Past and Present*, and in *The French Revolution*, though it is a wretched history." [2] Carlyle's view of history was entirely different from Lord Acton's. He viewed it as the "essence of innumerable biographies." "The history of the world is the biography of great men." That view has become popular to-day in the works of Lytton Strachey, Mr Philip Guedalla, and others. Carlyle's strength as historian was in vivid portraiture and dramatic pictures of photographic realism and intensity. He himself said, "The great business for me is recording the bodily concrete coloured presence of things." Mill said of *The French Revolution*, "It is not so much a history as an epic," and Jeffrey said, "It is like reading a story by flashes of lightning."

In 1837 Carlyle gave a course of lectures on "German Literature," in 1838 on the "History of Literature," in 1839 on "Revolutions," and in 1840 on "Heroes and Hero-worship." This he published in 1841, and it has been one of his most popular books. He disliked lecturing, and turned to writing again with *Chartism* (1839), his first book on politics. This was followed in 1843 by *Past and Present*, a fuller statement of his views. It was written at white-heat in the first seven weeks of 1843. Then he returned to history with *Cromwell*. He tried to write a history of the Puritan Revolution, but could not do it. His interest was in Cromwell himself, and he ended by editing Cromwell's letters and speeches, with connective comments. Rarely has a book changed opinion so much. He revealed and vindicated Cromwell the man, removed the dust and ashes of two centuries of misunderstanding, and in the extremity of his admiration made his hero perfect.

In 1850 Carlyle wrote a series of political papers, *Latter-day Pamphlets*, the final expression of his political ideas. In 1851 his delightful biography of John Sterling appeared, and

[1] An article in *Life and Letters* (December 1930).
[2] *Letters of Lord Acton to Mary Gladstone*, p. 70 (1904).

then, after long hesitation between Luther and Frederick the Great, he decided on Frederick, and for thirteen years he laboured and struggled with a very doubtful hero. He was in bad health, his wife was even worse, and his domestic difficulties were at their height. Moreover, he did not love Frederick. He said, "Frederick was the greatest administrator the world has seen, but I never could really love the man." "A questionable hero, with nothing of a Luther in him." Yet he idealises his hero, and sees no fault in him. He had become obsessed by hero-worship, and excused much that he ought to have condemned. Sir George Trevelyan said, "The greatest fault of Carlyle's *Frederick* is the absence of any moral reprobation of Frederick's brutalities." It is a great pity he did not choose Luther! The six volumes were finished in 1865, and Carlyle was exhausted. His wife's sudden death in 1866 was a terrible blow from which he never really recovered. His work was done. He wrote no more, except the *Reminiscences* and an article on the Reform Bill of 1867, "Shooting Niagara: and After?" It was the last scathing and violent attack on democracy. The fire died down. He lingered for some years in silence and weakness, till in 1881 he died.

III

Mrs Carlyle once said, "Carlyle was not one man but several." There was certainly a great difference between the early and late periods of his life. His idealism declined, and his pessimism grew with his years and his success. Professor G. M. Trevelyan draws a great distinction in his essay on "The Two Carlyles":

> There were two Carlyles, the first the author of *Sartor Resartus* and *Past and Present*, a poet tender as Shakespeare in his loving pity for all men; full of humorous charity for their failings, faults, and vanities; strong in sympathy with the poor and in just anger with their oppressors; one who was able, within forty years of the outbreak of the French Revolution, to write the first and still the only interpretation of it which, by reason of humorous insight and sympathy, set those loud events, now fallen so silent, fixed for ever in their place under the eternal stars. . . . Pity them all, for it went hard with them.

> The second Carlyle appeared about 1850, wrote in praise of negro slavery, the gospel of force, and Frederick the Great, uttering the while complaints about the trivial inconvenience of his own life, after he had obtained all those important goods the lack of which the first Carlyle had borne with silent courage.
>
> The transition is in Oliver Cromwell. Carlyle did much good to Cromwell, but Cromwell did much harm to Carlyle. He was tempted by hero-worship, and presents Oliver Cromwell as a perfect hero, always right in a world of fools and knaves. The doctrine that one strong man is likely to be right and all a nation wrong, and that it is well that he should rule them by the sword, is a bad doctrine. It is not the doctrine of William the Silent, of Cavour, or of Lincoln. It is the doctrine of Strafford, of Frederick, of Napoleon, and of Bismarck.[1]

This contrast has since been drawn even more strongly by Mr Norwood Young, who maintains that Carlyle's reputation and merit varied in inverse ratio to each other. His merit fell as his fame rose. With the exception of the *Life of Sterling*, he produced nothing of permanent value after the *Letters of Cromwell*, yet his fame steadily rose.[2]

I think that this contrast is broadly true, but rather overstated. The later Carlyle was implicit in the earlier. *Heroes and Hero-worship* was the bridge between the two. Yet the germ of *Heroes* appears earlier in the essay on Schiller and in *Sartor*, and came originally from Fichte. The difference is one of degree and emphasis. Carlyle preached silence, but was brilliant in conversation. Mrs Carlyle said, " I used to think my husband the most copious talker anywhere, but Macaulay beats him hollow—in quantity." [3] He was intolerant of opposition, and contemptuous of most of his contemporaries. He did not believe in tolerance. On one occasion, discussing the anti-slavery agitation with J. Sterling, he said, " When I look at this I determine to cast all tolerance to the winds," to which Sterling replied, " My dear fellow, I had no idea that you had any to cast." [4] Everything was to him right or wrong, white or black, and he could not tolerate a different point of view from his own. He took life too seriously, and scorned those who " sat at ease in Zion."

[1] *The Recreations of an Historian*, " The Two Carlyles " (1919).
[2] *Carlyle : his Rise and Fall*, p. 368.
[3] D. A. Wilson, *Life of Carlyle*, vol. iv, p. 395.
[4] *Ibid.*, vol. iii, p. 106.

Jeffrey said that he was "dreadfully in earnest." Dr Chalmers said of him as a young man, "He is more in love with earnestness than with truth."

IV

Carlyle was one of the pioneers of idealism. He belonged to the romantic reaction against the empty formalism and arid materialism of the eighteenth century. He vehemently rejected the 'cause and effect' philosophy and the utilitarian ethics and the *laissez-faire* political philosophy which were all dominant in his youth. Against these he passionately asserted the spiritual nature of man and the world, and the importance of *values*, of qualitative differences instead of quantitative.

Mr Muirhead regards Carlyle as the prophet of the idealist revolt against eighteenth-century naturalism, as Coleridge was its philosopher. They were the heralds of idealism. "To no less a degree than Coleridge embodied the romantic spirit Carlyle may be said to have been the living embodiment of the puritanic spirit."[1] "He was never a systematic student of philosophy, and relied largely on his intuitions, and they were extraordinarily accurate."[2]

He abandoned the Christian creed, but he remained a Puritan, and his faith in the moral order of the world was firm and permanent. He was a profound and convinced theist. God is ever on his lips, though often under fantastic names—"the Eternities," "the Immensities," "the Veracities." He was a Puritan without a creed. Froude called him a "Calvinist without Theology." Religion to him was profound and all-pervading, but it was the religion of the Old Testament rather than the New. He loved the Bible, especially the Old Testament, and was constantly quoting it. It was to him "the Book of Books for heartiness and sincerity." A story is told of him that is characteristic. He was staying at a country house, and the squire had family prayers after breakfast, with all the servants assembled. Carlyle was asked to read the Scripture. It was the first chapter of Job. Carlyle became engrossed in it, and read on and on till he

[1] *Platonic Tradition in Anglo-Saxon Philosophy*, p. 127 (1931). [2] *Ibid.*, p. 131.

finished the book. The servants had left one by one, but the squire dared not stop the reader.

Sartor Resartus is the core of his philosophical teaching and the germ of his political writings. Its style makes it difficult to read. It is chaotic, disjointed, vehement, and grotesque. With grim, satiric humour he develops a philosophy of clothes. The world is the garment of God—the only reality. All visible things are symbols of a spiritual universe. " The great soul of the world is just." Existence is an awe-inspiring mystery. Part of the book is autobiographical. It describes his own spiritual crisis, passing from the " Everlasting No " to the " Everlasting Yea." " Love not Pleasure; love God. This is the Everlasting Yea." Happiness will come only by renunciation, and peace only by active work. Do the duty which lies nearest to you, and do it with all your might. Renunciation, Duty, and Work are his gospel.

> " So true is it, what I then said, that *the Fraction of Life can be increased in value not so much by increasing your Numerator as by lessening your Denominator*. Nay, unless my Algebra deceive me, *Unity* itself divided by *Zero* will give *Infinity*. Make thy claim of wages a zero, then; thou hast the world under thy feet. Well did the Wisest of our time [Goethe] write: ' It is only with Renunciation that Life, properly speaking, can be said to begin.'
>
> " I asked myself: What is this that, ever since earliest years, thou hast been fretting and fuming, and lamenting and self-tormenting, on account of? Say it in a word: is it not because thou art not happy? Because the Thou (sweet gentleman) is not sufficiently honoured, nourished, soft-bedded, and lovingly cared-for? Foolish soul! What Act of Legislature was there that *thou* shouldst be Happy? A little while ago thou hadst no right to *be* at all. What if thou wert born and predestined not to be Happy, but to be Unhappy! Art thou nothing other than a Vulture, then, that fliest through the Universe seeking after somewhat to *eat*; and shrieking dolefully because carrion enough is not given thee? Close thy *Byron*; open thy *Goethe*."
>
> " . . . On the roaring billows of Time, thou art not engulfed, but borne aloft into the azure of Eternity. Love not Pleasure; love God. This is the Everlasting Yea, wherein all contradiction is solved; wherein whoso walks and works, it is well with him." [1]

[1] *Sartor Resartus*, pp. 132–133. This and subsequent references are to the Collected (Shilling) Edition of Carlyle's works (1888–90).

"... Most true is it, as a wise man teaches us, that 'Doubt of any sort cannot be removed except by Action.' On which ground, too, let him who gropes painfully in darkness or uncertain light, and prays vehemently that the dawn may ripen into day, lay this other precept well to heart, which to me was of invaluable service: *'Do the Duty which lies nearest thee,'* which thou knowest to be a Duty! Thy second Duty will already have become clearer." [1]

V

In *Signs of the Times* (1829), his earliest political writing, Carlyle denounces the mechanical spirit of the age in philosophy, politics, and industry. He protests that our social welfare depends on the mind within us, and not on external circumstances or legislative changes. It is dynamic, not mechanical; moral, not political. "To reform a world, to reform a nation, no wise men will undertake; and all but foolish men know that the only solid, though a far slower, reformation is what each begins and perfects on himself." [2]

In *Chartism* (1839) and *Past and Present* (1843) he applies the principles of *Sartor* to the social and political problems of his time. He protests against injustice, "which is but acted untruth," against *laissez-faire*, the selfish pursuit of wealth ("Mammonism"), and the indifference of aristocrats ("Dilettantism"). He denounces the materialistic spirit—politics without sincerity, democracy without reverence, economics without conscience, and philanthropy without discretion. He was the first to draw attention to the 'condition of the people' question, and much that he said powerfully influenced the public mind, and has been translated into action. He said he was a Radical—"the deepest, though perhaps the quietest, of Radicals," but he was not a Democrat, except in the sense that he recognised the worth of the individual apart from birth or origin. "A man's a man for a' that." "Is not every man a potential hero?—a spark of the Divine fire?"

In later life his opposition to democracy became so bitter that he was regarded as a Conservative. In this he was like Wordsworth and Burke. Some one has said, "He who is

[1] *Sartor Resartus*, p. 135.   [2] *Signs of the Times*, p. 252.

not a Radical in his youth is a knave; he who is not a Conservative in his age is a fool." It is impossible to label Carlyle. He is usually regarded as a strong individualist, yet Socialists claim him as one of their prophets. Keir Hardie, the founder of the Labour Party, said he was inspired by Carlyle's teaching, especially by *Latter-day Pamphlets*, the most fiercely anti-democratic of his writings! Carlyle was not a systematic thinker, and was more emotional than rational. He had a contempt for science generally, and especially for political economy, which he called "the Dismal Science." But he did not understand the economists, and was unfair to them. He confused economics and ethics, and had no conception of the positive point of view of economic science, which describes things as they are, and not as they ought to be. Economic laws are descriptions of what happens, not commands. They are in the indicative mood, not the imperative. Before action is taken the politician and the business man should consider the ethical aspect as well as the economic. They often failed to do this, and so merited Carlyle's scorn. But his condemnation is not valid against political economy as a science. He admired Adam Smith, but said of J. S. Mill's *Political Economy* that it was "well done, but not worth doing." It was really human selfishness and greed that he was denouncing. His criticism of *laissez-faire* as a policy was largely justified by events, and his advocacy of Government interference had great influence on legislation concerning factories, land reform, and public health. *Laissez-faire* declined in influence from about the time of Carlyle's death.

Past and Present paints the contrast between the order and prosperity of a twelfth-century monastery under a strong, wise man, Abbot Samson, and the disorder and poverty of England in 1842. The portrait of the abbot is one of the most vivid and attractive glimpses of medieval life in English literature. The industrial and social conditions of 1842 were deplorable. He wrote (and might not this be written with almost equal truth of the present day?):

> We have more riches than any Nation ever had before; we have less good of them than any Nation ever had before. In the midst of plethoric plenty the people perish; with gold walls, and full barns,

> no man feels himself safe or satisfied. Workers, Master Workers, Unworkers, all men, come to a pause: stand fixed, and cannot farther. Fatal paralysis spreading inwards, from the extremities. Have we actually got enchanted, then; accursed by some god? [1]

In this book, as in *Sartor*, he preaches his Gospel of Work. Here are some passages:

> All true work is sacred: in all true work, were it but hand labour, there is something of divineness; it is the noblest thing yet discovered under God's sky. One monster there is in the world—the idle man. . . .[2]
>
> The only happiness a brave man ever troubled himself with asking much about was, happiness enough to get his work done. . . . The night cometh wherein no man can work. . . . Our happiness, our unhappiness, it is all abolished. . . . But our work—behold that is not abolished—it remains or the want of it remains—for endless times and eternities remains. . . . Brief, brawling day, with its noisy phantasms, is gone, and divine, everlasting night, with her star diadems, with her silences and her veracities—is come! What hast thou done, and how? [3]

What does Carlyle mean by work? Not manual work only, but brain and spirit also—not money-making, for that is Mammonism. Is it any kind of effort, good or bad? No, it must be true work. Is it efficiency, order, justice, like good Abbot Samson's work? Partly, but not entirely. Probably the answer lies also in another great word of his—Duty. Duty to Carlyle meant right—an eternal law of the universe, or, in the language of religion, the will of God. We are here, not to be happy, but to obey God and serve our fellow-men. There is need for such a wise philosophy of work. The nineteenth century set it on a pedestal, the twentieth century regards it as a nuisance—a necessary evil. But Carlyle's teaching that work is duty and service is now again coming into favour with thoughtful people. A man's job is not merely making a living or a fortune, but his main channel of service to others. Work involves wages. Carlyle thought that wages should be proportioned to work—a sound economic view. "The giving and assuring to each man what recompense his labour has actually merited may be said

[1] *Past and Present*, pp. 5–6. [2] *Ibid.*, pp. 173–174.
[3] *Ibid.*, pp. 134–135.

to be the business of all legislation and government."[1] "The progress of human society consists in the better apportioning of wages to work."[2]

In *Heroes and Hero-worship*, *Past and Present*, and *Latter-day Pamphlets* Carlyle develops his fundamental doctrine of hero-worship. It is vitally connected with his views on democracy and liberty. He believed ardently in government of the people *for* the people, but not *by* the people. True government is by the wise and noble of the foolish and perverse, with or *without* their consent. They should obey the rule of the hero—the wise, strong man. His rule would always be right and just. "The vital point is not who decides, but what is decided on."[3] Democracy is a self-cancelling business. The vote is merely a "twenty-thousandth part of a talker in our National Palaver." "The majority are fools unfit to govern themselves." "Consider a body of 658 miscellaneous persons set to consult about business, with twenty-seven millions, mostly fools, assiduously listening to them, and checking and criticising them—was there ever any business accomplished in these circumstances?"[4]

Yet he saw that democracy is inevitable. "How is inevitable Democracy to be reconciled with indispensable Sovereignty—Despotism with freedom?" Carlyle answers, "Make your despotism *just*."[5] Justice, he held, could not be obtained by counting heads—mostly blockheads—but only by the rule of the wise hero. He confused right with might, and virtue with success. All the acts of his heroes were right—Abbot Samson, Cromwell, and Frederick. The end justified the means. Hero-worship degenerated into a gospel of force, and the extinction of freedom. Carlyle did not believe in liberty at all. He said of Mill's *Liberty*, "I don't agree with a single word of it." He defended slavery as an institution, and took the wrong side in the American Civil War. Here is Carlyle's definition of freedom:

> Surely of all rights of man the right of the ignorant man to be guided by the wiser, to be, gently or forcibly, held in the true course by him, is the indisputablest. If Freedom have any meaning it means enjoyment of that right.[6]

[1] D. A. Wilson, *Life of Carlyle*, vol. iii, p. 65.
[2] *Past and Present*, p. 17. [3] *Latter-day Pamphlets*, No. 4, p. 131.
[4] *Ibid.*, No. 6, p. 192. [5] *Past and Present*, p. 242. [6] *Chartism*, p. 144.

Here is another passage:

> The true liberty of a man, you would say, consisted in his finding out, or being *forced* to find out, the right path, and to walk thereon. To learn, or to be taught, what work he actually was able for; and then by permission, persuasion, and even compulsion, to set about doing of the same. That is his true blessedness, honour, 'liberty,' and maximum of well-being; . . . if liberty be not that, I for one have small care about liberty. You do not allow a palpable madman to leap over precipices; you violate his liberty, you that are wise; and keep him, were it in strait-waistcoats, away from the precipices! Every stupid, every cowardly and foolish man is but a less palpable madman; his true liberty were that a wiser man, that any and every wiser man, could, by brass collars, or in whatever milder or sharper way, lay hold of him when he was going wrong, and order and compel him to go a little righter.[1]

The right to be compelled to do what some hero thinks best for us! That seems to be the negation of liberty. Here he follows Cromwell, his ideal hero, who enforced righteous and efficient government, but would not allow self-government. He made righteousness compulsory, and it did not last. Sir Harry Vane tried to combine the two ideas and perished.

Carlyle's hero would be a despot. Wise and benevolent despotism may be good and efficient, but it extinguishes liberty. It has two faults. It is not educative, and it is not permanent. Power corrupts, and the despot may become a tyrant, or be followed by a tyrant. Carlyle would have approved of Mussolini, but what would he have thought of Lenin?

While constantly preaching, especially in the later years, that might is right, yet he explains that what he really meant was right is might. Probably he identified them or made the terms interchangeable. Quite late in life (1873) he said, in reply to a criticism of Lecky, "With respect to that poor heresy of might being the symbol of right, I shall have to tell Lecky one day that quite the reverse is my opinion, namely, that right is the eternal symbol of might."[2]

In the end "Good alone is deathless and victorious."[3] "Await the issue, . . . each fighter has prospered according

[1] *Past and Present*, p. 182.

[2] J. A. Froude, *Life of Carlyle*, vol. iv, p. 422.

[3] *Chartism*, p. 135.

to his right. . . . In exact proportion to all his right he has prevailed."[1] So Carlyle claims to be an optimist in spite of all his apparent pessimism. He never explains how to get the heroes; sometimes he expects them from heaven. He has at other times faith in an heroic people choosing them. "A whole world of Heroes; a world not of Flunkeys, where no Hero-King can reign: that is what we aim at!"[2]

Since Carlyle wrote democracy has come in full measure, and disappointed many. Some of his criticisms of it have come true. It is ignorant, fickle, and incompetent to handle the great and complex problems that confront us. To-day it is on its trial. Half Europe has turned to dictators—not perhaps heroes. The democracies of to-day, as Carlyle foresaw, are in desperate need of wise and inspiring leadership, and poor at getting it. Yet, as one of the wisest of modern statesmen, General Smuts, said recently,

> The consent of the governed is the only secure and lasting basis of government, and liberty is the condition of consent. Only free men can consent to their form of government. No enduring system can be established on the negation of liberty, even if it comes with the temporary gift of good government.[3]

He advocates changes in a direction Carlyle had suggested in *Latter-day Pamphlets* in 1850. The difficult economic problems of to-day cannot be settled by the electorate. They should be referred to the advice of the wisest and most capable experts, both nationally and internationally.

Carlyle was more of a stimulating critic than a practical guide. Yet he made some interesting suggestions, and showed remarkable foresight in some of his proposals.

He suggested, for example, though somewhat vaguely, an organisation of labour under "Captains of Industry," heroes in the business world. It was to be done, not by Parliament, but by masters and men together. "To be a noble master among noble workers will again be the first ambition with some few; to be a richer master only the second. . . . Love of men cannot be bought by cash payment, and without love men cannot endure to be together."[4] He foreshadowed

[1] *Past and Present*, p. 10. [2] *Ibid.*, p. 30.
[3] *Africa and Some World Problems*, pp. 175–176 (1930).
[4] *Past and Present*, pp. 232–233.

profit-sharing and copartnership. "The employer may find it necessary to grant his workers a permanent interest in his enterprise and theirs." [1]

In both education and emigration he proposed State systems long before they came into existence. He constantly insisted on the need for widespread education. "That one man should die ignorant who has capacity for knowledge, this I call a tragedy." [2] He proposed a national system of education in 1840, and we did not get it until 1870.

Carlyle was an imperialist in 1843, when most of his contemporaries regarded the colonies as a nuisance and a burden. He says, "Our little Isle is grown too narrow for us; but the world is wide enough yet for another six thousand years. England's sure markets will be among new Colonies of Englishmen in all quarters of the Globe." [3] With a very modern touch he adds, "Hostile tariffs will arise, to shut us out; and then again will fall, to let us in; but the sons of England, speakers of the English language, were it nothing more, will in all times have the ineradicable predisposition to trade with England." [4]

In *Latter-day Pamphlets* (1850) he expressed his final views on social and political questions. It is the most violent outburst of his absolutism and pessimism. It dismayed the admirers of his early idealism and passion for social reform. For a time it injured his reputation and popularity. He attacked democracy more fiercely than ever. He repeated his plea for "organisation of labour," but this time as a kind of industrial and military conscription—enforced by flogging or shooting. The few wise are to govern the many foolish, but he does not indicate how to get the wise, except that they are divinely ordained. He does not say how to distinguish between these and the self-ordained. The chapters vary enormously. In "Model Prisons" he goes back to the ferocity of the eighteenth century in his attitude to the criminal and his defence of revenge as a "divine feeling in the mind of every man."

In "Downing Street," on the other hand, he makes practical suggestions that anticipate some twentieth-century ideas.

[1] *Past and Present*, p. 241.
[2] *Sartor Resartus*, p. 158.
[3] *Past and Present*, p. 229.
[4] *Ibid.*

He advocates reform of the executive Government in preference to reform of Parliament or franchise. He says:

> What England wants, and will require to have, or sink in nameless anarchies, is not a Reformed Parliament, meaning thereby a Parliament elected according to the six or the four or any other number of 'points' and cunningly-devised improvements in hustings mechanism, but a Reformed Executive or Sovereign Body of Rulers and Administrators—some improved method, innumerable improvements in our poor blind methods, of getting hold of these. Not a better Talking-Apparatus, the best conceivable Talking-Apparatus would do very little for us at present; but an infinitely better Acting-Apparatus, the benefits of which would be invaluable now and henceforth. The practical question puts itself with ever-increasing stringency to all English minds: Can we, by no industry, energy, utmost expenditure of human ingenuity, and passionate invocation of the Heavens and Earth, get to attain some twelve or ten or six men to manage the affairs of this nation in Downing Street and the chief posts elsewhere, who are abler for the work then those we have been used to, this long while?[1]

These Ministers should be chosen by the Crown (through the Prime Minister) from the ablest men in the country, without regard to rank, birth, party, or power of getting into Parliament, where they would sit as the Crown's nominees. He says:

> Is not this proposal the very essence of whatever truth there is in 'Democracy'; that the able man be chosen, in whatever rank he is found? . . . All that Democracy ever meant lies there; the attainment of a truer *Aristocracy* or Government by the *best*.[2]

This illustrates the inconsistency and confusion of Carlyle's thought. 'Democracy' to him means 'Aristocracy.' 'Liberty' means being forced by others to do their will. He was paradoxical in many ways—a Scottish peasant who became one of the greatest writers of English, an idealist who turned pessimist, a brilliant talker who preached silence, a hero-worshipper who despised most of his contemporaries. He founded no school of thought, and had no disciples except Ruskin and Froude, but he profoundly influenced the political and economic thought of his age.

His Gospel of Work, Duty, and Self-denial is not as popular now as it was in his day, but there are elements in his teaching

[1] *Latter-day Pamphlets*, No. 3, p. 79.

[2] *Ibid.*, p. 102.

that are needed in our time, and will, I hope, recover their appeal. He fought the materialism and sentimentalism of the Victorian age, and they survive among us to-day. He put the man above the machine, moral values above material comfort, discipline above self-indulgence, work above slackness, duty above inclination, and quality above quantity. Dr Edward Caird has well said:

> His great power lies not in specific proposals or political analysis, but in constant preaching of the lesson that a moral regeneration of society is more important than any change of the machinery of Government, and is indeed necessary to make any such change effective. . . . No English writer of the nineteenth century has done more to elevate and purify our ideals of life, and to make us conscious that the things of the spirit are real, and that in the last resort there is no other reality.[1]

R. S. Dower

[1] *Essays on Literature and Philosophy*: "The Genius of Carlyle," p. 266.

BOOK LIST

A. Primary Authorities

Carlyle, Thomas:

1. *Works.* References are to the Collected (Shilling) Edition, 37 vols. 1888–90.
2. *Reminiscences.* Edited by J. A. Froude, 1881; edited by C. E. Norton, 1887; and recently reprinted in Everyman's Library.
3. *Letters to Mill, Sterling, and Browning.* 1923.

B. Secondary Authorities

Caird, E.: *Essays on Literature and Philosophy*: "The Genius of Carlyle." 1892.
Froude, J. A.: *Life of Carlyle.* 4 vols. Vols. i and ii, 1882; vols. iii and iv, 1884.
Garnett, R.: *Life of Carlyle.* 1887. (The best short life.)
MacCunn, J.: *Six Radical Thinkers*: "Carlyle." 1907.
Roe, F. W.: *Social Philosophy of Carlyle.* 1921.
Wilson, D. A.: *Life of Carlyle.* 5 vols. 1923–29.
Young, N.: *Carlyle: his Rise and Fall.* 1927.

III

HERBERT SPENCER AND THE INDIVIDUALISTS

IT is perhaps well that the eminent men whose social and political ideas we are investigating in these articles are not with us in person to state their cases in one another's presence. For among them were striking diversities of opinion, and several of them tended to express their views in highly explosive pre-Victorian language, displaying a veritable cave-man's irritation at opposition. In particular, Thomas Carlyle and Herbert Spencer were extremely antipathetic each to the other. Carlyle was a notable historian and a firm believer in the historic method; Spencer's method was the reverse of historic, and Spencer himself despised history as a subject fit only for the attention of "immature minds." To Carlyle the most fruitful of all human studies was biography; to Spencer biographies were but empty verbiage, and the only human study of value was "descriptive sociology." Carlyle's philosophy of society centred round the 'hero' or great man; Spencer, curiously for so strong an individualist, poured contempt upon the 'hero' and repudiated the great man theory as "ridiculous." Above all, Carlyle exalted the State and its autocratic rulers, while to Spencer the State was anathema—man's worst enemy and the irreconcilable foe of personal freedom. Finally, Spencer spoke of Carlyle as "arrogant" and "despotic," while Carlyle retaliated by describing Spencer succinctly as "an immeasurable ass."[1]

In truth neither of these two notable and typical Victorians was teachable or tractable. Both were prophets commissioned, the one by the Immensities and Infinities, the other by the Unknowable and Absolute, to instruct rather than to learn. They were better equipped to strike at each other's heads than to sit at each other's feet. Each had his vogue in Victorian

[1] D. Duncan, *The Life and Letters of Herbert Spencer*, p. 378.

days; each attained wide popularity and considerable influence. But both alike suffered swift and extensive eclipse as the twentieth century dawned. Carlyle's inequalitarianism offended the democratic sentiments of the Edwardian age, while Spencer's hard individualism outraged its soft collectivism. Carlyle was fortunate in dying before the decline of his cult set in; Spencer, unhappily, lived to see and feel his isolation in a new world of hateful institutions and alien ideas.

Until about 1860 Spencer was ahead of his generation: a pre-Darwinian evolutionist; a republican Radical with leanings towards Chartism, feminism, and Godwinian anarchism; a formidable, sceptical, unconventional, revolutionary reformer. After 1860, for some quarter of a century, while he was working out the great scheme of his synthetic philosophy, he was —as the arch-agnostic, and as the supreme interpreter of the universe (within the limits of time and space) in terms of evolutionary science—one of the prime representatives of his contemporaries. He marched with his generation, holding aloft their banner of scientific affirmation and religious negation. From 1885, however, when he sank into chronic invalidism, he fell out of the ranks of the progressives. Even as an exponent of evolution he, with his continued insistence on the inheritance of acquired characteristics, fell behind Darwin and Weismann. Still more did his pacificism, secularism, little-Englandism, and administrative nihilism alienate him from a new generation dominated by militarism, irrationalism, imperialism, socialism, and sentimentalism. Abandoning his juvenile adhesion to the causes of Chartism, feminism, and land-nationalisation, he became the exponent of a reactionary conservatism, the guide, philosopher, and friend of the leaders of the Liberty and Property Defence League.

He himself, it is true, changed singularly little. In his last book, *Facts and Comments* (1902), he repeated with senile emphasis many of the things that he had uttered with juvenile enthusiasm sixty years before in his first book, on *The Proper Sphere of Government*. He did not, indeed, change enough. He did not read enough. He did not sufficiently keep abreast of the swift movement of current thought. His ideas became fixed in middle life, and he lost the capacity to modify them. Nevertheless he was a great man and a notable thinker. Many of the principles to which he gave expression were principles of permanent validity and importance. Some, too, of the late Victorian and early Edwardian novelties to which he closed his mind were probably pernicious errors and dangerous aberrations. Certainly not a few of his painful prophecies have been fulfilled, and not a few of his solemn warnings justified by the course of events. There are many welcome signs that thoughtful men are beginning to open his books again in the search for social and political guidance in these difficult and anxious days. Just as the doings of modern democracy have vindicated many of the most mournful forebodings of Carlyle, so has the swift descent of recent socialism towards the abyss given a new relevance to the danger-signals hoisted by Spencer in the long series of his individualistic manifestos.

II

The life of Spencer need not detain us long, for it was singularly uneventful and unattractive. Spencer, indeed, was not so much a man as an intellectual organism, and his passage through this world was rather an existence than a life. It would be almost enough to summarise it under the five captions (1) Integration, April 27, 1820; (2) Evolution, 1820–60; (3) Equilibration, 1860–85; (4) Dissolution, 1885–1903; (5) Disintegration, December 8, 1903.

Spencer, said one of his early acquaintances, was "all head and no heart." He was never in love; he was never even married. Not till he was thirty-six years old, as he himself tells us, did he ever "give vent to an oath."[1] Now this was abnormal and unnatural. By the time a man is thirty-six he ought to be finishing, not beginning, his career as a venter of oaths. For the only excuse for the practice of swearing is the coexistence of violent emotion with a defective vocabulary. By the time a man has fulfilled three dozen years he should, on the one hand, have got his emotions under control, and he should, on the other hand, have acquired a vocabulary adequate to his needs. Hence, if for a person not to have emitted an oath when young argues emotional poverty, for him to continue to do so, or to begin to do so, when no longer young suggests

[1] *Autobiography*, vol. i, p. 486.

mental deficiency. This belated lapse into profanity, however, on Spencer's part indicates that in 1856 he had not become wholly dessicated and dehumanised. Fish, at any rate—for it was in pursuit of them that he vented his oath—if not men and women, were able to generate a passing flash of emotion. After 1860 he seemed entirely to dry up, and to become a mere organic machine for the production, in somewhat incongruous alternations, of synthetic philosophy and individualist propaganda.

But, although Spencer's life was flat, solitary, and uninteresting, it cannot be wholly passed over by any student who wishes to comprehend his social and political ideas. For if anyone ever inherited ancestral traits it was he; and if anyone ever retained throughout the whole of his career the impress of his early environment again Spencer was the man. He was a descendant on both his father's and his mother's side of a long line of Nonconformists and rebels—Hussite, Huguenot, Quaker, Methodist. His father, George Spencer, a Quaker schoolmaster of Derby, and his father's four brothers—and particularly one Thomas Spencer, a radical and individualistic clergyman of the Church of England—were all men of striking personality, pronounced independence of judgment, and extreme contentiousness. Their frequent and frank discussion of all political and religious problems of their day was undoubtedly the best education that Herbert Spencer received. For Herbert's father, although a schoolmaster, seems to have exercised no sort of discipline or restraint over his son—who was the only one of his nine children to survive infancy. He let him run wild; he left him to the guidance of Nature; he allowed him to evolve on much the same lines as Rousseau marked out for the ineffable Émile. This anarchic liberty in which George Spencer permitted the adolescent Herbert to grow up presents the sharpest possible contrast to that sleepless despotism which James Mill had, a few years earlier, exercised over the servile mind of the young John Stuart. All originality had been crushed out of John Stuart Mill by the ponderous loads of erudition with which his infant intellect had been burdened: he had read Greek at three; he had taught the classics to his brothers and sisters at eight; before he came of age he had mastered more subjects than most men are able to comprehend in a lifetime. Spencer, on the other hand, could not so much as read his own language when he was seven ; at thirteen he remained almost completely ignorant ; all his life he continued to be handicapped by a lack of knowledge of the merest rudiments of culture. There was never sufficient grist in his mill. For not all the lumber which his faithful collaborators collected and presented to him in sacks labelled " Descriptive Sociology " could take the place of the fine grain of thought stored in the garners of such master-minds as Plato and Aristotle, Augustine and Aquinas, Locke and Berkeley, Kant and Hegel. Nevertheless, in Spencer's case deficiency in ordinary education, aggravated in later life by an incurable indisposition to systematic reading, had its advantages. It was not wholly to the bad that a mind which proved itself to be one of the most powerful and original that the world has ever known should spend its energies in going over ground that—unknown to it—had been traversed and worked by a long line of the ablest predecessors. Of course, much waste of time and power was involved, and of course many long-buried errors were turned up again and displayed as epoch-making novelties. But, by way of compensation, many old truths were presented in new lights, and not a little new truth was discovered in regions regarded as exhausted. In short, on the whole it suited Spencer's strong and original genius to be allowed to roam at large in a world unclassified. As was said of a great contemporary of his (Benjamin Disraeli), whose education had also been unsystematic, " he escaped the permanent infantile paralysis which is often the consequence of a public school curriculum ; he evaded the premature senile decay that is sometimes the painful sequel to a university career." [1]

At the age of thirteen Herbert Spencer was not only almost completely ignorant, he was also disobedient, bad-tempered, and unsociable. Even his easygoing father felt that something ought to be done. So he sent him (1833) to the parsonage of his uncle, Thomas Spencer, at Hinton Charterhouse, near Bath, in order that the rudiments of discipline, decent behaviour, and learning might, if possible, be instilled into him. He at once ran away, and traversed the whole 115

[1] F. J. C. Hearnshaw, *British Prime Ministers of the Nineteenth Century*, p. 181 (1926).

miles from Hinton to Derby on foot in three days. But on being sent back he settled down, and for three years submitted to a process of semi-civilisation at his uncle's hands. He showed himself completely impervious to Latin and Greek; but he took to mathematics and physics as a fish takes to water, and he displayed a passionate interest in nature. His radicalism and individualism were nourished by his uncle's conversation and example; in particular he came to share his uncle's enthusiasm for the New Poor Law of 1834.

On returning home in 1836 he was faced by the problem of finding a career. Twelve years were occupied in unsuccessful experiments. He was a teacher 1836–37; an engineer 1837–41; a journalist and other things 1841–44; and again an engineer 1844–48. He made some money during the railway boom in the early forties; but he lost a good deal of it in the promotion of inventions which the public refused to patronise. His originality was at its height, and it manifested itself in the production of all sorts of ingenious novelties—a velocimeter, a dynamometer, a cyclograph, type-founding machines, sewing-machines, electromagnetic machines, pumping machines, planing machines, devices for binding music, devices for hurling mail-bags from moving trains—all sorts of contrivances for all sorts of purposes. But, if his pioneering genius was displayed by his inventions, not less clearly was his aloofness from his fellows revealed by the fact that not a single one of his inventions was a permanent success. Some subtle defect of inutility or over-elaboration or excessive expense made them all abortive. Hence in 1848 and at the age of twenty-eight he was still unsettled, impoverished, and at large.

Then in 1848 he took the step which put him into his right place and determined the remainder of his career. He secured, and for five years held, the appointment of sub-editor to *The Economist*, a magazine whose contributors included some of the most eminent men of the day. In the office of *The Economist* (340 Strand) and in the neighbouring parlour of Mr Chapman, the publisher, he met such men as Huxley, Tyndall, Froude, Francis Newman, G. H. Lewes, and Horace Greeley, together with such women as Anna Swanwick, Bessie Parkes (mother of Hilaire Belloc), Mrs Lynn Linton, Madame

Bodichon, and George Eliot. The conversation of these advanced thinkers did much to stimulate his inquiring mind; it also supplied him with material on which his mind could work. Spencer's originality as a thinker consisted largely in his ingenious development of novel ideas which he derived from the intellectual atmosphere wherein he moved during this seminal lustrum. And among all the sources of his inspiration none was more important than the ideas of one of his colleagues on the staff of *The Economist*—namely, Thomas Hodgskin, the amiable anarchist, disciple of William Godwin. He it was who suggested to Spencer the title of his first notable work, *Social Statics* (1851), and probably no small part of its contents owed their form to Hodgskin's anti-political bias.[1]

In 1853 Spencer felt his position in the literary and scientific world to be sufficiently strong to warrant his resigning his sub-editorship and embarking in his own canoe on the ocean of authorship. As events turned out, he found to his cost that he had cut himself adrift prematurely. For fifteen years he had a dire and doubtful struggle with adversity. His early works yielded him little or nothing in the form of money, and, but for the fact that three lucky legacies descended upon him to refresh him, he would almost certainly have been compelled to land and take to some terrestrial sort of work. Even as it was, he contemplated emigration to New Zealand. Nay, he was reduced so low as—after publishing *Social Statics*!—to consider the possibility of seeking employment in a Government office! Had not William Godwin eaten his principles, together with the necessaries of life, during the closing years of his existence, as yeoman-usher of the Exchequer? To make matters worse for Spencer, his health broke down in 1885. The number of his daily hours of work had continually to be reduced. Those who tend to criticise severely his *Synthetic Philosophy* should not forget that it was the product of insomnia, dyspepsia, and neurasthenia. He obviously did not manage his body well. If he had married, if he had read more and thought less, if he had taken more exercise, and, above all, if he had had his teeth attended to, he would probably have been a healthier, a happier, and a more permanently influential man.

[1] See C. H. Driver's article on Hodgskin in *The Social and Political Ideas of Some Representative Thinkers of the Age of Reaction and Reconstruction*.

In 1868, however, the tide of financial adversity turned. His books began to sell and to command good prices both in England and in America. He came into vogue as a contributor to the more weighty magazines. In 1868, too, he was elected to the Athenæum Club, and so was able to sleep in peace during the afternoons as well as to divert himself with billiards before going to bed. Finally he became rich enough to afford to live in lodgings in Brighton. Thither he moved in 1898, and there he died, in his eighty-fourth year, on December 8, 1903.

Of his character little need be said. It was estimable, honourable, but unattractive. There can be no doubt that Spencer's outstanding feature was his high intellectual power, his originality, his unconventionality, his independence of judgment, his disinclination to bow to any sort of authority. This intense individuality was accompanied by a courage, a sincerity, a hatred of shams, and a contentiousness that made him ready for any and every fray, rendering him, moreover, a formidable and persistent opponent. His famous controversies with Harrison, with Huxley, and with Weismann were particularly prolonged and acrimonious affairs. He was vain, egoistical, and sensitive. True, he had good grounds for vanity. For alone, and without any aid from education or patronage, he fought his way into the front rank of the intellects of his age. He possessed in a remarkable degree three powers not commonly found in combination—namely, the power of accumulating facts, the power of generalising from them, and the power of expounding his conclusions. He was dominated by two leading ideas which he expressed, iterated, and reiterated with almost fanatical zeal during sixty years of authorship. These two ideas were, first, in the sphere of politics, Liberty; secondly, in the sphere of science, Evolution. Such inconsistencies as marked his thought were due to the clashings of the corollaries of these two disparate principles. Of the two, his first love was Liberty; with this love he was born, and his early environment tended to foster it. His intellectual passion for Evolution was a later and an acquired characteristic. He saw in Evolution the veritable tree of knowledge; but to him Liberty was the incomparably superior tree of life.

III

Si monumentum requiris, circumspice. So Spencer might have said (if his uncle had been able to teach him Latin) when, at the close of his career, he surveyed the twenty substantial volumes that were the product of his pen. They represented the result of sixty years of arduous mental toil, or, as he would have preferred to call it, cerebration. In them he had worked out the implications of his two dominant ideas. They can be classified into two groups—namely, (*A*) the creative works written before 1860, (*B*) the explicative works written after 1860. To these must be added his posthumous *Autobiography*, written between 1875 and 1895, but not published until 1904. The following is a brief *catalogue raisonné* of his principal writings:

A. The Creative Period, 1842–60

1. *The Proper Sphere of Government* (1842). This juvenile work consisted of twelve letters written for *The Nonconformist*, a periodical inaugurated the year before, and edited, by Edward Miall, in order to advocate the cause of disestablishment. Spencer's unmitigated epistles maintained not only that the State had no business to meddle with religion, but also that it lay outside its proper function to regulate industry and commerce, to relieve the poor, to control education, to encourage colonisation, to enforce sanitation, and even (*mirabile dictu*) to wage war. Its sole concern, it would appear, was to administer justice and enforce contracts. This uncompromising utterance struck the keynote of all Spencer's political effusions. He himself has told us, in one of the most interesting passages of his *Autobiography*, how the apparent chance that led him to write these letters determined the whole course of his subsequent literary activity; for the letters gave rise to *Social Statics*, from that flowed *The Principles of Psychology*, and that in its turn generated the whole *System of Synthetic Philosophy.*[1]

2. *Social Statics* (1851), which has rightly been described as " one of the most original books since Plato and Aristotle," traversed the same ground as the twelve letters, but it surveyed

[1] *Autobiography*, vol. i, p. 212.

it more carefully, and it descended below the surface in its search for fundamental principles. The argument is as follows: Man is by nature—like Spencer himself—a solitary animal. Circumstances, and especially the growth of population, compel him to live in society. Hence his relations to his fellows need defining. As an aid to this necessary definition he is provided with a "moral sense." This moral sense enunciates four general principles of conduct—namely, the principles of (*a*) justice, (*b*) negative beneficence, (*c*) positive beneficence, and (*d*) self-realisation. Of these four principles the first is incomparably the most important. "What, then, is justice?" asks Spencer, apparently unaware that Plato has asked and answered the question in the greatest of his dialogues. To Spencer justice is that principle which ensures to each man in society, as though he were still living in solitude, the natural rewards of his energy and efficiency, and the natural penalties of his slackness and inefficiency. In order that this law of conduct and consequence may operate it is necessary that each individual should have the largest possible measure of freedom. The only legitimate limit, indeed, to the liberty of the individual is the equal claim to liberty of every other individual. Hence the primary and cardinal "law of equal liberty," which Spencer formulates in the words: "Every man has freedom to do all that he wills, provided he infringes not the equal freedom of any other man." [1] From this primary law of equal freedom (the first and foremost of the natural rights of the individual) are derived many secondary or particular natural rights, which Spencer then proceeds to specify—*e.g.*, the right to the use of the earth, the right to property, the right to freedom of trade, the right to free speech, and so on. The enumeration of the natural rights of the individual leads logically to a consideration of the proper limits of State action in a perfectly balanced society. Spencer no longer excludes war from the appropriate activities of government. On the contrary, he deliberately adds defence of the community against external foes to administration of justice and enforcement of contracts

[1] *Social Statics*, chapter vi. Criticisms of this 'law,' as thus inadequately formulated, leap to the mind. For instance, has every man freedom to brawl in church, to keep pigs in his garden, to walk naked through the streets, etc., etc., provided he infringes not the equal freedom of others to do the same? Obviously more definition is necessary.

within the community, to the proper duties of the political organ. But he repeats with emphasis his warning to the State to keep its freedom-destroying hands off commerce, religion, poor relief, education, colonisation, sanitation, and even off currency, banking, and the Post Office. The assumption throughout—not unlike that made by Mill in his *Liberty*—is that the individual and the State are necessary enemies, the one to the other; that any extension of State activity involves an inevitable restriction of personal freedom; and that the ideal condition of mankind is one of amiable anarchism. How different an assumption from that underlying the *Republic* of Plato, the *Politics* of Aristotle, and the works of the writers of the modern schools that look to Hegel as their lord!

3. *The Principles of Psychology*, regarded by Mr W. H. Hudson as Spencer's "greatest achievement," followed in 1855. Of its filiation to *Social Statics* we are informed by Spencer himself. "Had there been no *Social Statics*," he says, "those lines of inquiry which led to *The Principles of Psychology* would have remained unexplored."[1]

Although the connection may not at first appear obvious, it is nevertheless real. Spencer's social and political system, like that of Hobbes,[2] is based on psychology. Spencer, like Hobbes, starts from the individual man, his desires and apprehensions, his search for pleasure and his flight from pain. Hobbes, whose dominant emotion was fear, constructed his monstrous Leviathan as a safeguard against besetting perils: he did not object to regulation and regimentation, provided only he were protected from danger. Spencer lived in less alarming days. Amid the *Pax Victoriana* he felt secure and comfortable. He needed no Leviathan to defend him: a policeman, and he a long way off, and mainly active at night, was enough. Hence Spencer's dominant emotion was resentment at restraint. The passion for liberty possessed him, and his chief desire was to find a bit to place in Leviathan's jaw. And out of the same materials as Hobbes had employed in the construction of his Leviathan—namely, hedonism and contract—Spencer fabricated the chain of natural rights that should be capable of curbing the overgrown monster.

[1] *Autobiography*, *loc. cit.*
[2] And, one might add, those of Spinoza, Locke, and Rousseau.

Spencer's psychology—like that of Hobbes as set forth in his *Humane Nature* and in the first part of his *Leviathan*—was highly original. It was, indeed, mainly evolved out of his inner consciousness; for he had singularly little knowledge of what Hobbes or anyone else had written on the subject. It was based on a study of the nervous system and of the principles of phrenology. It included the study of the minds of children and even of animals. The whole conception of the work was evolutionary, although the evolution, unfortunately, was of the pre-Darwinian type, the inheritance of acquired characteristics and not natural selection being taken as the key to the evolutionary process.

But the most remarkable feature in this astonishing effort of genius was the way in which it suggested a mode of reconciliation between the sensationist and the intuitionist schools of mental philosophy. Sensationists, such as Locke, had maintained that the mind is originally a *tabula rasa*, and that all knowledge is derived from experience. On the other hand, intuitionists, like Descartes, had asserted the existence of innate ideas; or, like Kant, had contended that at least the forms of thought are innate. Spencer's reconciliation of their apparent incompatibles was effected by the brilliant and penetrating suggestion that ideas that transcend the experience of the individual are yet derived from the experience of the race and are transmitted by inheritance. The importance of Spencer's suggestion is well explained by Mr Hector Macpherson,[1] and also by Mr Hugh Elliot.[2] The latter ends an able summary with an eloquent paragraph that contains the words:

> Spencer's *Psychology* is of the first importance in the history of the subject; even now it is far better worth reading than the great majority of text-books that have been produced since his time. For the general point of view and the general method are quite beyond criticism: it is only minor points that have been affected by the progress of knowledge.

4. *Essays:* First Series (1858), Second Series (1863), Third Series (1874). Much of Spencer's time and energy

[1] H. Macpherson, *Herbert Spencer, the Man and his Work*, chapter vii, "The Evolution of Mind."

[2] H. Elliot, *Herbert Spencer*, chapter xi, "Psychology."

during these seminal years was spent in the production of a remarkable series of essays, which securely established his fame as a thinker. Twenty-four were written during the eight years 1852–60, and about one-half of these were published in a volume that was dated 1858. Their themes were very various, but all showed the workings of a mind of exceptional power and independence. Two principles dominated them: in the sphere of politics individualism; in the sphere of science evolution. Under the first heading may be mentioned *Over-legislation* (*Westminster Review*, 1853), *Representative Government* (*Westminster Review*, 1857), and *State-tampering with Money and Banks* (*Westminster Review*, 1858)—an essay full of warning, strikingly relevant to present-day politics. Under the second heading come *The Development Hypothesis* (*Leader*, 1852–54), *Progress: its Law and Cause* (*Westminster Review*, 1857), *The Nebula Hypothesis* (*Westminster Review*, 1858), and *The Social Organism* (*Westminster Review*, 1860)—an essay indicating that Spencer's politics and his science were getting painfully mixed up.

5. *Scheme of the Synthetic Philosophy* (1860). The same year as saw the publication of the notable essay on *The Social Organism*—the cardinal year of Spencer's existence—saw also the issue of the prospectus of his great projected *Synthetic Philosophy*, the elaboration of which occupied the major portion of his remaining forty-three years of successive equilibration, dissolution, and disintegration. The important point for us to note is that the whole colossal scheme was designed to elucidate and confirm precisely those principles of ethics and politics which Spencer had first enunciated in his letters of 1842 and his treatise of 1851. He himself tells us in his *Autobiography* (vol. ii, p. 314) that "the whole system was at the outset, and has ever continued to be, a basis for a right rule of life, individual and social." And he repeats this statement with emphasis in his preface to *The Data of Ethics* (1879). The scheme—which on the whole was closely followed during the succeeding thirty-six years—envisaged a series of volumes treating respectively of (*a*) first principles, (*b*) biology, (*c*) psychology, (*d*) sociology, including politics, and (*e*) ethics. The whole was inspired and unified by the idea of evolution.

6. *Education* (1861) really belongs to this same creative

period, for this volume, although issued in book form at the beginning of the next period, consists of four essays originally published in various magazines during the years 1854–58. The first essay is the ablest and most important of the four; when first published it struck a resounding blow at the classical curriculum of the day, and powerfully furthered the cause of scientific education. "What knowledge is most worth?" it asked. In reply it classified the aims of education as preparation successively for life, health, livelihood, parentage, citizenship, and the right use of leisure. It showed the uselessness of the ordinary grammar-school gerund-grinding for the realisation of any one of these aims, and advocated a new curriculum dominantly scientific.

IV

B. The Explicative Period, 1860–1903

7. *The Synthetic Philosophy* (1862–96). Spencer himself in his *Autobiography* has told us in minute detail the marvellous story of his achievement, in substantial completeness, of the gigantic task which he set himself in 1860. Hampered by chronic ill-health, harassed for many years by grave financial anxieties, depressed by the indifference of the reading public, irritated by the unfriendliness of the learned, distressed by the animosity of the pious—steadily he pursued his plotted path until he attained his projected goal. It was a pity that he called his system a "philosophy," for it was really only a synthesis of the sciences. It dealt wholly with the phenomenal, and not at all with the noumenal; it was concerned with processes, not with essences; its scope was less wide than even epistemology, from ontology it deliberately held aloof. It was a still greater pity that Spencer inaugurated his great series with a long dissertation on the Unknowable. The dissertation was irrelevant to his main concern, which was to interpret the known universe in general, and the moral and political phenomena of human society in particular, in terms of evolution. It needlessly offended theologians, who professed to have information respecting the Unknowable; it wantonly alienated metaphysicians, who considered that the

Unknowable should also be the Unmentionable. In any case, it said too much: it asserted, respecting the Unknowable, (*a*) that it exists; (*b*) that it is infinite; (*c*) that it is absolute; (*d*) that it is impersonal; (*e*) that it is inscrutable; (*f*) that it is unconditioned; (*g*) that it is indestructible. By the time the end of the dissertation is reached the reader feels that the Unknowable is an old familiar acquaintance. *First Principles* (1862) is unquestionably the weakest portion of the System of Synthetic Philosophy. *The Principles of Biology* (1864–67) also is not wholly satisfactory. For Spencer's knowledge of his subject was amateurish and second-hand, and he did no experimental work. He felt that he had to treat biology as a basis for psychology, but he had little interest in it for its own sake. Huxley, however, kept him from gross errors. Spencer's strength first fully displayed itself in *The Principles of Psychology*, which incorporated the work of 1855 and greatly extended it (1872). The crown of the system, however, consists of the series of five volumes comprising the *Principles of Sociology and Ethics* (1876–96). To the science of society and to the science of human conduct Spencer made contributions of real and permanent importance. Precisely what these contributions were we shall have to note in a later section.

8. *The Study of Sociology* (1873). While Spencer was at work on *The Principles of Sociology* he received a request from Professor E. L. Youmans, an American friend who had been of great service to him, asking him to contribute a volume on *The Study of Sociology* to the "International Scientific Series" which he was then inaugurating. After some hesitation Spencer decided to suspend for a short time his work on the *Principles*, and to comply with his friend's desire. He thought that it might be well, on the one hand, to unify his ideas by making a preliminary survey of the whole sphere of sociology, and, on the other hand, to prepare the public for his more detailed investigation of a subject that was then new to the orbit of science. Hence in 1873 he produced his highly original and intensely interesting monograph, *The Study of Sociology*. It treated, first, of the need for a science of society; secondly, of the possibility of such a science; thirdly, of its nature; fourthly, of the peculiar difficulties—objective and

subjective—that it had to face; and, finally, of the bases of sociology in biology and psychology. Spencer did not seem to realise that, in demonstrating the possibility of a social science, in stressing the constant factors in human nature and its terrestrial environment, in depreciating the influence of great men, and, above all, in treating society as akin to an organism, he was laying the axe to the roots of his individualism. Yet so he was. Nevertheless, in his next publication —apart, of course, from the successive sociological and ethical volumes of the *Synthetic Philosophy*—his individualism was once more set forth in its most naked and aggressive form. This publication was the four essays, originally contributed to the *Contemporary Review*, collected and issued under the title

9. *The Man versus the State* (1884). In the first essay, "The New Toryism," he laments the drift of the Liberal Party from individualism and defence of freedom towards collectivism and coercion; in the second, "The Coming Slavery," he demonstrates convincingly the trend of the times towards regimentation, bureaucracy, excessive taxation, and socialism; in the third, "The Sins of Legislators," he collects—with a bias amazing in an exponent of the science of society—examples of the disasters that have flowed from the meddling and muddling of politicians; finally, in "The Great Political Superstition," he attacks the theory of Parliamentary sovereignty, refurbishing, as a bit for the jaws of Leviathan, the antiquated illusion of "natural rights." The book is a powerful although partial one. It is replete with facts and arguments serviceable to those engaged in the tasks of maintaining the liberty of the individual and resisting the encroachments of socialism.

10. *The Nature and Reality of Religion* (1885) deals with matters outside our scope. It contains a record of a public controversy concerning agnosticism and positivism into which Spencer entered with Mr Frederic Harrison. It might have been entitled "The Unknowable *versus* Humanity." Mr Harrison objected to the publication of his letters without his knowledge or consent, and the volume was withdrawn from circulation.

11. *Various Fragments* (1897) and *Facts and Comments* (1902) consist of miscellaneous odds and ends. They are

interesting mainly as showing that Spencer had learned nothing and forgotten nothing since 1860. His remarks on State education, patriotism, party government, imperialism, re-barbarisation, regeneration, and sanitation bear the same marks of individualistic radicalism as had his utterances of 1842. But, by a strange process of social evolution, what was called individualistic radicalism in 1842 had come to be regarded as anti-socialistic conservatism in 1902!

12. *An Autobiography*, begun in 1875 and continued at intervals until 1893, should also be mentioned. It was undertaken as a relief from the more serious work of the *Synthetic Philosophy*. Although prolix and inorganic, devoid of literary charm and emotionally cold, it is well worth reading as a record of Spencer's intellectual development, and as an unconscious revelation of his harmless egoism and childlike vanity. He defined it as " a natural history " of himself. It should, indeed, be classed, not with biographies, but with works of descriptive sociology.[1]

As one surveys the writings of Spencer in the mass one cannot but concur in the justice of the judgment eloquently expressed by Mr Hugh Elliot in the concluding paragraph of his excellent volume on Spencer in the " Makers of the Nineteenth Century " series. He says:

> If we wish to estimate his real greatness, apart from the adventitious fluctuations of his environment, we shall enquire, not what was thought of him at different times, but what he did. We shall find that, without money, without special education, without health, he produced eighteen large volumes of philosophy and science of many diverse kinds; that he invented an entire new system of philosophy which for half a century filled the attention of all thinking people; that he led the chief controversies on evolution and biology without ever having received any tuition in those subjects; that he wrote perhaps the most important text-book of psychology of his century, without any acquaintance with the works of his predecessors, and scarcely any with those of his contemporaries; that he established the science of sociology

[1] Closely associated with Spencer's *Synthetic Philosophy* were the successive volumes of *Descriptive Sociology*, prepared under his direction by Dr David Duncan and other coadjutors. These ponderous volumes provided data respecting the customs and institutions of mankind drawn from world-wide sources. Eight volumes were published during Spencer's life (1873–81), at a loss of some £4000. The series was resumed in 1910, and it is still in process. The total number of volumes at the moment is eleven.

in England; that in all branches of so-called moral science he was recognised as a leader; that he became the philosophic exponent of nineteenth-century Liberalism; that he published a variety of mechanical inventions; and that on endless other subjects, great and small, he set forth a profusion of new and original ideas. A stable judgment will recognise in these achievements a true greatness that may withstand all passing gusts of popular opinion.

V

Spencer's general philosophic position does not call for our examination, except in so far as knowledge of it is needful for a comprehension of his social and political ideas. It may suffice to say that its outstanding features can be summarily indicated by the six words agnosticism, naturalism, dualism, intuitionism, evolutionism, and individualism.

First, Spencer was an agnostic who repudiated the investigations of metaphysics as useless and the revelations of theology as illusory. Into the ultimate realities that lay behind the phenomena of time and space he held that it was for ever futile for man to inquire. The finite human mind, necessarily restricted in its scope to the data provided by experience, was, he contended, devoid of capacity to comprehend anything beyond the reach of the senses. Hence, as we have already remarked, his "philosophy" was improperly so named. It was merely generalised science. It dealt wholly with relations; it knew nothing, and maintained that it was impossible to know anything, about the absolute.

Secondly, Spencer was a naturalist, in the sense that he held that observation and reflection constitute the only sources of human knowledge.

Thirdly, he was a dualist who accepted the equal reality of, and the fundamental difference between, the self and the not-self. As Mr Hector Macpherson well expresses it:

> What Spencer did was to start with two universal intuitions, which cannot be proved, and which must be accepted as necessities of thought—belief in personal identity, and belief in the permanence of the constitution of things which we call Nature. By starting with the intuitive beliefs—subjective existence and objective existence—Spencer escaped the sceptical conclusions of Hume and Mill.[1]

[1] Quoted by D. Duncan, in *The Life and Letters of Herbert Spencer*, p. 517.

Spencer's attitude was happily epitomised by the epigrammatist who exclaimed, "What is mind? No matter. What is matter? Never mind."

Fourthly, as Mr Macpherson indicates in the passage just quoted, Spencer was an intuitionist. He revolted against both the psychological sensationalism of Locke and the ethical utilitarianism of Bentham and the Mills. He revived the cult of innate ideas; he reasserted the authority of a moral sense; he reintroduced into the sphere of jurisprudence and politics the long-banished conception of natural rights. Not only, moreover, did he resuscitate these antiquated notions, he gave them—perhaps without knowing much about their antecedents—a new meaning, a new vitality, a new rationality. For he interpreted and explained them all in the light of his master-doctrine of evolution.

Fifthly, then, he was an evolutionist, although an evolutionist of a pre-Darwinian type. The doctrine of evolution, of course, was in the air during all the early part of the nineteenth century. Lamarck had introduced it into the study of biology; Hegel had made the gradual realisation of the idea of freedom the keynote of his philosophy of history; Newman had, in his masterly dissertation on *The Development of Christian Doctrine* (1845), offered an evolutionary defence of Catholic theology; and in many other spheres the conception of an unfolding by slow degrees had taken the place of the older idea of sudden creation or catastrophic change. To Spencer the evolutionary principle presented itself as the key to the whole cosmic process. As early as 1842 his *Letters on the Proper Sphere of Government* show that he conceived of society as a growth rather than a construction; that he attributed social changes to natural causation; and that he saw among the phenomena of ethics and politics the operations of uniform law. Still more clearly does *Social Statics* (1851) display the influence of the ideas of adjustment, adaptation, inheritance, survival, and so on in the interpretation of the doings of man in community. The famous essay on *Progress, its Law and Cause* (1857) is a sustained proclamation of the doctrine of evolution, and of its universal applicability. "From the earliest traceable cosmical changes down to the latest results of civilisation," it asserts, "we shall find that the transformation of the homogeneous into the heterogeneous is that in which progress essentially consists." And it proceeds to illustrate this general assertion by reference to the latest scientific views respecting the origin and development of the stars, the earth, plants, animals, man, the social organism, and human civilisation in all its branches. Finally, he devoted the thirty-six years of his mature manhood and old age to the explication of the evolutionary idea, in the successive volumes of his *Synthetic Philosophy*. He aimed at showing that all the transmutations in both nature and society could be explained as changes "from an indefinite incoherent homogeneity to a definite coherent heterogeneity, through continuous differentiations and integrations." Yet in spite of this evolutionism, which compelled him to regard society as an organism, he remained,

Sixthly, an individualist. In the sphere of practical affairs he continued to the end, as he had begun, a passionate devotee to the cause of personal freedom. He resented restraint; he repudiated authority; he denied that he was his brother's keeper; and he declined his brother's offer to keep (and control) himself. He looked forward to a day when State interference should be as obsolete as religious persecution; a day when every man would be wise enough and good enough to be allowed to do what he liked, and when amicable anarchism would prevail universally throughout the human race.

VI

It will already be evident that Spencer was the exponent of two different and incompatible systems of politics. On the one hand, he was an evolutionary sociologist, to whom the community appeared as an organism or quasi-organism, and to whom, therefore, the course of social development naturally tended to display itself as a gradual movement away from primitive, anarchic individualism towards the unity of a complete communism—a unity in which the legislature (the organ of social cerebration) would be omnipotent and omnicompetent. On the other hand, he was an anarchic individualist, or "administrative nihilist," continually on the alert to discover and denounce the "sins of legislators," regarding every act on the part of the State as an " interference " with the freedom of the subject, and constantly asserting the " natural rights " of the individual to be exempt from the molestation of the organised, but inorganic, masses of his fellows.

Now it is almost incredible that two systems so distinct and so conflicting as these could coexist for a lifetime in a mind so strong, so clear, so courageous, and so unconventional as Spencer's. Yet so they did. It is necessary, therefore, for anyone who would give a full account of Spencer's social and political ideas to expound the two systems separately. When this separate exposition is undertaken it will soon be found that the one system—namely, the individualistic system—is complete, coherent, fully realised, and set forth with passionate conviction by its author over a period of sixty years. It will be found, on the other hand, that the second system—namely, the sociological system—is incomplete, incoherent, imperfectly realised, and set forth with hesitations and confusions that are eloquent of intellectual uncertainty. In particular, when Spencer is asked (through his works) to say what sort of organism society is, or resembles, his various answers in their inconsistency and absurdities verge upon the comic. But of that more anon. We must first examine Spencer the individualist.

A. Spencer's Individualistic System

As we have already observed, Spencer's individualism was both innate in his blood and derived from his environment. He was, as his ancestors for many generations had been, by nature a religious dissenter and a political rebel. And his natural bent towards nonconformity and radicalism was increased by his early association with his disputatious and sceptical relatives, as well as by his later friendship with that notable Godwinian anarchist, Thomas Hodgskin. Hence,

1. *Man the individual* was the basis of this primary system of his. Like Hobbes, he regarded man as solitary, rather than social, by nature. Like Hobbes, too, and like Hobbes's disciples, the Utilitarians, he considered that happiness was the end or purpose of man's being. But he differed from both Hobbes and the Utilitarians in conceiving the prime source

of happiness to be, not the reception of agreeable sensations from without, but rather the development and exercise of faculties from within. The evolution of capacity, the employment of growing powers, the realisation of latent potentialities, the fulfilment of the purpose of creation—such he considered to be the deep fount of felicity. And for this process of self-realisation the one thing needful is freedom. Hence freedom is a natural right of the individual—indeed, the one supreme natural right, from which all other natural rights flow, and to which all merely civil rights are inferior.

2. *Natural rights*, then, returned to the fields of ethics and jurisprudence, whence they had been banished as "anarchic fallacies" by Bentham and his followers. They had, indeed, for many generations before Bentham's day played a prominent part in these and kindred fields, even if their tendency was, as Austin severely remarked, to "deluge them with muddy speculation." Originating, perhaps, in Greek sophistry and cynicism, the theory of natural rights had maintained itself in Stoic philosophy, Roman jurisprudence, and medieval Christian theology. Natural rights had been recognised by modern thinkers such as Hooker and Locke; even Hobbes and Spinoza had rendered them formal obeisance; they had formed the very foundation of Rousseau's system; they had been exalted and affirmed in the eighteenth century by both American rebels and French revolutionaries. But when the nineteenth century dawned the excesses of their devotees had discredited them, the squabbles of their defenders had cast doubt upon them, and the Utilitarians had utterly repudiated and rejected them. Spencer brought them back, knowing, it would appear, but little respecting, their historical antecedents. Certainly his attempt to demonstrate their existence and to maintain their authority is perfunctory and unsatisfactory in the extreme. The German jurists, it appears, admit them—or, at any rate, admit "the idea of *Naturrecht*," which, we may remark, is by no means the same thing. Moreover, the customs of savage peoples—the Bechuanas, the Korana Hottentots, the Araucanians, the Kirghizes, the Dyaks, the Chippewayans, the Ahts, the Comanches, the Esquimos, the Brazilian Indians, the peaceful Arafuras, the peoples of Java, Sumatra, Madagascar, and Ashanti—illustrate them (or, to be more

exact, something entirely different).[1] Spencer does not seem to realise that, if natural rights are to be reinstated in serious political speculation, arguments much more relevant and conclusive than these are necessary. He appears to take the natural right to freedom as granted, and from this postulate he deduces all the detailed secondary rights of which he treats at length in *Social Statics*, in the *Principles of Ethics*, and elsewhere. Such secondary rights are the right to physical integrity, to free motion and locomotion, to the use of natural media, to property, to reputation, to gift and bequest, to free exchange and free contract, to freedom of industry, freedom of belief and worship, freedom of speech and publication.[2] All these " natural rights " the natural man, isolated in an anarchic world, is supposed to possess independently of any organised society or any promulgated law. Society does not, according to Spencer, create these rights; it merely—when organised as a State, and when acting by means of a Government—defines and defends them. What, then, of society?

3. *Society* in this individualistic system is not an organism, or even a quasi-organism, but merely an organisation; not a growth, but a construction; not natural, but artificial. " The nation," says Mr A. W. Tillett, paraphrasing Spencer's argument, " is but an aggregate of individuals whose individual welfare is the only end to be subserved." [3] Society—this late and lamentable curtailer of personal freedom—came into existence by mere force of circumstances, and particularly owing to the growth of population. Since it is no longer feasible for people to keep out of one another's way, unrestricted liberty is no longer possible. Hence the problem arises: how to reconcile personal freedom with social harmony; how to adjust the relations between the individual and the community in which he inevitably finds himself.

4. *The Harmonisation of Man and Society.* The doctrine of natural rights inhering in the individual almost necessarily involves the doctrine of some sort of social contract as the basis of society. If the contract is not a formal and precise one, as

[1] See the article on " The Great Political Superstition " in *The Man versus the State*.

[2] Cf. *Social Statics*, chapters vii–xvii, and *Principles of Ethics*, Part IV, " Justice," pp. 64–147.

[3] A. W. Tillett, *Introduction to Spencer's Synthetic Philosophy*, p. 54.

envisaged by Rousseau, it is a tacit and implied one, as in the systems of Hobbes, Spinoza, and Locke. In Spencer's individualistic system, too, the contract is tacit and implied. It is founded on the universal recognition and acceptance of two primary principles or "laws"—namely, first, the "law of conduct and consequence," and, secondly, "the law of equal freedom." The "law of conduct and consequence" is thus formulated by Spencer:

> Each individual ought to receive the benefits and the evils of his own nature and consequent conduct, neither being prevented from having whatever good his actions normally bring to him, nor allowed to shoulder off on to other persons whatever ill is brought to him by his actions.[1]

The second law—namely, "the law of equal freedom"—to which Spencer constantly recurs, is briefly stated as follows at the beginning of Chapter VI of *Social Statics*—a chapter devoted to its exposition: "Every man has freedom to do all that he wills, provided he infringes not the equal freedom of any other man."[2] The extreme rigour of these two fundamental social laws is modified by two supplementary principles which Spencer terms respectively the "law of negative beneficence" and the "law of positive beneficence."[3] According to the first of these laws, each person in seeking his own self-realisation should refrain, so far as possible, from causing injury or unhappiness to his fellows. According to the second, he should actively aid and comfort his fellows, at any rate in so far as he can do so without inconveniencing himself. By observance of these ethical and prudential maxims, thinks Spencer, the nearest practicable approach to harmony between man and society will be attained, and the individual will reduce to a minimum the inconveniences that must necessarily ensue from the compulsion, placed upon him by circumstances, to mingle with his kind.

5. *The State*, according to this view, is an evil, even if, for the time being, a necessary evil. It originated in war, and its essence is force—that is to say, the very negation of individual

[1] *Principles of Ethics*, Part IV, "Justice," p. 17.

[2] Some embarrassing applications of this law, as thus stated, can, as we have already remarked, easily be imagined. See above, p. 62.

[3] Cf. *Social Statics*, chapter iii.

freedom. Hence in the ideal industrial and pacific society of the future it will vanish away. It is a temporary and transitional institution, needful only during the period in which man is passing from solitude to sociability, from savagery to civilisation, from the egoism of barbarity to the altruism of community. The first great step towards the abolition of the State will be its reduction to the rank of a voluntary society, corresponding to the modern Church. The Church was once a compulsory institution, which enforced obedience, promulgated positive laws, and levied taxes, punishing heresy and schism with excommunication and death. It no longer remains such: its imperative commands have given place to negligible exhortations; its devastating exactions have been mitigated to pathetic appeals; its ferocious penalties have been reduced to mild expressions of disapproval. The individual now can (and generally does) ignore the Church. In the idyllic future he will, says Spencer, be equally able to ignore the State.[1]

Viewed from this standpoint, the Aristotelian classification of States into monarchies, aristocracies, and democracies is almost meaningless. It relates to mere external forms, not to inward essences. The vital question to ask concerning any State is: Does it interfere much or little with individual freedom? According to this basis of classification there are two, and only two, distinctive kinds of State, namely, the militant type on the one hand and the industrial or pacific type on the other.

The militant type, the product of war, and the embodiment of all the most barbaric and primitive of men's passions, is necessarily despotic and authoritarian. It is organised for combat, and consequently it is characterised by rigid discipline, by regimentation, by universal regulation. It necessarily subordinates the individual to the community, the citizen to the soldier. It is stiff with status; and the features that mark its subjects are obedience, dependence, loyalty, patriotism, conservatism. On the other hand, the industrial type, towards which (in Spencer's earlier and more optimistic opinion) mankind is tending, is characterised by features diametrically opposite. It is marked by a minimum of governmental control. It is organised for peace and for voluntary co-operation.

[1] See *Social Statics*, chapter xix, on "The Right to ignore the State."

It is free from unnecessary rules and regulations, contract and not status determining the conditions of its members. Flexibility, not rigidity, characterises its institutions. The individual takes precedence of both soldier and citizen, and the outstanding features of the industrial individual are the meek and gentle virtues of the cosmopolitan, the pacifist, the philanthropist, the humanitarian, the free-trader, the free-thinker, the free-liver, the amiable anarchist of the type of Tolstoi.[1]

The industrial State, as described by Spencer, is obviously an extremely unstable and transitory institution. It is merely a momentary halt between militarism and anarchism. Its functions are reduced almost to vanishing-point: it must not interfere with commerce, religion, poor relief, education, colonisation, currency, banking, Post Office.[2] Indeed, its only proper duties are two—namely, first, to defend the community against external foes, and, secondly, to administer justice within the community. Hence when, on the one side, wars—those irrational relics of barbarism—cease, and when, on the other side, men obey the natural law of equal freedom, the State will have nothing to do, and so, by mere atrophy, will disappear. For

6. *Government*—the instrument of the State—*i.e.*, of society politically organised—is, in Spencer's individualistic view, an evil; a necessary evil due to the persistence in man's present communal condition of existence of those egoistic and purely selfish qualities proper to his condition of solitary savagery, the qualities of the cave-man. "Thus, as civilisation advances," he says:

> does government decay. To the bad it is essential: to the good, not. It is the check which national wickedness makes to itself, and exists only to the same degree. Its continuance is proof of still-existing barbarism. What a cage is to the wild beast, law is to the selfish man. Restraint is for the savage, the rapacious, the violent; not for the just, the gentle, the benevolent. . . . Magisterial force is the sequence of social vice; and the policeman is but the complement of the criminal. Therefore it is that we call Government a necessary evil.[3]

[1] For Spencer's detailed study of these two types of State see his *Principles of Sociology*, Part V, "Political Institutions," chapters xvii–xviii. It may be noted that he speaks of them under the heading of "Societies" rather than "States"; but as he is treating of political institutions States is the proper term to employ.

[2] See *Social Statics*, chapters xxii–xxix.

[3] *Ibid.*, Introduction, p. 25.

Such, in outline, is Spencer's individualistic system, the system that dominated all his political thinking from the day of his earliest publication (1842) to the day of his latest utterance (1902). It is obvious that it is based on a narrow and one-sided view of man; for man is not by nature a solitary animal. He is at least semi-social. If he sometimes wants to be alone, and can for a period remain self-sufficient, it is equally true that on other occasions he pines for fellowship, that he goes mad in isolation, and that he needs the presence and the co-operation of his kind. It is obvious, further, that this individualistic system of Spencer involves equally narrow and inadequate conceptions of Society, State, and Government. Society is not a mere congeries of human atoms; it is at least quasi-organic. The State is not mere coercion; it is also co-operation. Its action is not always "interference"; it is more commonly beneficent assistance. Government is not necessarily an evil or the product of evil; it is capable of becoming a good, and even the supreme instrument of good. Even if it vanishes as a means of coercion it will certainly remain and increase as a means of co-ordination: the policeman, even if no longer needed to arrest criminals, will continue to be needed to regulate traffic, to collect lost children, and to comfort cooks.

Spencer, himself, indeed, amid all the narrowness, rigidities, and aridities of his individualistic system, had curious and incongruous visions of a larger and more living world—a world in which the antithesis of Man *versus* State did not exist; a world in which organism took the place of organisation; and a world wherein the unity of communal life superseded the harmony of mere compromise between the individual and his fellow-individuals. To his second or sociological system we must now turn.

VII

B. Spencer's Sociological System

The intrusive idea that disturbed the tranquillity, broke the unity, and destroyed the finality of Spencer's individualistic system was the idea of evolution. In the doctrine of evolution, as we have already remarked, Spencer thought that he had found the key to all the processes of both physical and human nature. By means of it he attempted to explain the present constitution and condition not only of the starry universe, the planetary system, the face and figure of the earth, the flora and fauna of the world, together with the bodies of men, but also of the minds of men, the morals of men, the customs and institutions of men, and the forms of human society. Indeed, the primary aim of the *Synthetic Philosophy* was precisely the solution on naturalistic and evolutionary lines of the problems of ethics and politics. Hence the vitally important sections of *The Principles of Sociology* are those that treat of domestic institutions, ceremonial institutions, ecclesiastical institutions, and political institutions. Now if society is to be explained on evolutionary lines it must possess some sort of unity and some sort of continuity. It cannot be a mere fortuitous concourse of atoms devoid of all coherence or interrelation, without past and without future. And, since the phenomena of society are the phenomena of will, intellect, and emotion, it is clear that the unity of society must be either organic or quasi-organic—that is to say, if not organic in the strict sense of the term, it must be at least more akin to the organic than to the mechanical. Spencer, in his acquired and unnatural zeal to apply his evolutionary key to the phenomena of community, and to develop a science of sociology, did not hesitate to 'go the whole hog' and formally to proclaim society to be an organism. The idea of the "social organism" first appeared, most incongruously, in the midst of the extreme individualistic atomism of *Social Statics* (1851), which marked the dawning of the light of evolution in Spencer's mind.[1] The idea was fully and most elaborately explicated in the famous essay entitled *The Social Organism* (1860).[2] When Professor Huxley in *The Fortnightly Review* pointed out the disharmony between the "administrative nihilism" of Spencer's individualistic system and the collectivist implications of his doctrine of the social organism, Spencer tried, quite ineffectively, to reply in a supplementary essay, entitled *Specialised*

[1] *Social Statics*, chapter xxx, pp. 5 and 16.

[2] Spencer's *Essays*, Second Series, No. 5 (1863). *Cf.* also Spencer's *Autobiography*, vol. ii, p. 48.

Administration.[1] He recurred to the theme in *The Study of Sociology* (1873) and in *The Principles of Sociology*, Part II (1876). Finally, he reverted to it in his last work, *Facts and Comments* (1902). Thus we see that for over half a century this evolutionary conception of a social organism existed in Spencer's mind side by side with, and in unresolved antinomy to, the individualistic atomism of his primary political system.

If we ask Spencer to what sort of an organism society is to be likened he is in a difficulty. As an individualist who anticipates the ultimate disappearance of government he tends to compare society to an " indifferentiated jelly," in which individuals, like protozoa, float about. As an evolutionist who sees society in transformation from the incoherent, indefinite, and homogeneous to the coherent, definite, and heterogeneous, he is bound to compare it to one of the higher vertebrates, even if he refuses to go higher than the ass.

And if we ask him what is likely to be the future course of social evolution he is in a still greater difficulty. For as a politician he has definitely prophesied the disappearance of the militant type of State, with its high centralisation and unified control, and has predicted that the industrial type will universally prevail—the type which is marked by anarchic individualism. But as an evolutionist he is bound by all the analogies of nature to see the line of progress leading to increased unification, growing differentiation of function, closer interdependence of parts, and the final complete ascendancy of that " cerebral mass " the legislature.

The truth is that the conception of society as an organism cannot be made to accord with the radical *laissez-faire* individualism of Spencer. It is more in harmony with the conservatism of Burke, who, in spite of his lip-service to the contractual doctrine of Locke, viewed the nation as a living entity with the memory of a glorious ancestry and the hope of a splendid posterity. It is still more in harmony with the collectivism of Sidney Webb, the socialism of William Morris, and the communism of Karl Marx. For in all these systems the individual withers and the body politic or economic is dominant. It is for Webb, Morris, and Marx, rather than

[1] *The Fortnightly Review*, December 1871. Republished in Spencer's *Essays*, Third Series, No. 5 (1874).

for Spencer, the individualist, to develop the view that society is an entity; that it undergoes growth and decay; that it displays differentiation of structure and of function; that its parts are and remain mutually dependent; that it adapts its constitution to its environment; and that, generally, it follows the normal process of evolution and dissolution. Similarly, it is rather for Comte than for Spencer, the dissenter and rebel, to talk of a science of sociology, to dismiss the doctrine of free will as an illusion, and to treat the phenomena of man in community as coming within that sphere of positive and unvarying law wherein no volitions, human or superhuman, interfere. Again, it is for Buckle rather than Spencer—Spencer, the asserter of personality and the maintainer of the doctrine of the individual's natural right of self-realisation—to repudiate the "great man" theory, to denounce hero-worship, and to contend that the men who apparently make history are themselves but the products of their environment.

In short, in accepting and developing the dogma of the organic nature of society, Spencer, while he put the crown upon his system of synthetic philosophy, cut the ground from under the feet of his political individualism. And—if we may pursue the metaphor further—the sociological crown which he placed on the head of his philosophy was speedily appropriated by his chief enemies, the Socialists, and was by them melted up into weapons by means of which they were able to harass and destroy the individualistic disciples of Spencer.

Nevertheless, in spite of inconsistencies and confusions, Spencer was a great man and a notable thinker. His contributions both to the science and to the philosophy of the nineteenth century were of the highest importance. In the sphere of ethics and psychology he will be principally remembered as the man who found in evolution the key to the reconciliation of the inductive and deductive schools of thought. In the sphere of social and political ideas he will rank high, not as the founder of a science of a visionary 'sociology,' but as the dauntless champion in a collectivist and servile age of the claims of the individual and the cause of personal freedom.

F. J. C. Hearnshaw

HERBERT SPENCER

BOOK LIST

A. Primary Authorities

SPENCER, HERBERT:

The Proper Sphere of Government. 1842.
Social Statics. 1851.
The Principles of Psychology. 1855.
Essays, First Series. 1858.
Education. 1861.
The Synthetic Philosophy. 1862–96.
Essays, Second Series. 1863.
The Study of Sociology. 1873.
Essays, Third Series. 1874.
The Man versus the State. 1884.
Facts and Comments. 1902.
An Autobiography. 2 vols. Published posthumously. 1904.

B. Secondary Authorities

BARKER, E.: *Political Thought in England from Herbert Spencer to the Present Day.* 1915.
BEARE, J. J.: *Organic Morality, or the Ethics of Mr Herbert Spencer.* 1889.
COLLINS, F. H.: *An Epitome of the Synthetic Philosophy.* 1889.
DUNCAN, D.: *The Life and Letters of Herbert Spencer.* 1908.
DUNNING, W. A.: *A History of Political Theories from Rousseau to Spencer.* 1920.
ELLIOT, H.: *Herbert Spencer.* 1917.
HUDSON, W. H.: *An Introduction to the Philosophy of Herbert Spencer.* 1894.
LICHTENBERGER, J. P.: *Development of Social Theory.* 1924.
MACPHERSON, H.: *Herbert Spencer, the Man and his Work.* 1900.
MARTINEAU, J.: *Types of Ethical Theory.* 1885.
MORGAN, C. L.: *Spencer's Philosophy of Science.* 1913.
RITCHIE, D. G.: *Principles of State Interference.* 1891.
SIDGWICK, H.: *Lectures on Ethics.* 1902.
TILLETT, A. W.: *Introduction to Spencer's Synthetic Philosophy.* 1914.
WERNER, E. T. C.: *Herbert Spencer.* Shanghai, 1913.

IV

SIR HENRY MAINE AND THE HISTORICAL JURISTS

THE subject of the historical jurists is one which I approach with pleasure, since my own juristic work has always been cast in an historical rather than an analytical setting, while the subject of Sir Henry Maine's work I approach with peculiar pleasure, since I have striven, with fear and trembling, to extend his doctrines from the limited region of the Aryan world to customary law in general. Yet this subject fills me with doubt, since I regard it as an advocate, and not with a purely judicial mind. I am so persuaded that the right way to solve juristic problems is the historical way that I am afraid of being unfair to the noble field of analytical jurisprudence and to the great men who have thought that they can solve the tangled social problems of this world—which are really also juristic problems, problems of the relationship of men and women in the temporal sphere—by the application of pure thought and transcendental philosophy. I fully appreciate the great intellectual efforts of thinkers such as Immanuel Kant and his followers Rudolph Stammler and Hans Kelsen, of Hegel and Bernard Bosanquet, of Comte and Léon Duquit, and read them with sympathy and respect, but in the long run they throw me back with a sense of relief to historical methods and to the historical jurists, because the analytical jurists disagree with one another to an extent and with a violence that I should not have thought possible had I not studied the history of philosophy. The historical jurist is not troubled in this way. He sees the vision of Truth shining before him, and his task—a fearful one, no doubt—is to find the right path through the prickly gorse and jungle brushwood, the woods, the forests, the precipices, and mountains of pure fact, and to approach with reverence the one and indivisible altar where Truth dwells. The historical jurist is not troubled with the fear that he is seeking, with a neo-Athanasian mind, a multiplicity of truths which his utmost efforts cannot resolve into one; he has not the fear that these visions are not real at all and that the end of his journey—if it ever ends—is some black place where reason fails and there is no retreat.

A part of my theme must deal with what I may call the origins of the school of historical jurists. The origins as I see them are a product of the late fifteenth, the sixteenth, and the seventeenth century, of the Renaissance, in fact, centred in Francis Bacon, whom I regard as the father of comparative jurisprudence: of the French Civilians, of Selden, Hobbes, Filmer, and, in a certain sense, Grotius, Pufendorf, and Bodin. Selden, in his attack on tithes, published in 1618, directly uses the historical method to oust the claim of the divine origin of tithes. Mr Edward Manson says of John Selden that the "memory of his antiquarian and legal researches—preluding the historic method—has been perpetuated and honoured in the name of the Selden Society."[1]

Hobbes, Selden's dear friend and intellectual adversary, knew all that was to be known in the way of the theory, philosophy, and history of law in his day. The medieval law of nature was revived in a modern form by him, and "in a new and non-scholastic guise" was handed down to the jurists and philosophers of the eighteenth and nineteenth centuries. Yet all goes back to Francis Bacon, who based his empirical philosophy on his deep study of law, both in France and England, and to his deliberate revival of the Law of Nature. To him Selden, Hobbes, and Locke owed the bulk of their original thought. The association of the Law of Nature with the fundamental ideas of the historical jurists is plain enough, perhaps as plain as is the association of the Darwinian idea of progress with the ideas of Sir Henry Maine. The conception of the Law of Nature which was held by Francis Bacon, John Selden, and Thomas Hobbes was and is essential to the idea of natural social growth, which lies at the root of historical jurisprudence. Jean Bodin had already, we must remember, in his *Republic* and other works, based his economic, and, indeed, other, conclusions on the historical method a century earlier,

[1] *Great Jurists of the World*, p. 192 (1913).

and to a certain extent affected the method of the English thinkers. Bacon and Hobbes, his younger contemporaries, Samuel Pufendorf, and Sir Robert Filmer (who died before the English Restoration) had each of them some sense of historical jurisprudence, each, in their several fashions, striving to place impossible loyalties or possible social advances on the basis of a structure of historical kinship. When Filmer in 1642 wrote in his *Patriarcha, or the Natural Power of Kings*, of the " hereditary jurisdiction of Adam " he followed Bacon, and endeavoured to place the Divine Right of Kings on an historical basis, and takes the contrary view to the earlier *Vindiciæ contra Tyrannos* of Du Plessis-Mornay. In the case of Filmer's thesis I cannot do better than quote Dr Gooch :

> The origin of government, replies Filmer [to Hobbes's *De Cive*], was not a surrender of natural rights but an enlargement of the microcosm of the family. The State is an extension of the family, the King being the father, the people his children. Since Adam and the Patriarchs exercised regal rights over their children, the natural condition of mankind was not equality but patriarchal rule. Monarchy was at once a divine institution and in accordance with the teachings of nature. . . . But while the patriarchal hypothesis had no real relevance to the controversy between the Stuarts and their subjects, the conception itself was not less but more historical than the rival dogma of the social contract. Kinship has been the base of many communities, and chieftainship has often become hereditary in a single family. Again, in teaching that monarchy developed out of human relationships, it suggests that the State is an organism capable of development, not a mechanical contrivance.[1]

But the origin of the doctrine of the original and social contract was, at any rate in the hands of Du Plessis-Mornay, or whoever was the author of the *Vindiciæ contra Tyrannos*, in my judgment, not less historical than the patriarchal hypothesis. Dr J. Neville Figgis says that " the fundamental notion of the writer is that the State arises from the voluntary surrender by individuals of such portions of their natural liberty as are necessary for the purposes of peace and security."[2] That is, in a certain sense, historically sound. It was not a contract, but it was and is in every tribal society an implied

[1] *Political Thought in England : From Bacon to Halifax*, pp. 161–164 (1914–15).
[2] *Cambridge Modern History*, vol. iii, p. 761.

compact in some sense, even in the feudal society to which Du Plessis-Mornay traces his ideas. In the tribal and even in the feudal complex there is an understanding relating to property, obligations, and status which the members of the complex break at their peril, the peril of exclusion from the tribe or complex. It is significant that in 1672 Samuel Pufendorf (in the Appendix to Definition xviii), in the second edition of his *Elements of Universal Jurisprudence*, bases his argument as to moral action on the Decalogue and on the patriarchal principle. Pufendorf's view is governed by the historical outlook both of Grotius and Hobbes, and especially of Hobbes, who, whatever we may think of his conclusions, strove to detect the forces of natural law as the beginning of an historical process. Dr Figgis says, with respect to the opposing theories of the original social contract and the Divine Right of Kings, that

> nothing could be more superficial than to repudiate the debt which the whole modern world owes to both doctrines. . . . It is only as we realise how large an element in the mental atmosphere of the day was filled by the conception of natural law, soon to develop into that of natural rights, that a book like Mornay's becomes intelligible, and serves as a connecting link between the ideas of the medieval and the modern world.[1]

Mornay's book, moreover, shows that this new outlook came with the New Learning; that the historical method in the study of law is indeed one, and not the least, of the fruits of the Renaissance; and this is also in all the legal and philosophical thinking of Francis Bacon. As early as 1539, nearly four hundred years ago,

> Aymarus Rivallius issued the first-known history of the Civil Law, a work of importance which was supplemented by the vast labours of Jacques Cujas (1522–1590), who placed Roman Law on a new footing, and brought it into relation to the laws which it was destined to affect. In these two jurists of the Renaissance we see the historical and comparative methods operating together at a moment when Andrea Alciati had already given new life and literary form to the study of jurisprudence. A chain of eager workers, ending with Leon-Étienne Pütter (1725–1807), William Blackstone (1723–1780), Gustave Hugo (1764–1844), and Friedrich Karl von Savigny

[1] *Cambridge Modern History*, vol. iii, p. 763.

(1779–1861), the first great master of the historical method in law, placed the historical and philosophical study of law on a firm basis.[1]

The Renaissance origin of the whole movement is beyond doubt, though Bacon, Mornay, Hobbes, Filmer, and Locke were all working in the dark for want of some great principle or principles which could illuminate, like a rising sun, the classification of ascertained facts. These sixteenth- and seventeenth-century workers had neither the correlated facts as to human society nor the principles that only superb intuition could supply, but they were on the right track of historical thought, as were the famous French Civilians of the same period. Indeed, the great French jurists, in their treatment of the customary law of Paris, Normandy, Brittany, Maine, Anjou, Poitou, Touraine, Orleans, Burgundy, Auvergne, Angoulême, and the Basque areas, approached nearer to the historical method than any other pre-Darwinian thinkers. The names of Chasseneux (1480–1541), the mighty Charles Dumoulin (1500–66), D'Argentré (1519–90), Guy Coquille (1523–1605), Charondas (1536–1617), René Chopin (1537–1606), and Antoine Loisel (1536–1617) form an immortal group to whom Francis Bacon owes much. They borrowed from medieval and ancient times the idea of the Law of Nature, and worked with that as an instrument of thought on the imperfect, though vastly abundant, material that was available in France.

When John Milton said, " We are not bound by any statute of preceding Parliaments, but by the Law of Nature only, which is the only law truly and properly to all mankind fundamental " ; when John Selden said that it was for " the Master of the House " to give to Kings their privileges ; when Richard Hooker declared that " obedience of creatures unto the Law of Nature is the stay of the whole world "—they were one and all grasping the instrument which made possible the work of the historical jurists. That very great lawyer and prose stylist Sir William Blackstone kept the flag of the Law of Nature flying, and it was well that he did so, since the thought of John Austin, which had and has so disastrous an influence on Continental political and even juridical thought, was and is a direct threat to all true historical jurisprudence,

[1] J. E. G. de Montmorency, *The Natural History of Law*, p. 8 (1921).

and sought, with no mean success, to substitute the reign of Might for the reign of Law. It is strange that the brilliant Romanist, Rudolph von Ihering, the contemporary of Maine, strove to reconcile the doctrines of Savigny with those of Austin, maintaining that the essence of law is force, and yet delving into the mysteries of the early Aryan peoples and their laws. Fortunately, the old and drooping flag of the Law of Nature had suddenly, at the beginning of the nineteenth century, taken new life under the master-hand of Friedrich von Savigny.

> Savigny enunciated for all time that principle of continuity in law which is vital in any theory of the nature or origin of law. He showed the world that law itself is subject to law, that it is no arbitrary expression of the will of the law-giver, but is itself a thing obedient to a cosmic process. To show that law is itself the expression of a juristic process that runs through the ages was in itself an achievement of the highest order; but to go on to trace, as Savigny traced, the natural history of law, to exhibit its organic growth as a living thing, evolving with the evolution of races and tongues and kingdoms, was a still greater triumph.[1]

Savigny was an Hegelian, and in 1814 he laid down the doctrine of legal historical evolution in no doubting spirit. He declares that we must conquer the mass of juridical material, obtain the mastery over it by a thorough grounding in history, and thus appropriate to ourselves the whole intellectual wealth of preceding generations. Only through history, he says, "can a living connexion with the primitive state of the people be kept up; and the loss of this connexion must take away from every people the best part of its spiritual life." Savigny was a practical lawyer (Austin was not a lawyer in that sense of the term), and he tells us that the object of the strict historical method of jurisprudence "is to trace every established system to its root and thus discover an organic principle, whereby that which still has life may be separated from that which is lifeless and only belongs to history." Maine was destined to indicate that organic principle. Savigny was still at work until his death at the age of eighty-two in the year 1861, the very year in which Henry Sumner Maine published his *Ancient Law* and J. J. Bachofen announced

[1] J. E. G. de Montmorency, *The Natural History of Law*, pp. 8–9.

in his detailed study of Greek and Roman institutions the existence of matrilinear succession in Europe.

This background picture may seem too elaborate, but, for my own part, it is necessary if we are to understand the true significance and importance of the work of the great English jurist. Henry Sumner Maine was born on August 15, 1822, his father being a native of Kelso, and his mother an Englishwoman. His godfather, Dr Sumner, Bishop of Chester and later Archbishop of Canterbury, sent him to Christ's Hospital in 1829. In 1840 he won an exhibition to Pembroke College, Cambridge. He was the best classical scholar of his year; his university career was very distinguished; and he was senior classic in the tripos of 1844 and a senior optime. He was always delicate, and the exertions of these years overtaxed his strength. In 1847 he became Regius Professor of Civil Law, a chair which he held until 1854. The fact is important, as it turned Maine's attention to law. He married in 1847 his cousin, Jane Maine (who, with two sons, survived him), and was called to the Bar in 1850. In 1851 he began writing for the Press. In 1852 he was appointed by the Inns of Court as their first Reader in Roman Law and Jurisprudence. He never obtained much practice, either upon the Norfolk circuit or at the Chancery Bar, but he was rapidly gaining a reputation as a jurist. In 1855 he became one of the first contributors to *The Saturday Review*, an organ that had also the call on the services of the great statesman who became Lord Salisbury. In 1856 he contributed to a volume of Cambridge essays a paper on "Roman Law and Legal Education." In 1861 he published his first famous work, *Ancient Law*. He was appointed legal member of Council in India in 1862, where he made great mark, and returned in 1869 to take up the Corpus Professorship of Jurisprudence just founded at Oxford. His first group of lectures was published in 1871 under the title *Village Communities*. In 1871 also he was given the dignity denoted by the letters K.C.S.I. and a seat on the India Council. In 1875 he published his third legal volume, entitled *The Early History of Institutions*, a second series of Oxford lectures. In 1877 Maine was elected Master of Trinity Hall, Cambridge, and he resigned his Oxford chair in 1878. In 1883 he issued the last of his legal lectures under the title *Dissertations on Early Law and Custom*, but in 1885 he produced a volume on *Popular Government*, in which he applied the historical method to current political institutions. The volume aroused the wrath of Mr John Morley. In those years he was a frequent contributor to *The St James's Gazette*. In 1887 he succeeded Sir William Harcourt as Whewell Professor of International Law at Cambridge. He died on February 3, 1888, crowned with a great reputation and many honours. He was a man who succeeded in everything in which he thought it worth his while to succeed. To the last, in spite of physical feebleness, he did work of the highest order, but he was not a laborious scholar. He relied on a great memory for his accuracy, and, unlike Macaulay, very rarely went wrong. Mr Leslie Stephen notes in his life in *The Dictionary of National Biography* the almost complete absence of authorities in his books. Drudgery he could not abide; it was method that he was after, and he wrought his work by the light of method.

It is true that many workers in the legal field that Maine chose for his own have extended the confines of that field and also have dug deeper into certain parts of it. It is true also that there were contemporaries of Maine's working hard at similar problems, and certainly Maine did not despise workers such as L. H. Morgan, his American contemporary, or J. F. McLennan, though he refused to decide between their conflicting theories of the origin of institutions with a certain judicial aloofness. At this very date McLennan enunciated the theory that exogamous tribes who developed the dangerous art of marriage by capture brought us into the region of patriarchy, while the practice of endogamy, or marriage within the group, gave birth to non-patriarchal institutions based on Mother-Right. Maine contented himself with praising the invention of the words exogamy and endogamy, and refused even to condemn Morgan's theory of group marriage. Moreover, in the last of his law books, *Dissertations on Early Law and Custom*, he took the trouble to indicate the lines on which the problems of patriarchy and matriarchy could be solved, the latter being in his judgment the result of a deficiency of women in some remote islands or other places where only the sturdiest of women—twentieth-century women, so to speak—could survive. In Maine's judgment the sexual character of the original population determined the character of the institution, but he is quick to remind the student, in the light of the earliest inscriptions, that patriarchy was secured, in the bulk of early movements, by the simple expedient of a conquering host: the killing of all the males and the carrying off of all the females. Whether the problem is as simple as that it is not for me to say. But the method is certainly right in the case of the mysterious traces of matriarchy and matrilinear descent, which so troubled the mind of J. J. Bachofen in the very year that *Ancient Law* was published that he announced with rash dogmatism that group marriage was the earliest institutional stage—which a curious passage in Cæsar's *Commentaries* seems to support in the case of the ancient Britons—that matriarchy came second, and that patriarchy is the final—if anything is final when woman is becoming more and more dominant and threatening—stage of our institutional life. There were other Continental contemporaries, and especially Adolphe Pictet, who in 1859–63 endeavoured to reconstruct the common civilisation of the Aryan race, while B. W. Leist strove to reconstruct the fundamental rules of common Aryan law before the separation of tongues and nations.

These Continental thinkers were overwhelmed by the immensity of the task that they set themselves with insufficient material and without any guiding method. Maine was fortunate in having one of the great thinkers of all time, Charles Darwin, as his fellow-countryman. Charles Darwin shows in his "Historical Sketch on the Progress of Opinion on the Origin of Species," which appeared in the first edition of his famous work published on November 24, 1859, that England and the Continent were humming with the conception of evolution in the decade before the publication of *Ancient Law*. Saint-Hilaire, Naudin, and Lecoq in France, Bronn, Schaaffhausen, and von Baer in Germany, Herbert Spencer, Wallace, and Huxley in England, gave the idea of evolution permanent vogue. Maine applied the Darwinian idea of evolution to the special field of what we may call institutional law. But he did so in no dogmatic spirit. Sir Frederick Pollock says truly that certain learned critics

> . . . missed that symmetrical construction of a finished system to which their training had accustomed them. Now it is to be observed

that no words of Maine's own ever gave his readers the promise of a systematic doctrine. Not one of his books professed on the face of it to account for the ultimate origin of human laws, or to settle the relations of jurisprudence to ethics, or to connect the science of law with any theory of politics or social development.[1]

Sir Frederick goes on to say:

Maine's dignified and almost ironical reserve about his own work has certainly made it rather difficult for a student approaching it for the first time to form any general notion of what it has really done for legal and historical science. Although Maine himself was the last person from whom the answer to such a question could be expected, we who are in no way bound to reticence must say that he did nothing less than create the natural history of law. He showed, on the one hand, that legal ideas and institutions have a real course of development as much as the genera and species of living creatures, and in every stage of that development have their normal characters; on the other hand, he made it clear that these processes deserve and require distinct study, and cannot be treated as mere incidents in the general history of the societies where they occur. . . . Maine has taught us that the way to impart a historical habit of mind to lawyers is to show them that law has an important history of its own, not at all confined to its political and constitutional aspects, and offers a vast field for the regular application of historical and comparative method.[2]

All that is true, and after the seventy years which have passed since *Ancient Law* was published we still may ask with the famous editor of the latest edition

in what books, legal or historical, of earlier date than *Ancient Law* he could have found adequate perception or any distinct perception, of such matters as these: the sentiment of reverence evoked by the mere existence of law in early communities; the essential formalism of archaic law; the predominance of rules of procedure over rules of substance in early legal systems; the fundamental difference between ancient and modern ideas as to legal proof; the relatively modern character of the individual citizen's disposing power, especially by will and freedom of contract; and the still more modern appearance of true criminal law.[3]

Yet we must not overstate the case for Maine's commanding position. Darwin in 1859 carefully traced what he and

[1] Introduction to *Ancient Law*, p. xiv.
[2] *Ibid.*, pp. xv-xvi. [3] *Ibid.*, p. xvii.

Wallace owed to contemporary and earlier thinkers, and Maine himself was very much of Darwin's mind and outlook. He owed a great deal both to contemporary and older thought, and one reason for his reserve in making any claims to originality was that he was fully aware that he was not the only man who was struck with the applicability of the idea of evolution to the whole field of law. Leslie Stephen, writing not long after the death of Maine, said that he lives by his law books:

> They were among the first examples of the application of the genuine historical method to such inquiries. Coming soon after the publication of Darwin's great book, which had made the theory of evolution a great force in natural philosophy, he introduced a correlative method into the philosophy of institutions. A scientific writer is liable to be superseded in proportion to the fruitfulness of his own discoveries. But Maine's admirable style and skill in exposition will make his works models of investigation even if their statements of fact require modification.[1]

That is a very judicial summing up of the whole position. Leslie Stephen did not claim for Maine any exclusive foundation of a new theory of law. In Maine's perhaps greatest law book on *Early Law and Custom* he says that he, the author—abolishing the egoistic 'I'—

> . . . endeavours to connect a portion of existing institutions with a part of the primitive or very ancient usages of mankind, and of the ideas associated with these usages. In the first four chapters he attempts, with the help of the invaluable series of "Sacred Books of the East," translated under the superintendence of Professor Max-Müller, to throw some light on that close implication of early law with ancient religion which meets the inquirer on the threshold of the legal systems of several societies which have contributed greatly to modern civilisation. In the chapters which follow he treats of another influence which has acted strongly on early law, the authority of the King. In the later portions of the book he examines certain forms of property and tenures, and certain legal conceptions and legal classifications, which have survived to our day, but which appear to have had their origin in remote antiquity.[2]

Maine's easy style, his quiet humour, and his method might be illustrated by many passages, but I choose one—though

[1] *Dictionary of National Biography*. [2] Preface.

I disagree with the alleged facts—for its singular happiness. It is contained in *Early Law and Custom*. He writes:

> There is reason, in fact, to believe that at some period of human history a revolution took place in the status of aged men, not perhaps unlike that which is still proceeding in the case of women. There is abundant testimony that tribes, long pressed hard by enemies or generally in straits for subsistence, systematically put their members to death when too old for labour or arms. The place from which a wild Sclavonic race compelled their old men to leap into the sea is still shown. And the fiercer savage has often in many parts of the world made food of them. Nevertheless, the ancient records of many communities, especially those of Aryan speech, show us old age invested with the highest authority and dignity. . . . There is a story of a New Zealand chief who, questioned as to the fortunes of a fellow tribesman long ago well known to the inquirer, answered, "He gave us so much good advice that we put him mercifully to death." The reply, if it was ever given, combines the two views which barbarous men appear to have taken at different times of the aged. At first they are useless, burdensome, and importunate, and they fared accordingly. But at a later period a new sense of the value of wisdom and counsel raises them to the highest honour.[1]

For quiet humour this passage deserves to be famous. What undergraduate or graduate under the age of thirty could fail, however stupid, to appreciate those words of a man over sixty who was giving them such fountains of good advice on the subject of law? It was, in effect, a word of warning to elder statesmen, such as Mr Bright or Mr Gladstone or even Mr Disraeli, to all the eminent Victorians who lived and lived and lived, and talked and talked and talked. It was a plea for youth from a man who was indeed an elder statesman himself. The cryptic passage about women is also suggestive in a university to which women had not yet penetrated. Is it a suggestion that up to the year 1883 women got old as men got old, and were sacrificed because they gave so much good advice, but that there would come a time when women, eternally young, clad in the garments of a new Paris, would neither give advice nor receive it? It must be remembered that Maine's book was published in the year after the passing of the Married Women's Property Act of 1882. As to the facts

[1] Pp. 23–24.

of Maine's theory about old men and women I am very doubtful. It reminds the reader of Othello's recital of his adventurous life:

> . . . of antres vast and deserts idle,
> Rough quarries, rocks and hills whose heads touch
> heaven,
> It was my hint to speak—such was the process;
> And of the Cannibals that each other eat,
> The Anthropophagi, and men whose heads
> Do grow beneath their shoulders. This to hear
> Would Desdemona seriously incline.

So the wide-eyed students of faithful Oxford would "seriously incline" to Sir Henry Maine's most excellent irony. But the fact that the aborigines of Australia, despite ceaseless want of food, depend upon their old men, live by them and not on them, restores my belief in elder statesmen even in these strange political and social times, when Bread and Circuses are all to seek.

One thing nothing but an earthquake or other act of God can take from us, even if the gold, silver, lead, and tin or paper standards all pass away, and that thing is land. Maine knew well enough that the relationship of man to land was the beginning of civilisation, and so in his *Early History of Institutions* he developed his irrebuttable theory. He says:

> We at length know something concerning the beginnings of the great institution of Property in Land. The collective ownership of the soil by groups of men either in fact united by blood-relationship, or believing or assuming that they are so united, is now entitled to take rank as an ascertained primitive phenomenon, once universally characterizing those communities of mankind between whose civilization and our own there is any distinct connection or analogy.[1]

This earliest phase stands out distinct from what Maine terms "that comparatively modern combination of primitive and Roman law which we call feudalism."[2] He is, of course, referring to European feudalism, which was beginning to take effect soon after the fall of the Western Empire. We know now that every society which has emerged from the group stage passes through, as Mexico and Peru and many empires in the South Pacific passed through, a stage of feudalism on the way to despotism or so-called representative government or both.

[1] P. 1. [2] P. 5.

Maine is lecturing on the Irish Brehon law, "the oldest institutions of the portion of the human race to which we belong,"[1] and he exposes to full view the archaic but comely vestiges of Irish tribal law which foreran the coming of Irish and Norman feudalism. He makes the great theme yield thoughts to console us in our present discontent. He writes:

> Even if the worst that has been said by Englishmen of the Brehon law down to our own day were true, we might console ourselves by turning our eyes to spheres of inquiry fuller of immediate promise to the world than ours, and by observing how much of the wealth of modern thought has been obtained from the dross which earlier generations had rejected. Meanwhile, happily, it is a distinct property of the Comparative Method of investigation to abate national prejudices. I myself believe that the government of India by the English has been rendered appreciably easier by the discoveries which have brought home to the educated of both races the common Aryan parentage of Englishman and Hindoo. Similarly I am not afraid to anticipate that there will some day be more hesitation in repeating the invectives of Spenser and Davis, when it is once clearly understood that the "lewd" institutions of the Irish were virtually the same institutions as those out of which the "just and honourable law" of England grew.[2]

The elegance of phrasing, the fruitful thought, the delicate irony, the superb pathos, and the great statesmanship of this passage must strike the imagination of all. The scientist who knows that the dust-heaps and dross from the Cornish tin-mines have given the world the rarest metals, which we thought were only existent in the sun itself, will appreciate what Maine (who did not know these things) means when he says, "How much of the wealth of modern thought has been obtained from the dross which earlier generations had rejected." The delicate irony which contrasts the "lewd" and "unreasonable" customary law of Ireland, denounced in the seventeenth century by Sir John Davis, with the "just and honourable law" of England; the pathos which by implication contrasts the views of Edmund Spenser, the poet of eternal beauty, with Edmund Spenser, the Irish administrator, who, though discerning, as his great intellect could not fail to discern, some greatness in the Brehon laws, yet condemned them "in many things repugning quite both to God's law and man's": irony

[1] P. 11. [2] Pp. 19–20.

and pathos could go no further in such a passage, but Maine turns to statesmanship, and says, quite frankly and simply, that it is the distinct property of the comparative method of investigation to abate national prejudices, and points to India as an example—the India that draws our gravest thoughts to-day—and to Ireland. That was three years before the conversion of Mr Gladstone. Curiously enough, at this very hour there is a movement among English lawyers to co-operate with the Continental jurists in making comparative law a force tendency for righteousness, an effort, as Maine says, "to abate national prejudices." English and Continental lawyers met at The Hague in August 1932 for this very purpose, and that meeting will not be the least of the fruits that the world is gathering from the Tree of Life that Henry Maine planted.

I dare not quote further, not even the great passage in which Maine destroys, as I think, Austin with his own weapons. I have said enough to indicate the present position of Maine in the region of juridical and historical thought. I am disinclined to say anything of his successes in the region of evolving jurisprudence, partly because they are many and are frequently speaking for themselves. It was necessary to trace in detail the predecessors of Maine in order to show the bedrock on which he stands.

I might well discourse at length of the work of the late Professor Maitland and Sir Frederick Pollock; of workers across the Atlantic such as Holmes and Roscoe Pound; or of men like Bryce. I must mention Vinogradoff, because not only has he worked directly and immensely and fruitfully on the problems of evolving jurisprudence, but he has created a noble school of workers on the same subject, of whom, perhaps, Miss Eleanor Lodge and Professor de Zulueta are the most prominent living examples. But the names of the workers in two worlds are legion, and I want to say one word in conclusion as to the significance of their labours to our sad but dogged post-War world.

The purpose of jurisprudence is useless unless it teaches us how to live, since that is its object. If Law is separated from the Humanities, if Law does not lead to a region where peace and not war is the objective of nations, does not lead to that *Humanitas* of which the great Romans dreamed, if Law has not the meaning which Dante put into the lips of the great lawgiver in one immortal line—

Cæsar I was, and am Justinian

—then the history of jurisprudence will have failed in its purpose. In many ways we are savages still, despite all our knowledge. We can measure the universe and weigh the stars in their courses; we can apply history to biology and trace our ascent from God's first germ; we can review the march of law from man's first instinctive striving for social peace. We have knowledge, but not discipline. Mark Pattison in 1855, when Maine had just resigned his chair of law at Cambridge, wrote of true learning, "It is not a knowledge but a discipline that is required."[1] Law and the Humanities cannot be separated. The study of the growth of discipline is the business of the historical jurist, and in that business Maine, who was first and foremost a Humanist, blazed a way that we all must follow.

J. E. G. de Montmorency

[1] *Essays*, vol. i, p. 425.

BOOK LIST

A. Primary Authorities

Maine, Sir Henry S.: *The Conception of Sovereignty and its Importance in International Law.* 1858. (The Juridical Society, 1855.)
—— *Ancient Law.* 1861.
—— *Village Communities.* 1871.
—— *Early History of Institutions.* 1875.
—— *Dissertations on Early Law and Custom.* 1883.
—— *Popular Government.* 1885.
—— *International Law.* 1888. (Whewell Lectures, 1887.)

B. Secondary Authorities

Duff, Sir M. E. Grant: *Sir Henry Maine: a Brief Memoir of his Life.* 1892.
Pollock, Sir F.: Introduction and Notes to Maine's *Ancient Law.* 1930.
Vinogradoff, P.: *The Teaching of Sir Henry Maine.* 1904.

The *Dictionary of National Biography* contains a useful list of Maine's publications, but it omits the very brilliant essay of 1855 on the conception of sovereignty, in which the jurist prophesies the end of Negro slavery in America. In this essay Maine strongly compliments Austin on his famous treatise.

V

ALEXIS DE TOCQUEVILLE AND DEMOCRACY

WHO does not know Tocqueville cannot understand liberalism. A case of unanswerable power could, I think, be made out for the view that he and Lord Acton were the essential liberals of the nineteenth century. For liberalism is the expression less of a creed than of a temperament. It implies a passion for liberty; and that the passion may be compelling it requires a power to be tolerant, even sceptical, about opinions and tendencies you hold to be dangerous, which is one of the rarest of human qualities. To be conscientious about facts which tell against your desire, to be calm and detached in the presence of events by which, within yourself, you are deeply moved, to admit the inevitability of change and, as a consequence, the impermanence of all matters of social constitution, to recognise that history gives no sanction to any dogmas which claim an absolute value—these, I venture to think, are of the very heart of the liberal temper. Acton and Tocqueville seem to me to have embodied these qualities with a fullness to which no other thinkers of that age can pretend.

The significance of Tocqueville as an observer, indeed, is likely to seem greater rather than less as the years go by. His calm and reflective insight saw with remarkable profundity into the secret of his time. He was the first writer of the nineteenth century able to survey the phenomena of democracy, not, indeed, without passion—beneath the gravity of his sentences any careful reader can detect his depth of emotion—but with something of the detachment that a physicist brings to the study of atomic structure. Compare the inferences he drew from his American voyage with those of any contemporary traveller; set his *Ancien Régime* alongside the narratives of Thiers or Mignet, Quinet or Louis Blanc, and the penetrating quality of his vision becomes at once apparent.

With the single exception of Marx, he seems to me to have seen more profoundly the inevitable consequences of the French Revolution as they met the results of industrialisation than any other thinker of the period.

To understand his work, even more, to appreciate its quality, we must grasp for a moment the character of the man himself. He was an aristocrat who recognised that the day of his order was done. He was an aristocrat who realised that the new forces threatened at every turn the qualities in life he most deeply cherished. Sensitive, timid, indifferent to public applause, proud, but unwilling to stoop to conquer the objects of his ambition, made for reflective solitude, yet with a constant yearning to play his part on the theatre of great events, a man of the study who longed to be the leader of a party, yet wholly devoid of all the qualities by which a man can grow into political leadership, it was his fate to watch, with a full understanding, events he did not know how to control. He could see their import; he could not communicate his insight nor lead men to act upon it in the world of affairs. He who longed to be an actor in the drama was given only those qualities which make the supreme commentator upon the play. So that there is a note of sadness, of contempt even, in all his public utterances; they are the work of one who is agitated by his inability to influence a policy he feels he understands more deeply than his fellows. He lacked altogether the essence of the leader's art—the faculty of giving oneself. He was never of the crowd, but always aloof from it. His temperament drove him to reflection instead of action, to the obligation to analyse instead of the capacity to convince. He lacked altogether that joy in taking decisions, that ardour for combat, that art of clothing general truths with the pungent sense of direct immediacy, without which no politician can lead a party. He could be positive enough about the direction of an era; he had nothing of the politician's gift for being positive about the direction decisions must take in the next fortnight. He could propound a philosophy; he did not know how to recite a creed.

I do not mean to imply that Tocqueville was not highly regarded. He was a magistrate held in affectionate respect. For a dozen years he was a deputy whose speeches were invariably treated as significant pronouncements. For a few brief months he was Foreign Minister under Louis Napoleon, despite his passionate hostility to that tragic comedian. Each of his books was regarded as a European event; he made something of the sensation with them that Montesquieu had made with the *Esprit des lois* nearly a century before. He was the centre of a little group of friends, all of them men far out of the common run, who looked upon him with something of the disciple's reverence for the master of genius. Not least, to men like John Stuart Mill and Nassau Senior he seemed of little less than prophetic stature. The world he cared for recognised to the full his devotion, his disinterestedness, his cold grandeur of soul, his zeal for truth. But I cannot explain a certain remote disdain in Tocqueville except by the assumption that the recognition he received, great though it was, was not the recognition he wanted; that the career upon which his heart was set was the career for which, within himself, he knew himself to be unfitted. It would not be true to say that he regarded himself as a failure, for he knew—how could he help knowing?—the significance of his books. But it is, I think, true to say that he would have forgone gladly the glory they achieved for Guizot's chance, or Thiers', of adjusting principle to action. The political philosopher yearned to play the statesman; and something of the melancholy realisation that the part of each is different accounts for not a little of the temper in which his books are written. He never reconciled himself to the recognition that the value of the thinker depends upon his ability to take long-term views. Though he looked upon humanity from an eminence, it is clear that his heart was always in the dusty conflict of the arena, whose fortunes he yearned to control.

II

I cannot pretend here to summarise the *Democracy in America*. I can seek only to make some general remarks about it, and to draw attention to some of the more salient principles it lays down. And the first thing one is tempted to say is that the book is not really about America at all. The New World has merely served to provide Tocqueville with materials through which to emphasise the truth of a message he had seen already in the experience of the Old. The book itself, his own journals and correspondence, show us that, in fact, his acquaintance with the United States in general was rather superficial, with its governmental system particularly so. What he saw there, what interested him in its life, was the spectacle of a society freed from the control of an aristocracy. He sought, in terms of a profound observation of the French scene, to deduce from the American condition the lessons of the French Revolution.

The abrogation of privilege, he argued, means an inevitable trend to an equal society. The consequences of this change are momentous. They mean rapid innovation, because the barriers of status are withdrawn. They mean a constant instability of social structure, since the absence of privilege will mean a decreased authority for established families. A democratic society will not, like its predecessors, have natural leaders to whom a public career will remain the highest obligation. Men will have to battle for political position; their power will be built upon the interests they can persuade to support them rather than the principles they seek to fulfil. The abrogation of privilege, indeed, may make it difficult for superior men to emerge, for the passion for equality tends to make men look for identity rather than difference of outlook. They are jealous of difference because it destroys equality; they desire to see the society made in terms of the greatest common measure. The leaders most likely to emerge are those who can best interpret the common mind to itself, rather than the older type who will seek, from the very elevation of their position, to draw ordinary men to their own level.

For equality confers power upon public opinion; and the rule of public opinion is the rule of the commonplace. It may be honourable, virtuous, disinterested; but it is all these things in a petty way. It may avoid the vast errors of an aristocracy; it rarely attains the loftiness of its virtues. For the rule of public opinion is the rule of the man in the street. He is preoccupied with his own affairs. He has little leisure for contemplative analysis. He is so immersed in the daily routine that he cannot live upon the heights. His danger, indeed, is the cardinal danger that he may not know of the heights upon which to dwell. He has a system of values derived from his own petty experience; and he tends, inevitably, to make those values the method by which he judges all experience alien from his own. In such a society, therefore, the exceptional man is rarely understood, and seldom welcomed. His perceptions are so different that men repulse them as alien. The rule of the mass may mean more individualism, but it also means less individuality. More individualism because, when the barriers of privilege are down, there is a wider avenue upon which the energetic may march; but less individuality because, in such a society, the love of equality means an insistence upon conformity, and the condition of success is the willingness to accept the standards average men may impose.

There is a special reason for this. An equal society tends, from its very nature, to discover a plane of behaviour upon which identity of outlook is at its maximum. This plane is that of material welfare. That standard of progress is immediately and widely intelligible. Its appeal to a democracy is profound. Higher wages, better housing, shorter hours of labour—these are objects of ambition which every one can understand. They bring with them their own scheme of values. They make of material success a goddess. They abandon simplicity because ostentation, being the proof of success, is also the proof of virtue. And material welfare, as an ideal, transforms all social institutions into its own image; their development is conditioned by its demands. In a democratic society religion, foı instance, loses its unworldliness, and ceases to be a critic of material standards. It renounces that interference with the daily life of men which was its medieval habit, and becomes, instead, a way of escape from the hard facts of the practical world about it. Its priests declare their aloofness from politics; they offer consolation rather than counsel. They do not anathematise; they cease to become a militant order. They assume the colour of their environment, which transforms them into men who offer an avenue of relief to those who are fatigued by the energy of the struggle.

Much the same is true of the arts and sciences. It is untrue, Tocqueville argues, to say that democracy is the enemy of either. What it does is to change their direction for its own purposes. Science in an aristocracy is a search for the abstract principles of the universe; the arts are an attempt to discover ultimate principles of beauty which a small and wealthy class has the leisure to contemplate. But a democracy is not interested in abstractions. Aiming at material welfare, its effort is necessarily to extract from human ingenuity the maximum service it can render to this end. The observer will find, accordingly, that its emphasis is laid upon their practical character. Men seek for principle only as it issues into application. It is science as it gives the mastery of nature; science as it leads to invention which increases comfort; science as it minimises the cost of heavy toil, which is revered. Democracy is unlikely to produce men like Newton; but it will produce a hundred inventors who shape principle to useful ends.

So, also, with the arts. There is a greater audience for them, but the range of their understanding is smaller. More artists appear, but the merit of their production is diminished. The handicraftsman can rarely live in an equal society, as he could live in an aristocratic, by supplying the lofty taste of a few; he searches for means which will enable him to make more things more quickly. Inevitably, he becomes the ally of the machine; and the unique products of a past age are replaced by commodities which satisfy a general rather than a particular taste. Where an aristocracy demands the diamonds and pearls of nature, a democracy manufactures them. The rare becomes the commonplace; and it is the characteristic of the commonplace in art to replace what is profound by what is elegant and pretty. So in an aristocracy Raphael sought through his portraits of man to catch a glimpse of divinity; but David and his followers, depicting with wonderful fidelity the models before their eyes, did not seek to imagine anything beyond them. So, too, with literature. In a democratic society it will, in general, be the object of authors to attract rather than to convince. "Authors," wrote Tocqueville,

> will aim at rapidity of execution rather than perfection of detail. . . . There will be more wit than erudition, more imagination than profundity; and literary performances will bear marks of an untutored and rude vigour of thought, frequently of great variety and singular fecundity. The objects of authors will be to astonish rather than to please, to stir the passions more than to charm the taste.

A democracy, in a word, wants a literature suited to its leisure hours; and because that is where material success is to be secured the bent of the writer will be turned in that direction.

This is, I hope, a fair summary of what Tocqueville considered the moral ethics of democracy. Clearly enough, its inherent principle is the setting of standards in terms of the wants of the mass. It is clear enough that not a little of his view is shaped by a half-conscious nostalgia for an aristocratic system. He yields to the inevitability of a democracy without comfort in the values it will create. And this hesitation is apparent even more decisively when he discusses the economic and political aspects of its future. Because a democracy is built upon the elevation of material welfare it naturally tends to an emphasis upon the importance of commerce. In a society where the barriers of privilege have been broken down the manufacturer is king; and because equality, on the horizons he can foresee, is limited to the political sphere its consequences are of a character which fill him with grim foreboding.

In the political sphere it leads to centralisation. The people is sovereign, and the more power it possesses in its organised expression the more sense it has that its sovereignty is real. The tendency, therefore, of every democracy is a concentration of authority in the central government. Men come to regard it as a Providence to the capacities of which they set no limits. The more it does on their behalf the greater the material welfare each believes himself to possess; the wider the scope of its activities the less the distance between citizen and citizen. The tendency is a dangerous one. It enervates the society by making men look rather to the exertions of Government than to their own for their improvement. It weakens the sense of civic responsibility by persuading them that a Government's interests are naturally coincident with their own. It diminishes the interest in public affairs by a continual diminution in the numbers of those who participate in public business. The result is an *étatisme* fatal to the spirit of liberty and independence. From a citizen the individual is transformed into the mere recipient of orders from the administration. His way of life is increasingly regulated for him. The range of pressure and restraint to which he is subjected becomes so wide and so profound that he is deprived of the chance to experiment with himself. The variety of life is stifled; his will is softened and bent; he and his fellows are so compressed and stupefied that they are "reduced to be nothing better than a flock of timid and industrious animals, of which the Government is the shepherd." Liberty, in a word, is sacrificed to the demand for equality; and it is the tragedy of a democratic society that the masses are persuaded to accept the erosion of individuality by the administration as a benefit for which they should be grateful.

Nor is this all. In the establishment of political democracy there is a contingent contradiction which men too rarely perceive. The field is open to the talents; the barriers of privilege have been withdrawn. But because democracy makes material comfort its ideal the field in which talent finds the main outlet for its energy is commerce; and the opportunities afforded there lead rapidly to great inequalities of fortune. In the circumstances of large-scale manufacture these have an impact different from their effect in an aristocracy. In the latter inequalities are the product of an hereditary condition. Ranks and classes are stable; man and master are bound together by reciprocal ties softened by a shared experience to which long tradition lends glamour and even beauty. In an industrial society the relationship is different. The operative in the factory may have contact with his master; he has no sense of partnership with him. Their lives are not passed in common; they are linked together by a mere cash nexus from which no permanent relations can be born. More, such a society is much less stable, so much more subject to rapid and profound fluctuation, that the interests of worker and master can never achieve an organic harmony.

Manufactures, in brief, develop an aristocracy of wealth without social or political function. The worker has been taught that in the political field he is his master's equal; in the industrial his patent inferiority is brought home to him every day. And, since he learns from the effect of centralisation that he should use his political power to increase his material welfare, it is inevitable that he should ask himself why the equality of political life should not be paralleled by an equality in the economic field. The contrast of his position as a citizen with his subordination as a worker arouses in him a sense of indignation and envy. He begins to demand that legislation shall equalise the results of the industrial process; and when he is told that the rights of property stand in the way he sees no reason why the rights of property, also, should not be the subject of control by popular sovereignty.

Tocqueville's foresight in this regard seems to me one of the major prophecies of the nineteenth century. His sense that an individualistic economy and a political democracy are incompatible has been justified by all subsequent history. His own experience, after 1840, only confirmed the tenacity with which he held this view, and when, after the grim days of 1848, he sat down to write his final reflections upon his age and its outcome it was to this antithesis that his mind most constantly returned. There is a passage in the *Recollections* so remarkable in its prescience, so profound in its insight, that it is, I venture to think, worth quoting to you at some little length. I shall not comment upon it; the brilliance of the analysis seems to me to carry with it its own quite final commentary.

Tocqueville explains that the socialist element in the Revolution of 1848 ought not to have surprised the observer.

> Had it not long been perceived that the people had continually been improving and raising its condition, that its importance, its education, its desires, its power, had been constantly increasing? Its prosperity had also grown greater, but less rapidly, and was approaching the limit which it hardly ever passes in old societies, where there are many men and but few places. How should the poor and humbler, and yet powerful classes not have dreamed of issuing from their poverty and inferiority by means of their power, especially in an epoch when our view into another world has become dimmer, and the miseries of this world become more visible and seem more intolerable? They had been working to this end for the last sixty years. The people had first endeavoured to keep itself by changing every political institution, but after each change it found that its lot was in no way improved, or was only improving with a slowness quite incompatible with the eagerness of its desire. Inevitably, it must sooner or later discover that that which held it fixed in its position was not the constitution of the Government, but the unalterable laws that constitute society itself; and it was natural that it should be brought to ask itself if it had not both the power and the right to alter those laws, as it had altered all the rest. And to speak more especially of property, which is, as it

were, the foundation of our social order—all the privileges which covered it and which, so to speak, concealed the privilege of property, having been destroyed, and the latter remaining the principal obstacle to equality among men, and appearing to be the only sign of inequality —was it not necessary, I will not say that it should be abolished in its turn, but at least that the thought of abolishing it should occur to the minds of those who did not enjoy it? . . . Will socialism remain buried in the disdain with which the socialists of 1848 are so justly covered? I put the question without making any reply. I do not doubt that the laws concerning the constitution of our modern society will in the long run undergo modification; that they have already done so in many of their principal parts. But will they ever be destroyed and replaced by others? It seems to me impracticable. I say no more, because the more I study the former condition of the world, and see the world of our own day in greater detail, the more I consider the prodigious variety to be met with, not only in laws, but in the principles of law, the more I am tempted to believe that what we call necessary institutions are often no more than institutions to which we have grown accustomed, and that in matters of social constitution the field of possibilities is much more extensive than men living in their various societies are ready to imagine.[1]

III

It was said of *Democracy in America* by no less a judge than Royer-Collard that there had been nothing like it since Montesquieu; and John Stuart Mill did little more than provide a magistral proof of that lapidary verdict. When the tyranny of Napoleon III drove Tocqueville once more into private life he turned from America to the French Revolution, but with a purpose unchanged. " To explain to men how to escape tyranny," he wrote to a friend, " that is the idea of both my books. To work in this sense is a holy mission for which one should spare neither money, time, nor life." Lord Acton has judged the result of his effort with an authority to which no other writer can pretend. " Of all writers," he remarked, " he is the most widely acceptable, and the hardest to find fault with. He is always wise, always right, and as just as Aristides."[2]

[1] *Recollections* (English translation), p. 99.
[2] *Lectures on the French Revolution*, p. 357.

Lord Acton wrote as a liberal whose own sympathies were fully with Tocqueville's thesis. Let us seek for a moment to summarise the purpose of the book. On the basis of a fairly wide study of provincial archives he sought to trace the transformation of the *ancien régime* into the Revolution. What he demonstrated was the gradual character of the transition. Ideas, principles, hopes, institutions, underwent no startling change. One arbitrary system was exchanged for another. The aristocracy deserved to lose its privileges, because, by misusing them, it made a revolution inevitable. But the root of the change was less the depth of the oppression than the fact that improvement made its burden seem less tolerable. Its tragedy was the acceptance by the new epoch of all the centralising tendencies of the old. Thereby, like its predecessor, it chose equality in subjection instead of liberty. But to establish equality by the abrogation of privilege it had to pass through a period of anarchy; and, like its predecessor, it found that only despotism can stem those forces of disorder which anarchy lets loose. It began with generous hopes; it ended by making of Frenchmen the soldiers of Napoleon. It made the laws equal, the administration uniform, the power centripetal; but to attain these things it sacrificed local liberty and civic individuality. The citizen became *l'administré*.

For Tocqueville, therefore, the Revolution did no more than complete the structure of the *ancien régime*. The latter had sought to destroy feudalism by making the Crown the equal master of all its subjects; it succeeded, but only at the price of maintaining the feudal privileges of nobility and clergy. To do so it destroyed local independence—that intermediate power in society which Tocqueville held to be the key of freedom—and transformed the aristocracy from an order which enjoyed privilege in return for function into a leisured and idle caste. The Revolution abolished the privilege, and replaced the Crown by the nation itself. But so much had the privilege been hated that men mistook the attainment of equality for the victory of freedom. Feudalism was destroyed, but its place was taken by a new system of authority more powerful and more brutal than the old.

It was said by Scherer of Tocqueville that his history did for the Revolution what Lyell had done for geology; he substituted evolution for catastrophe. In a sense that is true; and this aspect of his work has marvellously stood the test of time. Indeed, it may be doubted whether any great historical work, Gibbon apart, has been less materially altered by subsequent research. But what remains outstanding in Tocqueville as an historian is the intensity of feeling his work displays. Behind the assumption of calm objectivity it is not difficult to discover the real passion by which it is informed. It is not that he condemns the Revolution even while he understands it; no one has ever written of the Revolution, one way or another, in the way in which a naturalist can describe his specimens. It is rather that, perhaps despite himself, he could not avoid what he intended to be dispassionate science transforming itself into an exalted defence of liberalism. The real clue to his book is its sadness. There, as always, he is an aristocrat driven to accept defeat because he recognised that his order had proved unworthy of its principles. There, as always also, he recognises the inevitability of a new social system even while he is convinced that its results are bound to be disastrous. The history, as it were, is really the prelude to the *Democracy in America*, even though the latter is earlier in date. Like all true liberals, the essence of his creed is unchanging. It is an insistence on the right of the individual at all costs to affirm his own essence, a sad indignation at those implications of social life which, by their nature, subordinate the individual to the mass. It was, I think, John Stuart Mill who said of him that he mistook the consequences of civilisation for the principles of democracy. I should not express the difficulty quite in that way. But I should argue that, both as observer and as historian, Tocqueville is so essentially the aristocrat that he is unable to accept without pain the collectivist discipline involved in societies of the modern scale. He wanted a degree of uniqueness for men of generous ability, such as himself, that is only capable of purchase upon terms which demand the sacrifice of ordinary humanity to a privileged order. He wanted it; but he knew it to be impossible. Hence, as I think, the pervasive and sombre warning that is the constant undercurrent of all his speculation.

IV

It is said that in our own day Tocqueville is but little read. The history apart, most of his works are out of print, and, in England, difficult to procure. He remains a venerated figure; but, like his own master, Montesquieu, the dust on the shelves which contain his works is rarely disturbed. The generation to which he seemed a prophet, the generation of Scherer, Taine, Boutmy, and Prévost-Paradol, has left no successors. Partly, no doubt, the reason for this oblivion lies in the mental climate of our epoch. Liberalism is essentially an aristocratic creed, and a period of insecurity is unfavourable to its emergence. Tolerance, individuality, freedom—these need the atmosphere of peace and economic well-being if they are to be welcomed as virtues by classes which contest fiercely for the seat of political power.

Yet I take the essence of Tocqueville's teaching to be even more vital for our day than it was for his own. He was right in his perception that the union of political equality and economic inequality is an unhappy one. It enthrones, as he saw, material well-being as the ideal; it shapes all principles to that single end. Out of it, as he insisted, there emerges a conflict certainly as profound, and probably more decisive, than that which enthroned the middle class in power in 1789. The real lesson of his book is the argument that once a people has set its foot on the path of equality in the realm of material well-being there is no logical end to its journey until it has abolished significant differences within that realm. He saw that the privileges of property are an inherent contradiction of popular sovereignty, and that they involve either surrender by their possessors or challenge by those excluded from them. He realised that the natural conclusion of popular sovereignty is the deliberate use of the legislative power to mitigate the sharp differences between men's economic position. A democratic and centralised society comes, sooner or later, to mean the social service State.

But, with a foresight that seems to me remarkable, he saw also that there is a point in the history of that State where its development is either halted or slows down. Some failure in the continuity of economic expansion makes taxation of the rich for the benefit of the poor a more difficult, perhaps even an impossible, adventure. At that point, as he argued, the very progress of the poor in well-being makes them, as in 1789, more resentful of the privileges of the rich than they were in an earlier period when their own advantages were smaller. Before they were prepared to accept privilege on the condition that their own position was consistently improved; now they are led to challenge the very basis of privilege itself. Of the outcome of this challenge, of its wisdom even, the passage I have ventured to quote at length shows that Tocqueville remained uncertain. That it would be made he was clearly confident; and it would be an interesting task to trace the ways in which, in the last generation, it has been so remarkably fulfilled.

I must end, however, on a different note. If I had to find a pedigree for the ideas Tocqueville represents the line of his intellectual ancestry would, I think, be fairly clear. His roots are in Royer-Collard and the Doctrinaires of the Restoration, and, through them, he goes back to Burke, and particularly to that side of Burke which Montesquieu so profoundly shaped. It is, I believe, curious that few of the commentators on Tocqueville have noticed the relation between the *Reflections on the French Revolution* and the *Democracy in America*. The one, no doubt, is conceived in passion, the other in gravity; the one, also, is a pamphlet fighting for victory while there is still time, the other a pamphlet registering with sadness a defeat. But, at bottom, different as they were in temperament, I think Burke and Tocqueville would have agreed in basic desires. A disposition to preserve and an ability to improve would have been, with each, the essential standard of a statesman.

There is another element in Tocqueville to which it is worth while to draw attention. Few men have seen more clearly how economic systems produce their own schemes of values, or how profoundly these control the thoughts and ideals of men. However different their ways of expression, however antagonistic the purposes they served, Tocqueville would, I suspect, have subscribed to a good deal of what we call the Marxian interpretation of history. Many of his conclusions bear a striking resemblance to those of *The Communist*

Manifesto; with, of course, the important difference that what for Marx represented victory for Tocqueville represented defeat. But Tocqueville saw hardly less clearly than Marx the disharmony of interest between masters and men in a capitalist democracy. He underlined hardly less emphatically its probable issue in revolution. He lacked, indeed, that positive—dare I say Utopian?—element in Marx which made the latter welcome the advent of that revolution as the maker of a society in which freedom and equality were reconciled; he was insistent that revolution can never be the parent of freedom. He was too sceptical to believe that a change in the system of production can effect a final improvement in the relations of men. Like Burke, there is, at the foundations of his being, an element of religious mysticism which made him find in a supernatural ideology the only ultimately effective canons of right conduct in men. And there is, of course, the final difference between them, that Marx's interest was in the massed legions of humanity, where Tocqueville's passion is always for a solitary figure, incapable of assimilation by the herd, devoted to high thoughts upon a lonely eminence. There is a fascinating sense in which the whole effort of his thought was to discover the secret of a social order in which there was scope for the manner of man he himself was. Yet that difference must not be allowed to conceal an important resemblance between thinkers so wholly alien in objective.

"Our business," wrote Odilon Barrot to Tocqueville in 1842,

> is somehow to make democracy capable of governing and of being governed; as it is to-day it is rather a great instrument of revolution and of despotism. . . . It would be a great task, worthy of your powers, to seek to change this condition; it would be even worth the devotion of all your life.

Tocqueville, I think, could claim with justice that he had responded with ardour to his friend's appeal. For from his earliest days it was his own ambition. As a young man he had written: "I do not know any way of life more honourable or more attractive than to write with such honesty about the great truths that one's name becomes known to the civilised world. I would wish, if only in a small degree, to serve the great cause."

He may claim to have realised it. None of those who inherited directly the results of 1789 saw more clearly the strength and weakness of its implications; none, certainly, strove more earnestly or more disinterestedly to make them of service to his contemporaries. He was always loyal, and invariably scrupulous. He put into the work he did all the energies of a remarkable mind and a generous heart. The quality of his effort dignified the great intellectual tradition whose boundaries he so notably enlarged.

HAROLD J. LASKI

BOOK LIST

A. PRIMARY AUTHORITIES

DE TOCQUEVILLE, ALEXIS: *Œuvres*, edited by G. Beaumont. 9 vols. Paris, 1863.

—— *Souvenirs*. 2 vols. Paris, 1893.

ANON.: *Memoir, etc., of A. de Tocqueville*. 2 vols. Boston, 1862. (This contains much material not in the French edition of the collected works.)

B. SECONDARY AUTHORITIES

BRYCE, J.: *Studies in History and Jurisprudence*, Essay VI. London, 1901.

D'EICHTHAL, G.: *Tocqueville et la démocratie libérale*. 1894.

FAGUET, E.: *Politiques et moralistes*, 3rd series. Paris, n.d.

MARCEL, P.: *Essai sur Tocqueville*. Paris, 1913.

MILL, J. S.: *Dissertations and Discussions*, vol. iii. London, 1867.

RUGGIERO, G.: *History of European Liberalism*. Oxford, 1927.

SAINTE-BEUVE, C. A.: *Causeries du Lundi*, vol. xv. Paris, n.d.

SOLTAU, R. H.: *French Political Thought in the Nineteenth Century*. New Haven, 1931

VI

KARL MARX AND SOCIAL PHILOSOPHY

KARL MARX was born at Trèves, in Germany, on May 5, 1818, three years after the Treaty of Vienna had seemed to stabilise the continent of Europe on a basis of semi-feudalism, and within a year of the publication of Sismondi's attack on the new industrialism and of the socialist critiques of Saint-Simon and Robert Owen. He was destined to revive the doctrines of eighteenth-century communism and to transplant them in the soil of the new institutions of the industrialist epoch. He was, moreover, to seek a new justification for the communist ideal by making it the pivot of a great philosophical system, if not as universal as that of Hegel, from which it was derived, more urgent and influential than any other offshoot of that last and most fertile of philosophies. Almost as a by-product of this activity, he created the beginnings of a scientific outlook in social studies. But his main work was to rehabilitate the intellectual defence of the revolutionary method in politics. He has given his name to a social revolution of incalculable significance, which aims at transforming the most tenacious of the social institutions we have inherited from the remote past, in conformity with the secular aspiration towards human equality.

The chief events in the life of Karl Marx are well known. His father, a middle-class Jewish lawyer professing the Christian faith, sent him to the universities of Bonn and Berlin. He took his doctorate in the latter place in 1841. Owing to his heterodox philosophical opinions—he was already a Left Hegelian—he could not realise his ambition of teaching in a university, and entered the world of radical journalism instead. In 1843 he both married and became a socialist. He went to Paris immediately afterwards, where he mixed with the German radicals and with French socialists like Proudhon. Here he wrote his first work, *An Intro-*

duction to the Criticism of Hegel's Philosophy of Rights (1844). He fell more and more under the influence of communist theory, particularly those elements which emphasised the *rôle* of the working-class movement, and in 1844 began his friendship with Friedrich Engels,[1] which was lifelong, affectionate, and fruitful.

In 1845 he left Paris with the expelled German radicals and went to Brussels, where he studied economics and economic history and wrote *The Holy Family* (1845) and *The Poverty of Philosophy* (1847), a reply to Proudhon's *Philosophy of Poverty*. He was instrumental in reshaping the policy of the Federation of the Just, a semi-secret communist society, and wrote for it *The Communist Manifesto*. This was in January 1848. Next month the revolutions broke out, and Marx took part in the struggle in the Rhineland, engaging in ardent journalistic warfare. On its failure he returned to Paris, but was soon expelled, and came to London in 1849, where he resided until his death. After ten years of bitter poverty he was able to lead a fairly comfortable exile, mainly owing to the bounty of Engels. He began work on *Capital*, whose great design his health and energy did not allow him to complete. He threw himself with great fervour into the work of the First International, which he induced for a time to accept his views of socialist strategy. But in 1871 the failure of the Paris Commune, combined with the attempt of Bakunin and the anarchists to capture control, led to its rapid decline. The effort exhausted Marx, although he wrote a

[1] Engels (1820–95), the son of a rich manufacturer of Barmen, had experience of English factory conditions and of the Chartist movement. Already he had written *The Condition of the Working Classes in England in 1844* and accumulated a library of works on economics and English Blue Books. Like Marx, he was a Left Hegelian and a socialist. After his meeting with Marx he devoted himself almost entirely to the work of expounding and illustrating Marx's characteristic doctrines and of persuading German socialists of the significance of truly revolutionary action. He collaborated with Marx in *The Holy Family* and *The Poverty of Philosophy*, wrote the first (and very inferior) draft of *The Communist Manifesto*, and assisted him in his unfinished philosophical studies—*e.g.*, in *The Theses to Feuerbach* (1845). Marx in turn contributed the chapter on the history of political economy to Engels' *Anti-Dühring* (1876), his most important work, which is probably the best place to find a systematic exposition of Marx's fundamental philosophy. Bolshevik writers generally regard Engels as being of almost equal importance to Marx in the foundation of revolutionary communism; but this is probably an exaggeration. See D. Ryazanoff, *Karl Marx and Friedrich Engels* (1927).

stirring defence of the Communards in *The Civil War in France* (1871). His other best-known works are *The Critique of Political Economy* (1859), *The Eighteenth Brumaire of Louis Buonaparte* (1852), and *The Letter on the Gotha Programme* (1875). The first volume of *Capital* was published in 1867, the remaining two by Engels after his death (1885 and 1894). Subsequent publications of his literary fragments include the important *Theories of Surplus Value*, edited by Karl Kautsky (1905–10).

Marx died in 1883, and lies buried in Highgate Cemetery.

II

The present time is a propitious one for the renewed study of the doctrines of Karl Marx, not only because of the world-crisis in the economic system, which bears at least a superficial resemblance to that predicted by Marx, but also because of the growth of cultural relations between Communist Russia, where Marxism is the official social philosophy, and a hostile but increasingly curious world, whose social thought appears to languish for want of a similar certitude. It was easy fifty years ago to dismiss most of Marx, as did the Austrian school, as mere dull, turgid nonsense appealing only to the ignorant and discontented, and to regard the task of refutation as more a political than an intellectual duty. But to-day the apparent partial conversion of economic historians and sociologists, even of biologists and psychologists, to one or other of Marx's views, combined with a new attitude in economic theory itself, fatal to the objections of the Austrians, makes it urgent to attempt a new assessment of the Marxian system.

The need exists, but the difficulties have multiplied. I do not refer merely to the unsystematic and often obscure and inconsistent nature of Marx's argument. The glosses made by Lenin and his followers upon the theories of Marx have enormously complicated the task of historical criticism. Marxism is a developing system, as Christianity was in the first century. It is not easy to decide in every case what can be legitimately attributed to the founder of the religion and what may be understood only by reference to a historical context which he could not possibly have foreseen. I have not hesitated to avail myself of the help provided by neo-Marxist thought where its application to later experience seems to throw light upon the fundamental concepts of Marx's own work. But I have endeavoured to remind myself that the historian of ideas cannot allow himself the luxury of reinterpreting a thinker's words in terms not logically incompatible with them when, in the light of his intellectual antecedents and social environment, actual and predictable, he could not reasonably have meant them.

The three great intellectual influences on Marx's thought were the philosophy of Hegel, French and English socialism, especially the materialist schools of eighteenth-century communism, and political economy. I have been compelled to omit from this article any account of Marx's economic doctrines, because an adequate consideration of them is beyond my powers.[1] I am here concerned only with the philosophical groundwork of his thought.

Psychologically, socialism came first with Marx. It cannot be derived directly from anything in the Hegelian system; it was a foreign importation into it. Had Marx remained a liberal he would have had no occasion to invent the doctrines of historical materialism and class war. Marx became a socialist during the summer and autumn of 1843, at the age of twenty-five, by a process of which we know hardly anything. It is difficult to attribute any influence to his racial ancestry, while his paternal class was typically liberal. There is no trace in Marx, save in a faint anti-Semitism, of any beliefs which might possess a compensatory value for a racial inferiority complex. An exile in the flesh, he was no wanderer in the spirit, but retained a faithful intellectual domicile in the national tradition of Germany. Still less can his philosophy be explained by his own social environmentalist doctrine, for

[1] The same applies to the economic prophecies contained in the three volumes of *Capital*. I am not sure enough of the orthodox view of their ineptitude to repeat it, nor have I the opportunity to controvert it. For discussions of the Labour Theory of Value the reader may be referred to E. von Böhm-Bawerk, *Karl Marx and the Close of his System* (translated 1898); to H. W. B. Joseph, *The Labour Theory of Value in Karl Marx* (1923); and to the eminently more profound treatment in A. D. Lindsay's *Karl Marx's "Capital"* (1925). An interesting rehabilitation, at least in part, of Marx's essential economic views is to be found in H. D. Dickinson, *Institutional Revenue* (1932), and M. H. Dobb, *Capitalist Enterprise and Social Progress* (1926), Part I.

he was born in a small market town in the economically backward Rhineland, and learned his socialism from the thinkers of a France which was but little more developed industrially.

Equality had a long pedigree, and had been recently a doctrine much discussed. Industrialism could be read about and seen approaching over all Europe. There was even something conservative about Marx's dislike of it; he wanted the existing form of it to be transformed as soon as possible, in the hope that its next stage would differ much less from his ideal—an ideal whose simplicity and orderliness resembled more what could be made out of the materials of the best of past civilisations than what could be inferred as proceeding from industrialism as Marx knew it. Might it not also be said that the intellectual, other things being equal, tends naturally to rationalist and perfectibility doctrine, to the ideal of a society simple, understandable, uncapricious and predictable, where a comparatively small number of generalisations will describe the behaviour of events, and where the chaos and complexity of actual living is subordinated to the interests of those who wish to regulate and reform it? Howsoever this may be, Marx's theoretical development seems certainly to illustrate the partial autonomy of the rationalising abilities of man.

From the very beginning, as his correspondence proves, Marx was influenced more by the communist tradition of eighteenth-century France than by the newer socialist schools of Saint-Simon, Enfantin, and Fourier, who were not essentially egalitarians, but rather humanitarian critics of a system which seemed inevitably to produce poverty and injustice. Marx's well-trained historical mind and his acquaintance with natural rights philosophy, together with his vivid sense of the continuity of intellectual tradition, made him regard socialism rather as the logical projection into the economic sphere of rational principles of human equality than as an *ad hoc* remedy for new abuses. Nowhere does Marx explicitly acknowledge his debt to this tradition. In *The Holy Family* [1] there are appreciative references to Babœuf as a

[1] *The Holy Family* has been reprinted in the *Nachlass*, vol. ii. See particularly p. 239 *et seq.*

founder of proletarian political strategy, and in *The Communist Manifesto* he is exempted from the criticism of early socialists, which is one of its most interesting features. In *The Holy Family*, too, we find Marx tracing the influence of Helvétius on the materialism of Gay and especially Dézamy, as well as on Bentham and Owen. It is probable that the formative influence on Marx's socialism came from Babœuf, Gay, and Dézamy, along with Cabet and Weitling, who became the models of the diluted philosophical socialism of men like Moses Hess, by whom it is known Marx was at first greatly impressed.

It was from this literary communism that Marx revolted even before going to Paris late in 1843. He criticised it strongly in *The Communist Manifesto* on the ground that in translating it into Hegelian phraseology the "philosophical socialists" had also emasculated it with their master's idealism and quietism, lacking any materialist, historical background or class impulse. Further, Engels, in the preface to the 1890 German edition of the *Manifesto*, explains that Marx and he, when founding the Communist League, chose the term "communist" rather than "socialist" to distinguish them from the Owenites and Fourierists, and to indicate their greater sympathy with Cabet and Weitling. It must be remembered, moreover, that Marx had begun as a politically minded radical, whose Hegelian training made him respectful of the claims of actual society and hostile to Utopianism. He often uses this term in a confused way, to refer sometimes to Utopia-builders and sometimes to non-materialist communists, although it was as the latter that he had appeared himself in his first published essay, *An Introduction to the Criticism of Hegel's Philosophy of Rights*.

A Hegelian dialectician, of course, could not be the exponent of a natural rights philosophy. From 1844 Marx seeks to defend communism as being historically inevitable,[1] and manifests no further interest in the formulation of an

[1] "When the proletariat proclaims the dissolution of the existing order of things it is merely announcing the secret of its own existence, for it is in itself the virtual dissolution of this order of things. When the proletariat desires the negation of private property it is merely elevating to a general principle of society what it already involuntarily embodies in itself as the negative product of society."—*Zur Kritik der Hegelschen Rechtsphilosophie*, reprinted in the *Gesamtausgabe*, vol. i, p. 620.

ethical indictment of capitalism, nor in the preparation of a bill of human rights, an attitude which was confirmed by his new materialistic doctrine. Few social reformers have been so little occupied with speculation as to the values wherein lies man's true happiness. The passage in his writings that seems best to illustrate his hopes comes in *The Letter on the Gotha Programme.* Criticising in 1875 Lassalle's faith in the right of every man to enjoy the whole fruits of his labour, Marx writes as follows:

> Equal right we indeed have here; but it is *still* a '*bourgeois* right,' which, like every 'right,' *presupposes inequality.* Every 'right' is an application of the *same* measure to *different* people, who as a matter of fact are not similar and are not equal one to another; and therefore 'equal right' is really a violation of equality and an injustice. . . . To avoid all this, 'rights,' instead of being equal, should be unequal. . . . In the highest phase of communist society, after the disappearance of the enslavement of man caused by his subjection to the principle of the division of labour; when, together with this, the opposition between brain and manual work will have disappeared; when labour will have ceased to be a mere means of supporting life, and will itself have become one of the first necessities of life; when, with the all-round development of the individual, the productive forces, too, will have grown to maturity, and all the forces of social wealth will be pouring an uninterrupted torrent—only then will it be possible wholly to pass beyond the narrow horizon of *bourgeois* laws, and only then will society be able to inscribe on its banner: "From each according to his ability; to each according to his needs."

The other elements in Marx's thought were philosophical and economic. He turned first to the task of entrenching it in the solid foundations of history and logic, and finally to that of providing it with the artillery of economic criticism.[1]

[1] If we examine closely Marx's reasoning in *Capital* we find that he always distinguished, though far from clearly, between two tendencies, both of which would lead to the downfall of capitalism. The first arises from the inherent contradictions of capitalism as a mode of production. The second consists of the conscious hostility, the rebellious pressure, of a proletariat enjoying parliamentary rights, organising in trade unions, and making demands upon capitalism which the latter could not possibly satisfy. To quote Marx's words, capitalism developed in a society "where the notion of human equality had already acquired the fixity of a popular prejudice" (vol. i, p. 29). The whole work of Marx is a striking tribute to the power of the secular movement towards an equalitarian ideal, the nature of which still awaits investigation. Marx himself implies that it is not merely an automatic result of economic changes.

KARL MARX

III

Marx's philosophical theories are generally known by such names as 'historical materialism,' 'dialectical materialism,' 'economic determinism,' and so on. But these descriptions are highly unsatisfactory. I wish to suggest, without adhering to obsolete modes of speech, that Marx in effect elaborated four doctrines. The first is a dialectical theory of moral and political action, designed to justify the right of revolution in terms different from those of the classical Protestant doctrine; the second constitutes an environmentalist social psychology; the third calls attention to the *rôle* of technical and economic changes in transforming the nature of society; and the fourth maintains the view that those group forces which he called "classes" played the determining part in the process of political history, and thus in the production of social thought.

Fundamental to Marx's entire philosophical system is his use of the dialectic of Hegel. The philosophers who followed Kant had begun to inquire whether the natural world did not exhibit the rule of that reason which Kant had shown to be the surest ground of human knowledge. The natural sciences were growing in achievement, and seemed to afford the required proof that reality was rational. It was Hegel's ambition to bring the content of this knowledge into closer relation with the rational methods by which man investigated the world. The use of the triadic formula first appears in the thought of Fichte and Schelling. Hegel adopted it and made it central to his system. The 'argument' of the external universe corresponds to argument among human beings designed to elicit new truths. The world of nature conformed to the pattern of logic; thus reality was rational.

Hegel named his metaphysic-cum-logic after the Greek art of discourse and rejoinder. In this dialectical procedure the assertion of propositions was followed by their criticism and contradiction. Out of the haze and dust of controversy a new view appeared, contained in neither of the contesting views, but comprehending and transcending them. This result appeared to the antagonists (or to their audience) as being more true than the previous propositions before they had undergone their trial by combat. The new view was recognised to be a new whole, not a mere sum of pre-existing parts, although constituted by them; it was qualitatively and not merely quantitatively different. Moreover—and this is significant—it had been reached by a process of opposition, of conflict, in which there was the possibility that brute force, the non-rational assertion of Nature, would importantly affect the decision. Hegel is thus in a sense the real founder of German *Machtphilosophie*, and Marx, who was the first to make the political deduction from it, the real father of that *Machtpolitik* whose authorship is often attributed to Nietzsche.

Hegel behaved as if he understood this logic to be the logic of natural science. Following Schelling, who had adduced the example of magnetism, electricity, and chemical substance in support of the triadic formula, he filled his later works with presumptive evidence of the universal validity of the sequence thesis, antithesis, synthesis. But this was not what interested the young Marx in 1844. As a socialist he attached more weight to his master's application of the dialectic to human history. Employed to exhibit a teleological rather than chronological order, Hegel's formula runs as follows: the Oriental, or despotic, stage of human development, characterised by a primitive governmental absolutism (corresponding in the cosmic triad to the antemundane rule of abstract universals, the Idea), is brought into intimate opposition with the classical stage, represented by the growth of unconscious group solidarity (the unconscious sphere of nature), out of which we pass into the synthetic stage of Germanism, in which men attain a life of full individuality within a rational state (the Spirit, enjoying a richer absolutism than the mere logical idea, by contact with art and society, science and religion).

It was on this model that Marx constructed his plan of human history, his argument that the development of external, 'material' events, largely economic in character, caused successive qualitative changes in social structure, his theory of class struggle, and his attempted demonstration of the irreconcilable contradictions inherent in capitalist society. It is on the validity of this method of proof that Engels and all later Marxists have staked the certitude of their political beliefs.[1]

A generalised theory of the process of social development cannot be found in Marx's writings. This is partly because of the absence in his time of ethnological and anthropological studies that would have necessitated a longer backward view, and partly owing to the lack of any social science with claims to explain exhaustively the nature of man's social behaviour, deriving from a basis of experimental knowledge predictions that might give a more accurate picture of the social future. It would also be true to say that Marx, no more than Hegel, shared the modern sceptical temper of science, with its perspective of eons of time, man being regarded as only in the beginning of his journey. The full repercussions of the Copernican revolution have been felt only in very recent years among other than physical thinkers. Marx was still anthropomorphic enough to believe that the millennium lay, not, indeed, in the present of the Prussian State, where Hegel placed it, but just round the corner in the communist society of to-morrow. There is abundant evidence that he held the view, common to the rationalist perfectionists of the previous century and to the anarchists of his own, that under communism not only would classes and divisions of economic power entirely disappear, but there would be no more scarcity or inequality or injustice in the world. In this connection his thought was teleological, and when he spoke of evolution he meant development (*Entwicklung*) to a goal already known or decided in advance to be desirable, not a verifiable and potentially modifiable generalisation of what had occurred under certain conditions, would hold in the future only under the same conditions, and had not, by itself, any ethical status at all.

Marx's exposition of the dialectical process, therefore, refers exclusively to that historic stage in which private property had made its appearance, and with it class division. A

[1] The readoption into the Marxian system of the Hegelian logic as applied to the interpretation of the natural sciences seems to have been the work not of Marx himself, but of Engels and Joseph Dietzgen. Marx in his old age greeted it with approval. The "back to Hegel" movement, so conspicuous a feature of Lenin's *Materialism and Empiriocriticism* and of contemporary Russian philosophy, is the tribute paid by communist apriorism to the cultural prestige enjoyed by science in the modern world.

reference in the third volume of *Capital* [1] and another in the preface to *The Critique of Political Economy* [2] are not genuinely capable of a wider application. Marx's historic triad may be reconstructed thus: The Thesis corresponds to the period of private property proper, where no exploitation exists and no classes. The labour theory of value obtains in its pristine purity; the form of society may be designated "classless individualism," [3] or what Marx and Engels, following the argument of Morgan's *Ancient Society*, later described confusedly as "primitive communism." The Antithesis is private capitalism, where labour is exploited and the distribution of property takes the form of wages and surplus value. It is the period of first feudal and then *bourgeois* rule and permanent class struggle, overt or concealed. There are two sides to the Antithesis, feudalism and the *bourgeoisie*, or the frank negation of the Thesis, on the one hand, and, on the other, the proletariat, or the negation of the negation, which must ultimately shatter the whole of the Antithesis and inaugurate the Synthesis. The character of the Synthesis is communism, where common ownership of capital prevails, classes have been abolished, and there is no exchange value, properly speaking, at all. Wealth is a social product, and is distributed according to the formula "From each according to his ability; to each according to his needs." [4]

[1] Pp. 420–421.—"In so far as the labour process operates merely between man and nature, its simple elements are common to every form of its social development."

[2] Pp. 11–13.—"In the social production of the means of life, human beings enter into definite and necessary relations which are independent of their will—production relations which correspond to a definite stage of the development of their productive forces. The totality of these production relations constitutes the economic structure of society, the real basis on which a legal and political superstructure arises, and to which definite forms of social consciousness correspond." Note the emphasis upon "legal and political." Later in the same passage Marx refers to property relationships as a "legal expression" for "productive relationships." He is not, in short, explicitly applying his concept to societies which have not yet achieved legal and political organisation.

[3] M. H. Dobb, *Capitalist Enterprise and Social Progress*, p. 143 *et seq.*

[4] Marx, like Ricardo, regarded the problem of distribution as the central theme of political economy. The final conquest of scarcity and the simplicity of communist distributive arrangements would thus render economics superfluous. Hence Marx refused to recognise that there was any "science" of economics at all, in the sense in which we speak of a science of physics or astronomy. According to him, economic categories and ideas merely reflected, described, and rationalised historical, transitory economic relations. There is an evident element of truth in this view (*cf.*

It is extraordinarily difficult to assess the merit of such forms of reasoning. The progress of natural science is now seen to depend upon a wholly different kind of logic from that of Hegel, a logic which may be described as exclusively quantitative or incremental, and which denies the final utility of qualitative concepts over an ever-increasing field of practical investigation. Scientific logic appears to be the ideally satisfactory method of investigating the world, since it not only provides us with a rational account of it, but enables us also to control the world, and with the world ourselves, in the way that most exactly, economically, and dependably ensures the fulfilment of our desires. Certain conditions are requisite for the success of this method. In addition to the prime condition of disinterestedness in the pursuit of explanation, the phenomena investigated must possess the character of experimental tractability, which in turn demands the prior existence of extensions to human sense-perception in the shape of scientific instruments, etc., whose properties are known and verifiable. It is this that enables us to formulate our descriptions of events in atomistic and mathematical terms, and thus to create artifacts which 'work' very finely for our purposes.

No one can pretend, I think, that every legitimate universe of discourse is equally amenable to these refined methods of observation and control. The question then arises of the validity of alternative types of logical inquiry in providing us with the best available rational account of other fields of knowledge. Is there such a realm in which the dialectical logic is most relevant?

Marx is undoubtedly in a strong position when he claims some utility for the Hegelian dialectic in the fields of social science and history. In spite of the progress of comparative and experimental methods in the social sciences, it is idle to assert that they are yet equal to the task of returning adequate answers to many of the chief questions raised, and to which it is imperative that we should have some provisional answers, in order to take action on matters that we cannot evade. This is clearly the case with social

L. Robbins, *An Essay on the Nature and Significance of Economic Science* (1932), p. 18, who, starting from very different social premisses, reaches a strikingly similar conclusion).

psychology, politics, and ethics. The prime condition of disinterestedness, of the absence of a wish to believe, of pragmatic neutrality, is progressively more difficult to satisfy the more vital are the problems involved. The second prerequisite of experimental tractability and refined verification is, by hypothesis, almost entirely lacking. History can never become an experimental discipline. (For that reason even economics, like physics and biology, seeks to dispense with the aid of historical studies.) The method predominantly employed in historical studies is the comparative, which helps to dispel erroneous interpretations and to narrow down competing hypotheses to a small number, perhaps even to two. But in the absence of the definitive experimental criterion our choice of which of the surviving hypotheses to adopt may often be determined by what we wish to believe true, in terms of national or class bias or temperamental or moral prejudice. This is the chief reason why history is the happy hunting-ground of the Marxist as of the *bourgeois* social theorist.

In the absence of a developed model of an atomistic social science there was little in the experience of mankind to suggest that its actions, past or present, would permit an explanation which stressed the element of continuity. When applied to human history the dialectic revealed the duplicate of its own internal relations—namely, the influence of conflict processes in determining change and development, and the emergence out of conflict of qualitatively different social levels. In a word, it implied a theory of the discontinuous evolution of human society. The agency of discontinuous social evolution which Hegel had found in the growth of 'spirit' Marx regarded as the rise and development of successive classes based on the possession of the prevailing sources of economic power.

So considered the dialectic constitutes a kind of governing idea which may set in motion activities designed to obtain evidence in support of it as a type of final, interpretative hypothesis. It does not seem to enable us to force or discover new observations of a particular kind. To a great extent Hegel simply imposed a ready-made scheme of interpretation upon already discovered data. What trustworthiness Marx's historical reasoning may be held to possess derives entirely from its conformity with the ordinary technique of such investigations. From the moment he started to illustrate his *a priori* principle he was obliged to rely upon the ordinary rules of evidence and on a logical method which owed much more to Aristotle than to Hegel. Marxists frequently make the mistake of imagining that their master learned the topography of the British Museum in a dialectical manner, or used exclusively the method of contradiction in pursuing his studies in economic history. The truth seems to be that the dialectic is not a logic of investigation at all, but only an *a priori* statement of what investigation shall reveal as to the structure of the universe.

In the second place, Marx had no wish to believe in a theory that postulated incremental change as the agency of the social or historical process. Marx saw in the dialectic a defence of a certain kind of social action. When he turned the dialectic of Hegel "right side up" he not only used it in a materialist instead of an idealist way; he used it in a revolutionary instead of a conservative way. "Up to the present," he wrote in *The Theses to Feuerbach*, "the philosophers have but interpreted the world; it is, however, necessary to change it."

The dialectic is essentially a statement about the way in which untrained or unrefined human perception is constituted. Distinctions of quality are the first to arise: discontinuity rather than continuity seems to be the pattern of our world. Whether we find continuity or discontinuity depends upon our knowledge of the field and upon our time perspective; the more we know of a thing, the longer the period over which we observe it, the more likely are we to discover incremental, as opposed to discontinuous, processes. It is most conspicuously when we come to *do* anything that the limitations of our known world become of critical importance. Scientific thought is co-operative, cumulative, relatively timeless; human life is isolated, brief, and urgent. We are not free to do anything that is logically conceivable, nor to wait until we have proved our intended action to be the best. We cannot wait until the long run, for in the long run we are all dead. An interpretation of history which emphasises the discontinuous character of the social process and the *rôle* of conflict in promoting sudden and qualitatively different changes in social organisation may thus produce a logic of action, a political morality which defends the use of conflict methods in social affairs, on the ground that revolution is the characteristic mode of human development.

As I see it, Marx was trying to maintain that there was no need to base a revolutionary philosophy upon a doctrine of natural rights. No 'rational' defence of the waging of revolutionary strife was possible or necessary; it was simply an inevitable part of our world. But it is easy enough to conclude that what he really succeeded in doing was to reinterpret and rehabilitate the doctrine of natural rights, basing it not on *a priori* ethics, but on an *a priori* philosophy of history. For absolutism in ethics he substituted the equally absolutist conception of historically inevitable goals of human action.

One other observation may be made. I have already suggested that Marx's notion of evolution is not identical with the standpoint of natural science.[1] He cannot justly be regarded as the Darwin of social philosophy. Nor is his theory of socialism 'scientific' in the sense often claimed by his followers. Engels wrote a pamphlet entitled *The Development of Socialism from Utopia to Science*, but Marx's socialism remains obdurately *a priori* for all that. Indeed, it is likely that no body of ethical or political doctrine immediately conceivable deserves to be described as scientific, although it may assuredly be rational and systematic in its own field. Marx's faith in his untutored intuitions of ethical knowledge, illustrated in his unquestioning adherence to the goal of communism, his philosophy of history, and his assertion of the unique efficacy

[1] Marx was favourably disposed to Darwin's *Origin of Species*, which appeared in the same year as *The Critique of Political Economy*, but it must not be supposed that he maintained in human history the standpoint that has since been described as evolutionary in biology. Compare also Lenin's remarks in his article on Marx: "In our own times the idea of development, of evolution, has almost fully permeated social consciousness, but it has done so in other ways, not through Hegel's philosophy. Still, the same idea, as formulated by Marx and Engels on the basis of Hegel's philosophy, is much more comprehensive, much more abundant in content, than the current theory of evolution" (*The Teachings of Karl Marx*, p. 14). From what he goes on to say it is evident, in fact, that the notions of "evolution" and "development" are quite distinct. Both, of course, introduced into European thought the concept of slow, secular change, which has done so much to undermine anthropomorphic ideas. But the Hegel-Marx theory is older, still *a priori*, less careful of the world of objective fact, and thus more capable of an extremist application in politics and ethics.

of the method of revolution in social development are examples of an apriorism which is the essence of idealism.[1] No amount of superadded materialism can make Marx in this respect less of an idealist.

IV

On the other hand, Marx stands at the beginning of that sceptical, investigatory tradition in social psychology and economic history which has still, perhaps, to gain its victory. It was probably not chance that made him write his doctoral thesis[2] upon the philosophy of the Greek materialists, Democritus and Epicurus, but because his interest in the naturalistic tradition proceeded from his perception that the introduction by Hegel of the natural world as a semi-autonomous province of reality demanded further inquiry into its behaviour. In the course of his reading for this essay he made the acquaintance of seventeenth- and eighteenth-century materialism and environmentalism, which a few years later was to become the chief source of his philosophical beliefs, and put him on a road which led very far away from Hegel's objective idealism. His interests soon led him beyond the speculations of the Left

[1] By the term which we now translate as 'natural science,' *Wissenschaft*, Marx meant criticism with the purpose of promoting the development of the historic dialectical process, the law of which he knew before ever he set out. It is not without reason that most of his principal works are entitled "Critiques."

Apriorism, however, is fundamentally authoritarian and very often conservative, since it is incurious, not disinterested, and exalts intuitions which are as often as not inimical to change. It is an extraordinary fact that the philosophies with which modern Russian dialectical materialists have most in common are holism, emergent evolution, *Gestaltpsychologie*, and the 'indeterminism' of some mathematicians. These are almost always socially conservative. Western materialist science is regarded as gradualist, and hence tending to defeat the ends of revolution.

The dangers of the dialectical method in social theory are best illustrated in Marx's double use of the Labour Theory of Value, from which, I think, the felt precariousness of many of his economic prophecies derives. The main reason that led Marx to employ the Labour Theory was that he wished to *épater les bourgeois* economists by turning their own doctrine against them. He succeeded in showing that not only was it radically self-contradictory, but also fatal to the moral pretensions of private property. In order that it should be able to demonstrate this the theory required only to be inconsistent and of the nature of a boomerang. But Marx went on to make predictions about the future trend of capitalist industrialism on the basis of the same theory, for which purpose it had also to be *true*. Marx here was hoist with his own petard, a frequent fate of the unwary militarist.

[2] This is available in the *Marx-Engels Gesamtausgabe* (1927), vol. i, pp. 1–144. It has not yet been translated.

Hegelians and of humanists like Strauss and Feuerbach. From an early period they lay in explaining the impact of the social environment and tradition of mankind upon its political and moral beliefs, and it is in this sphere that his enduring contribution to social philosophy is to be found.

The germs of his theory are to be found in *The Holy Family*, written at the end of 1844. There are scattered accounts of it in *The Poverty of Philosophy*, *The Eighteenth Brumaire*, the famous preface to *The Critique of Political Economy*, and in *Capital*, especially in the preface to the second (1873) edition of the first volume. The *Anti-Dühring* and other works by Engels also contain a more extended exposition which can be roughly said to represent the views of Marx. In the two first-mentioned works there are abundant references to the theories of Hobbes and Diderot, Helvétius and Holbach, Condorcet, Bentham and Owen, which serve to indicate the groundwork of his thought.

In 1873 Marx wrote:

> My dialectic method is not only different from the Hegelian, but is its direct opposite. To Hegel, the life-process of the human brain, *i.e.*, the process of thinking, which, under the name of 'the Idea,' he even transforms into an independent subject, is the *demiourgos* of the real world, and the real world is only the external, phenomenal form of 'the Idea.' With me, on the contrary, the ideal is nothing else than the material world reflected by the human mind, and translated into forms of thought.
>
> The mystifying side of Hegelian dialectic I criticised nearly thirty years ago, at a time when it was still the fashion. But just as I was working at the first volume of *Das Kapital* it was the good pleasure of the peevish, arrogant, mediocre Επίγονοι, who now talk large in cultured Germany, to treat Hegel in the same way as the brave Moses Mendelssohn in Lessing's time treated Spinoza, *i.e.*, as a 'dead dog.' I therefore openly avowed myself the pupil of that mighty thinker, and even here and there, in the chapter on the theory of value, coquetted with the modes of expression peculiar to him. The mystification which dialectic suffers in Hegel's hands by no means prevents him from being the first to present its general form of working in a comprehensive and conscious manner. With him it is standing on its head. It must be turned right side up again if you would discover the rational kernel within the mystical shell.[1]

[1] Preface to *Capital*, vol. i, pp. xxx–xxxi (translation of Moore and Aveling, 1886).

Elsewhere he declared, " It is not the consciousness of men which determines their existence, but, on the contrary, their social existence determines their consciousness." [1]

And again :

> Does it require deep intuition to comprehend that man's ideas, views, and conceptions, in a word, man's consciousness, changes with every change in the conditions of his material existence, in his social relations, and in his social life? . . . When people speak of ideas that revolutionise society, they do but express the fact that within the old society the elements of a new one have been created, and that the dissolution of the old ideas keeps even pace with the dissolution of the old conditions of production.[2]

There can be no doubt that Marx and Engels maintained the then fashionable materialist position that the universe, and with it the mind, consisted of matter in motion, and that they conceived matter to consist of irreducible atoms of palpable substance, whose description could be exhausted in terms of the five senses. They retained the then universal Cartesian dualism, and may be classified as epiphenomenalists. Marx did not amplify his views on this subject, and it is unlikely that they would have been very interesting. What is important to observe is that he was not concerned to account for the nature of the thinking or mental *process*, but rather for the source of ideas, beliefs, and rationalisations—what are called "presentations"—as they actually come to be held by men at different times and places.

The magnitude of the revolution wrought by Marx in the form of the environmentalism he inherited from French tradition has never been properly appreciated. His views differ widely from those of, say, Helvétius, Godwin, or Robert Owen. Deriving their epistemological theory largely from Locke, adherents still of an associationist psychology like that of Condillac, they held an essentially individualist view of the way in which man came to have knowledge. Man was still the passive recipient of sense impressions which were assumed to come from stimuli in the physical world, rarely from the organic, and hardly ever from the social world. (This attitude can be correlated with the rise throughout Western Europe at

[1] Preface to *The Critique of Political Economy*, p. 11 (translation).

[2] *The Communist Manifesto*, p. 11.

the same time of individualist doctrine in social affairs.) It is true that Helvétius and Holbach stressed heavily the *rôle* of the intellectual and moral tradition in moulding men's beliefs, but, like Rousseau in *Émile*, they exaggerated the extent to which these beliefs were determined in the course of personal education and training, narrowly considered; while the chief ambition of the anarchists whom they influenced was to enable man to emancipate himself from the tyranny of custom and society. If we except Hegel, Marx was the first to lay bare the more indirect social processes which profoundly influence our thinking, and which have become preponderant in an age of industrialism, when the tutor and the family have ceased to be the exclusive agencies of social and institutional conditioning. For Hegel the social unit *par excellence* was the nation, for Marx the international class.

Marx had a strong sense of the co-operative character of society, of its interdependence, and of the significance of group unities and forms of social control. He thus made a departure from the individualist psychology of his day. In contradistinction to the Utilitarians, he denied that men were moved by a sense of their own self-interest. Materialists like La Mettrie, who held that man was a machine, believed also that he was a calculating machine. Marx saw him rather as a social animal, influenced more often than not quite unconsciously by his intimate and inescapable relations with his fellows; he saw resemblances rather than differences; stressed, like the modern Behaviourist, the eminent plasticity of men under the impact of social forces; and held that varying norms of character and interest were the result not so much of natural differences in desire and capacity as of subjection to different types of social tradition and function. The substantial accuracy of this view has since been firmly established. On the other hand, Marx had no adequate theory of those individual differences, genetic in origin, that help to produce innovation in social and economic organisation.[1] It led him

[1] Compare Lancelot Hogben, *Genetic Principles in Medicine and Social Science* (1931), p. 169. There would seem to be two reasons why Marx ignored both genetic factors and the limitations imposed by gross disparities of geographical endowment. They were inimical to the revolutionary purpose, and they did not operate significantly in the comparatively recent history of the more civilised parts of the world, with which, as a politician, he was more immediately concerned.

to exaggerate the ease with which a homogeneous class-consciousness can develop within a social group as a result of its uniform economic basis.[1] It caused his optimism and his faith in the facility and smoothness of the revolutionary method in politics. Trained in the school of Hegel, he was necessarily occupied with the "idea," and neglected the "will," or the impulsive aspect of human behaviour,[2] the study of which was to dominate one branch of post-Hegelian philosophy and psychology from Schopenhauer to Bergson, Freud, and McDougall, and culminate in a new and greatly exaggerated emphasis upon "instinctive" and "racial" factors making for variability in social behaviour.

V

Briefly, Marx's theory of the growth of social relations and ideologies may be put thus. Men, in their expanding interaction with the world of nature and their fellows, modify the

[1] In addition to the more direct and rational interests of economic activity, men display an attachment to other kinds of values, which cause them to enter into relations with their fellows. These relations also give rise to social institutions and to characteristic ideologies. Marx neglects the historical consequences of nationalism and religious bellicosity, restricting his interest in them to a description of their correlations with economic movements and class struggles. Later Marxists have developed the economic interpretation of wars and of imperialism, but remain curiously blind to the non-economic factors involved. Marx took the view that only technical and economic changes were truly dynamic and developmental; religion and nationalism were merely conservative and static. He held that there was an immanent progressive force in human affairs which, rational and economic in origin, expressed itself in the contributions of successive class and revolutionary movements. As a historian he was compelled to take some account of the resistance offered to change, though he came perilously near believing that it was due primarily to the self-interest, in the Benthamite sense of the word, of the ruling classes. As a politician Marx continued to imagine that neither religion nor nationalism had any weight divorced from their class affiliations. *Cf.*, for the influence of nationalism, Bertrand Russell, *Principles of Social Reconstruction* (1916), chapter ii, and *The Prospects of Industrial Civilisation* (1923), chapters iv and v, and C. E. Playne, *The Neuroses of the Nations* (1929), *passim*. The interaction of economic affairs with religion is well discussed in Weber's *Die Protestantische Ethik und der Geist des Kapitalismus* (in his *Gesammelte Aufsätze zur Religionssoziologie* (1920)), by Troeltsch in his *Soziallehren der Christlichen Kirchen* (1912), and by R. H. Tawney, *Religion and the Rise of Capitalism* (1926).

[2] In spite of the reference in the *Theorien über den Mehrwert*, vol. i, p. 381, to "the mutual interactions of mental and material production," I cannot find in Marx that well-developed pragmatist epistemology which Lenin and Bukharin claim for Marxism. See, for example, the latter's "Theory and Practice from the Standpoint of Dialectical Materialism," in *Science at the Cross Roads* (1931).

external conditions of their existence by creating artifacts. Man is typically a tool-using and tool-perfecting animal. Tools and machines and fixed capital in general, including bridges, harbours, roads, and the like, constitute the inanimate "productive forces," a notion that Marx might have got from the Physiocrats.[1] Human labour and abilities comprise the "personal production forces." Next in logical order come the "conditions of production," or, as Marx often put it, the "social relations" of production. These include the institutions of economic society, the division of labour, the habit of extended economic intercourse between nations, the system of monetary credit, the juridical notions of contract and inheritance, as well as the general machinery of the State, and, most important of all, the institution of property, the distribution of the product in wages, rent, interest, and profits.[2] These "relations" or institutions are, of course, entirely man-made. They are continually being modified, in ways which Marx endeavoured to explain. It was his view that they acquired their form from the requirements of the technical basis of society, and that they changed in response to men's perception that new technical advantages demanded new ways of organising to exploit them best. The *personnel* associated with the exploitation of the technical equipment of society at a given stage of development naturally assumes the position of a ruling class, and transforms the institutions of the law, the State, and so on, in order to sustain its hold upon the instruments of production, which enable it to exploit not only nature but other men.

Under primitive communism the tie of blood relationship served to maintain a homogeneous society, but, with the weakening of this tie after the growth of external trading contacts and the appearance of land scarcity, society, in the absence of any new social bond, was split up into classes corresponding to the manner in which men got their livelihood. Since land and the other means of production were limited,

[1] The Marxist Loria described these forces compendiously as "technique." The concept has proved very fruitful since Marx. It enabled a geographer like Réclus, for example, to get away from the purely physical preoccupations of Buckle.

[2] "In a word, land-rent, profit, and all the economic essentials of private property are *social relations*, corresponding to a particular phase of production."—*Der Heilige Max* [Stirner], reprinted in E. Bernstein, *Dokumente des Sozialismus*, vol. iii, p. 363.

they fell into the hands of those best fitted by reason of their social opportunities to exploit them and maintain their claim to ownership. Thus private, exploitative property and class division arose. Feudal society is based on the possession of land, commercial capital, and industrial monopoly (in the gilds). The further development of trade, the extended use of money, and the growth of machinery led to the economic dominance of the *bourgeoisie*, who, in order to obtain unfettered control of their possessions, destroyed the institutions of feudal society, inaugurating the middle-class national State. But the new system of large-scale private capitalism is essentially an employing system; it calls into existence the proletariat. This in turn moves into the position of being able itself to administer the new technical equipment of society, which now necessitates international economic intercourse and productive units nation-wide in scope, best fitted to be controlled by a whole people in association.

On this account technical progress, the growth of knowledge as applied to the satisfaction of the primary biological needs of mankind, is the driving-force of social development. The action is all one way. Science, philosophy, religion, and, in a lesser degree, art are the necessary ideological reflections of the social relations appropriate to a given level of material culture.[1]

A detailed discussion of this formidable doctrine is not

[1] "With the change of the economic foundation the entire immense superstructure is more or less rapidly transformed. In considering such transformations, the distinction should always be made between the material transformation of the economic conditions of production, which can be determined with the precision of natural science, and the legal, political, religious, æsthetic, or philosophic, in short, ideological forms in which men become conscious of this conflict and fight it out."—From the preface to *The Critique of Political Economy*.

Here, as elsewhere, Marx writes as if he held that the forces he calls "economic" were coextensive with those he describes as "material" in the wider sense. Engels, however, made a distinction between the two theories of "economic determinism" and "historical materialism," when he modestly claimed in 1885 coauthorship of the former, declaring at the same time that Marx alone invented the latter. (See *The Communist Manifesto*, edited by D. Ryazanoff (1923), Introduction, pp. 7–8.) Engels' subsequent admission that perhaps he and Marx had stressed the economic influences too much cannot therefore be regarded as involving a recantation of their main doctrine. (See the letters of October 1895, quoted in E. R. A. Seligman, *The Economic Interpretation of History*, pp. 142–143.) As I understand Engels, he still maintains that economic factors are the most prominent. So, without question, did Marx. He regarded them, not as constituting the sole category of social fact, but as the leading species of a larger genus—namely, that of material factors in general.

possible here, but several points may be mentioned as being essential to its proper understanding. Firstly, the word 'material' is not used in the narrow sense of physical objects. In the writings of Marx it denotes the external referent of the Hegelian 'idea,' the objective 'real' which provides the thinking subject with the particulars of sense experience which are worked up by the mind into universals. Material forces thus include economic and social institutions, or the ways in which men relate themselves in society, and social *mores* in general, when they are accepted as a result of environmental impacts. It is here that Marx sought to give his social environmentalist doctrine its historical confirmation.

Secondly, this part of the Marxian system has nothing whatever to do with modern mechanist views of the identity of 'mental' with brain and nervous processes.[1] It is logically quite compatible with vitalist or emergent theories. Marx was interested in the conditions that produced *change* in social behaviour, not in the original character of the thing that suffered change, nor in the conservative forces resisting it. I cannot do better here than quote the words of Mr Beer:

> Marx . . . does not aim in the first place at the discovery of the origin of thought, of rights, of religion, of society, of trade, etc.; these he takes to be historically given. He is rather concerned to find out the causes, the impulses, or the springs which produce the changes and revolutions of the essentials and forms of the mental and social phenomena, or which create the tendencies thereto. In a sentence: What interested Marx here was not the *origin*, but the development and change of things—he is searching for the dynamic law of history.[2]

Again, the method he applies is the dialectical. As I understand him, he is not attempting to deny that the ideological superstructure has no relatively autonomous life of its own, that there are no sciences, say, of morals, politics, and æsthetics, with 'laws' of their own. But he was anxious to minimise the influence exerted by independent intellectual systems, and to regard their internal developments as belonging in importance to the second order of small quantities. These developments were liable to be set aside or surpassed by the onrush of basic social changes, rooted in technology and

[1] *Cf.* Bertrand Russell, *The Practice and Theory of Bolshevism* (1920), pp. 119–120.
[2] *The Life and Teaching of Karl Marx*, p. 66.

social institutions in more immediate servitude to gross human desire. The dialectical temptation, moreover, to deal in sharply contrasted historical epochs, beginning and ending in sudden and conspicuous revolutionary events, prevented Marx from appreciating the element of continuity in intellectual and religious life.

Thirdly, Marx seems to be in error if what he asserts is that the pursuit of ' biological ' ends, as he conceived them, necessarily determines most significantly the structure and ideology of all societies. Primitive peoples no doubt live on the very margin of subsistence and spend the bulk of their time in the search for the biological necessities of life. But it is not the direct, logical consequences of their productive system that are responsible for primitive magic and religion or commensalism, sexual and marriage taboos and ceremonies, which powerfully affect their institutional and ideological existence. Marx's theory, invented in a progressive and more logical age, is more true of historical periods in which, to use Max Weber's phrase, a " rational ethic " prevails. The very perception that men primarily pursue 'biological' ends has to wait for the growth of a rational biology. Even to-day the expression is tautological. We mean merely that men pursue what they are made by nature to pursue directly and economically, instead of in a roundabout and intellectually confused manner.

There is some doubt as to whether Marx wished to elevate this theory into a general sociological law. It was to him the key to a philosophy of recent history, which is a very different thing. He believed that economic determinism would cease to be true with the consolidation of the " highest phase " of communism ; he even speaks of the present epoch as " the closing chapter of the prehistoric stage of human society." He could only have meant by this that changes in that future time, *if changes there would be*, would obey different laws. It is too often overlooked in this connection that Marx was a perfectibilitarian. It is completely to misconceive his doctrine to hold that it is derogatory to human freedom or that it is fatalist. His real philosophy has been put thus :

> If, at any given moment, the character of the economic forces at work in social life can be discerned and understood, if observation can lay bare the hidden dialectic of any given system, reveal the stage of

> its movement and the contradictions it contains, then the character of the next stage, the direction of the changes implicit in the existing system, can be predicted, and, as it were, the programme and policy of human life arranged accordingly.[1]

Marx wished not to inaugurate but to destroy social necessitarianism.[2] The dialectic was to be the good fairy which was to unite mankind and enable it to live happily ever after.

VI

We have seen that Marx maintained that our social beliefs were conditioned not so much by our individual experiences as by our experience as members of a social group. In practice, true to his dialectical principle, he neglected the effect of all other social groups but the group he called a class. His materialism is essentially a theory that ideologies are determined by membership of one or other of the two social classes which exist at any given moment; that, especially, the growth and change of ideas is a reflection of the changing character of the class struggle.

The Communist Manifesto begins with the unequivocal assertion that "the history of all hitherto existing society is the history of class struggles." The entire work is inspired throughout by this conception, which is applied in turn to the analysis of historical development, the discussion of socialist strategy, and the criticism of previous socialist theory.

> Freeman and slave, patrician and plebeian, baron and serf, guild-master and journeyman, in one word, oppressor and oppressed, standing constantly in opposition to each other, carried on an uninterrupted warfare, now open, now concealed; a warfare which always ended either in a revolutionary transformation of the whole of society or in the common ruin of the contending classes.
>
> In early historic epochs we find almost everywhere a complete organisation of society into various degrees, a manifold gradation of social rank. In ancient Rome we find patricians, knights, plebeians, slaves; in the Middle Ages, feudal lords, guild-masters, apprentices, and serfs, and within almost all of these classes again further divisions.

[1] *Encyclopædia of Religion and Ethics*, edited by J. Hastings (1920), article on socialism, vol. xi, p. 642.

[2] "Freedom is the recognition of necessity. Necessity is blind only in so far as it is not understood."—Engels' *Anti-Dühring*, p. 112.

> Modern *bourgeois* society, springing from the wreck of feudal society, had not abolished class antagonisms. It has but substituted new classes, new conditions of oppression, new forms of warfare for the old.
>
> Our epoch, the epoch of the *bourgeoisie*, possesses, however, the distinctive characteristic that it has simplified class antagonisms. All society is more and more splitting up into two opposing camps, into two great hostile classes: the *bourgeoisie* and the proletariat.

It is further stated that "political power, properly speaking, is the organised power of one class for the purpose of oppressing another." "The modern State is but an executive committee for administering the affairs of the whole *bourgeois* class."[1]

Two later passages in the same work confirm the view that Marx was using the term 'class' in several different senses.

> The little middle class, the small shopkeepers, tradespeople, peasant proprietors, handicraftsmen, and peasants, all these classes sink into the proletariat, partly because their small capital is not sufficient for modern industry and is crushed out in the competition with the large capitalists, and partly because their specialised skill is depreciated by the new methods of production. Thus is the proletariat recruited from all classes of the population. . . . Of all the classes which stand at present in opposition to the *bourgeoisie* the proletariat alone is a truly revolutionary class.

From this account it can be inferred, in the first place, that a class is a social group that stands in some relation to the distribution of social power and privilege in unequalitarian societies: there will be as many classes as there are well-marked degrees of social status. In the second place, these groupings also have an occupational reference: men of similar social status tend to be found in similar occupations and to have the same *industrial* status. This follows from the leading Marxian conception of the intimate association between the possession of the strategic technical and industrial positions in society and social and political power in general. Thirdly,

[1] This view has since been made familiar through the work of Gumplowicz and F. Oppenheimer. The former sees the essence of the State in "a division of labour made and maintained by coercion among a number of social elements organically united into a whole. The development of this composite unit proceeds by a struggle among its constituents for the purpose of determining their relative powers—the issue in each case being expressed in law and statutes."—*Die Soziologische Staatsidee* (1892), p. 55. Compare also his *Grundriss der Soziologie* (1885), p. 115.

The best gloss on Marx's views is to be found in Lenin's *The State and Revolution*, which is very well criticised in H. J. Laski's *Communism* (1927), chapter iv.

there seems to be a tendency for many of these classes, so distinguished, to coalesce at critical periods, so that we have the spectacle of two main classes in conflict with each other.

It is often alleged that these different meanings of the term 'class' are inconsistent with each other, and that, in particular, the notion that there are only two classes cannot be upheld by economic analysis. Such criticism displays a fundamental misunderstanding of the governing conception of Marx's whole work. It is vital to observe that the emphasis is always placed, not on classes as statistically distinguishable groups, for which better names would be occupational or functional groups,[1] but on class *struggle*, the movement or trend of group alignments and conflicts. The interest of Marx in social studies was primarily historical—that is to say, dialectical. He sought the laws of change and conflict, the nature of the development of the great triad of human history. Thus the sociology of Marx is always subservient to the needs of revolutionary prophecy. He was only secondarily interested in periods in which the movement was slow, the conflict temporarily suspended; and in his own time looked only for those characteristics of group behaviour which would throw light upon the problems of ultimate proletarian unification and the time of the final class war. It was this purpose that motivated his studies of economic and technical developments and—*e.g.*, in *The Eighteenth Brumaire*—of shifting class alignments.

"The history of all hitherto existing society is the history of class struggles." Had Marx been forewarned of the need for terminological exactitude he would have restricted the meaning of the word 'class' to denote those two segments of society which could be seen to form the matrices of two opposing forces in a revolutionary crisis. The historian has no difficulty in working backwards from some given social revolution to describe the gradual coalescence of groups into the two sides who ultimately fought it out. The observer of contemporary affairs, less happily placed, can only predict events with the aid of the principle of "economic determinism"

[1] A class in Marx's sense is not an occupational group *tout simple*. The criterion is industrial—and hence for Marx *social—status*, not the nature of the trade which men follow. This classification cuts horizontally across occupational groupings.

and a dialectical faith in the final and inevitable victory of the communist ideal.

Marx's theory of the fundamental part played by class struggle in social development states that the *personnel* associated with the exploitation of the prevailing technical basis in a given social epoch naturally engrosses for itself the best environments in society, and thus occupies the position of a ruling class, adapting and devising political and legal instruments to consolidate its hold and exercising a powerful influence over the social beliefs of men. It goes on to argue that in time the ruling class is challenged by a new body of persons who determine to control the means of production, which are now more appropriately administered, considering their technical nature, by a new type of class with a different experience. The old economic system has in the course of its development brought into existence a new technique, elaborated from that which it had seized or inherited in the past, and with it a new class of producers who, in the early phase of the system, had been non-existent or negligible in numbers and experience. This is the dialectical notion of immanent development, the unfolding of new evolutionary forms out of the old in a process of conflict.[1]

Thus the feudal order created the need for merchants and craftsmen, who developed slowly, by means of the growing use of money and credit and the growth of more productive methods in general, into commercial and industrial capitalists, and ultimately wrested political control from the landed aristocracy in the *bourgeois* revolutions of the eighteenth and nineteenth centuries. So also, continued Marx, the industrial capitalists bring into existence the proletariat or wage-earning class, which will grow similarly in power and capacity to administer the new industrialist society. In fact, for various

[1] In the preface to *The Critique of Political Economy* Marx writes: " In broad outlines we can designate the Asiatic, the ancient, the feudal, and the modern *bourgeois* methods of production as so many epochs in the progress of the economic formation of society. The *bourgeois* relations of production are the last antagonistic form of the social process of production—antagonistic not in the sense of individual antagonism, but of one arising from conditions surrounding the life of individuals in society; at the same time the productive forces developing in the womb of *bourgeois* society create the material conditions for the solution of that antagonism. This social formation constitutes, therefore, the closing chapter of the prehistoric stage of human society."

economic reasons described in *Capital*, a democratically organised and economically equal society of producer-consumers can alone solve the distributive problems raised by international, large-scale capitalist industry. When this fact is seen the proletariat will revolt and "expropriate the expropriators." After a period of dictatorship, necessary as a temporary political expedient to liquidate the reactionary forces that still survive, it will inaugurate the wholly classless society of communism.

This account contains many ambiguities. (1) What is the precise nature of the connection between the new technical equipment of society and the rise to power of a new class? Marx nowhere states explicitly that the *personnel* of the new ruling class is drawn from those best fitted by reason of their technical proficiency in the new methods to exploit them.[1] Economic progress simply provides new places and powers for individuals or groups most able to secure them. Where, on account of the operation of existing social institutions, there is little mobility between classes, there need be little change in the family composition of the ruling class. In other cases physical prowess, qualities of leadership, the arts of deception and mass-suggestion, a *coup d'état* or a military rising, may serve to bring new men on top, provided they possess a minimum of technical or administrative competence. On this view technical and economic progress determines the *material character* of the enjoyments and methods of consumption available to mankind, while the prevailing social institutions and qualities making for political domination decide their *distribution—i.e.*, determine the *personnel* of the rulers and the ruled.

Here is revealed a twofold interpretation of the great triad of human history. Marx attributed enormous influence to the effect of economic factors on institutions and ideologies. His theory of the class struggle also requires the recognition of the power of the dominant social class to mould social

[1] It is often implied that the actual *personnel* was different without a distinction being made between two possible causes of this, viz., that economic experience of a certain kind itself gave its possessors immediate access to power, or that the old *personnel*, grown slack, was ousted by a more vigorous group using violent methods. It is the business of historical investigation to establish the different sets of facts relating to different revolutionary eras.

relationships. Inequality as such, which seems to constitute the essence of class relations, cannot be regarded as exclusively economic in origin. The forms of class superiority and inferiority may be significantly determined by the economic means at hand, but the amount and trend of inequality in a given society depend also upon other relationships and institutions, many of which are changed only very slowly through the pressure of the material environment. In a broad view of history the purely economic interpretation breaks down. In estimating the trend of contemporary events it must be supplemented by other considerations.

(2) On what logical basis does the prediction of the inevitable victory of the proletariat rest? Marx seems to ground it on the demonstration that the nature of the developing economic order requires it. This seems in turn to depend on a view of the necessary connection between economic function and social power which as a historian he had not clearly established. The requirements of the economic system will only lead to the triumph of the proletariat on the assumption that men rationally follow whither their economic noses lead them. It cannot be denied that Marx in many places writes as if he believed this to be true. In his work rationalist optimism lives uneasily alongside the more disinterested recognition of historical truths. Recent economic developments in capitalist industry are only one set of factors in the problem of the future of class alignments.

(3) Can we say with confidence, again, that it is the working class, the wage-earners, who are uniquely fitted to administer the material basis of the Great Society? Might not Marx have been mistaken in thinking that, on his dialectical theory, it was the proletariat which constituted the significant new class thrown up by the *bourgeois* system of production? Might not the " negation of the negation " be a wholly different class, whose existence he did not foresee or whose function he failed to appreciate? I refer to the distinct modern group of administrators, officials, managers, educators, entertainers, editors, scientists, etc. In a word, is there any further evidence of the truth of the great triadic formula than that the wish was father to the thought? The fallacy into which Marx fell proceeds from two causes. As a perfectibilitarian

communist he believed that a classless society, being inherently desirable on ethical grounds, must therefore be the next stage in social evolution. As an agitator and revolutionary he saw in the working-class movement the only available instrument for the achievement of his aim in the immediate future, and consequently was tempted to regard it as the final "negation of the negation." Moreover, it must be borne in mind that Marx, like Hegel, was satisfied, as a philosopher of history, with one great dialectical process whose end was in sight; it was never intended to be a process outgrowing into an endless future. For this reason, if for no other, it is inaccurate to compare Marx with Darwin as a pioneer in the field of historical evolution. It was not primarily as a naturalist that Marx studied history. It was as an idealist moral philosopher.

While Marx's thought contains very prominently the ideas later known as "economic determinism," it also stresses, though implicitly and confusedly, the belief that "men make their own history." I have suggested that he did not overcome the inconsistency between his economic theory and his view of the character of class struggles in history. It is through the doctrine of the class struggle that Marx asserts the function of the human will. His theory is a mixed one: besides standing in some close relation to the prevailing sources of economic power, classes are also thought of as comprising the *personnel* of the conservative and of the revolutionary forces in society independently of their economic affiliations. The theory is designed to show how revolutions are made as well as how social development as a whole takes place. Marx, indeed, held that revolution was the fundamental mode of social development, not the incremental, cumulative, and co-operative march of technology and science, although he made a valuable contribution to social science in stressing the significance of these factors. It is an irony that modern sociologists, under the guidance of natural science, should single out as Marx's main contribution to the thought of the nineteenth century what he himself regarded merely as an adjunct to his essential doctrine.

It has been German social democracy which has fathered the notion of "economic determinism" as a complete sociological law, not Karl Marx. The doctrine of Kautsky, the

German equivalent of English Methodism, assured the exploited masses that the social millennium would come without any effort on their part, simply by the irresistible march of economic events. The views of Marx, as Lenin has succeeded in proving, were not so necessitarian. They were saved from that fatal political defect by the conception of the dialectic and by the theory of the class struggle, which the modern Communist holds, with some justice, to be the central part of Marx's teaching.[1]

Marx thought of the class war as something to be waged, in which propaganda and strategically selected strikes and other forms of coercion were to be employed and, when the time was ripe from both the economic and the military point of view, civil war itself. It does not matter whether Marx failed to reconcile his metaphysical materialism with his dialectical ethical theory; the fact remains that he believed in the power of the human will to force the pace of social change, to bring a revolution about in one place rather than another, at one time rather than another. The dialectic is not a determinist philosophy. It is a statement of the general pattern of the process by which men change the world. Like most ethical philosophies, it is uncertain which to stress the most, the world that men are given or the extent to which they can transcend its limitations.

The emphasis laid by Marx on technical and economic factors seems to have been devised in order to refute the Utopian socialists and anarchists, who held either that socialism would come " like a thief in the night " (to quote Robert Owen), by the spontaneously rational conversion of the existing ruling classes, or that the assassination of a king or

[1] The Leninist emphasises above all Marx's theories the doctrine of the class struggle precisely because it leaves a loophole for the revolutionary will striving to assert itself in seemingly unpropitious circumstances. The doctrine does this by providing an historical demonstration of the ability of certain groups, *under certain objective conditions*, to seize social power by virtue of their employment of an efficient technique of revolutionary action. These objective conditions in the case of the Bolshevik Revolution of 1917 certainly did not comprise a developed capitalist system involved in inherent contradictions. The conditions of the triumphant dialectical process include, therefore, *all* factors relevant to the success of revolutionary measures. The Russian State is not a logical, if assisted, outcome of a late, exhausted stage of capitalism. It is a new culture, forced upon the existing economic relationships and planned *de novo*. *Cf.* M. H. Dobb, *Russian Economic Development since the Revolution* (1928), especially pp. 7–19.

president, with a *coup d'état* the same day, must succeed in establishing any kind of new social order you please. It is criticism of this kind that forms the central theme of *The Communist Manifesto*. Inconsistent though he was, Marx was aware of the need to transplant into the field of political philosophy that concern for objective observation and measurement which is characteristic of natural science.

Marx surely wished to put revolutionary action on a more scientific basis, but he remained none the less a revolutionary. This meant that he had to take the validity of some ethical goal for granted, not pausing to re-examine the foundations of his beliefs, because man's life is short, and the desire for a better society urgent and of the heart. It is this necessity to act on undemonstrable assumptions that we call 'free will.' As long as we continue to know less than everything about the world, so long must much of our action partake of this character. It may even be held to be our duty to act in this manner, no less than to urge on the progress of scientifically demonstrable knowledge. It is the singular merit of the social philosophy of Karl Marx that it exhibits this eternal, ever-fresh dilemma in the acutest form, and thus engages our minds and our enthusiasms. Marx may be damned not only by the prevailing *bourgeois* bias of European thought, to whose existence he was the first to draw attention, but because of his apriorism, foreign to the empirical temper of modern science, his eschatology, his ethical incuriosity, his dogmatism, obscurity, and rank errors. But he is the greatest subversive force in the modern world. The aspiration towards human equality, perhaps the most significant feature of the modern mind, draws its chief nourishment from him. In factories and workshops, farm, office, and mine, in barracks and battleships, common-rooms and parliaments, the words of no political thinker are so often on the lips of men. A social revolution has been waged in his name.

J. L. Gray

KARL MARX

BOOK LIST

A. Primary Authorities

(Where works have been translated the date is the date of the translation.)

Marx, Karl:

1. *The Poverty of Philosophy*, translated by H. Quelch. 1900.
2. *The Critique of Political Economy*, translated by N. I. Stone. 1904.
3. *Selected Essays.* 1926.
4. *Capital: a Critique of Political Economy.* Vol. i, translated by E. and C. Paul, 1930; vols. ii and iii, Chicago, 1909.
5. *Theorien über den Mehrwert.* 3 vols. Edited by K. Kautsky. 1904–9.

There are numerous editions of *The Communist Manifesto, The Eighteenth Brumaire, The Civil War in France*, and other briefer works by Marx. Very important also are the two German collections, *Aus dem literarischen Nachlass von Karl Marx und Friedrich Engels*, edited by Franz Mehring, 4 vols., 1923 (which contains *Die Heilige Familie*), and *Der Briefwechsel zwischen Friedrich Engels und Karl Marx*, edited by A. Bebel and E. Bernstein, 4 vols., 1921. The *Marx-Engels Gesamtausgabe* is now being issued from the *Marx-Engels Archiv*, Frankfurt, edited by D. Rjazanov.

B. Secondary Authorities

Beer, M.: *The Life and Teaching of Karl Marx.* 1921.

Bernstein, E.: *Evolutionary Socialism.* 1909.

Eastman, Max: *Marx, Lenin, and the Science of Revolution.* 1926.

Engels, Friedrich: *The Condition of the Working Class in England in 1844.* Translated. 1892.

—— *Landmarks of Scientific Socialism.* 1907. An abridged edition of *Herrn Eugen Dührings Umwälzungen der Wissenschaft* (*Anti-Dühring*). 1876.

Hammacher, E.: *Das Philosophischökonomische System des Marxismus.* 1910.

Kautsky, K.: *Ethics and the Materialist Conception of History.* 1913.

—— *The Economic Doctrines of Karl Marx.* 1925.

Laski, H. J.: *Karl Marx: an Essay.* n.d.

—— *Communism.* 1927.

Lenin, N.: *The Teachings of Karl Marx.* This contains the most useful bibliography in English. 1931.

—— *Materialism and Empirio-criticism.* 1929.

Lindsay, A. D.: *Karl Marx's "Capital."* 1925.

Luxemburg, Rosa: *Die Akkumulation des Kapitals.* 1913.

Mehring, F.: *Karl Marx* (German). 1908.

Plekhanov, G. V.: *Fundamental Problems of Marxism.* 1929.

Portus, G. V.: *Marx and Modern Thought.* 1921.

Ryazanoff, D.: *The Communist Manifesto of Karl Marx and Friedrich Engels.* 1930.

—— *Karl Marx: Man, Thinker and Revolutionist: a Symposium.* 1927.

Ruehle, O.: *Karl Marx: Leben und Werke.* 1928.

VII

T. H. GREEN AND THE IDEALISTS

THIS article is concerned with a group of Balliol men, most of them teachers in the University of Oxford, who were responsible for a philosophical movement of considerable importance in political theory. Their influence was prevalent in most of the university teaching in this country at the end of last century. The three earlier teachers of the group were T. H. Green, Edward Caird, and William Wallace. To these should perhaps be added some names in a younger generation, D. G. Ritchie, Arnold Toynbee, and Bernard Bosanquet, though Bosanquet's special work on political theory came a good deal later, and was so important that it would require another article for its proper consideration.

Green was born in 1836, was a Fellow and tutor of Balliol from 1860 to 1878 and Whyte's Professor of Moral Philosophy in the University of Oxford from 1878 till his death in 1882. His *Lectures on the Principles of Political Obligation* were first delivered in 1879, and published after his death.

Caird was born in 1835, became a Fellow of Merton in 1864, was Professor of Moral Philosophy in the University of Glasgow from 1866 to 1893, and Master of Balliol from 1893 till 1907. He died in 1908.

William Wallace was born in 1843, studied at the University of St Andrews, and went up to Balliol in 1864. He became a Fellow of Merton College in 1867 and Whyte's Professor of Moral Philosophy on Green's death in 1882. He died in 1897.

D. G. Ritchie was born in 1853, became a Fellow of Jesus in 1878, and died in 1893. His writings on political theory, *Darwinism and Politics*, *Principles of State Interference*, *Darwin and Hegel*, and *Natural Rights*, were published between 1889 and 1895.

Arnold Toynbee was born in 1852, and died in 1883. He was a Fellow of Balliol from 1878 till his death.

Bernard Bosanquet was born in 1848 and died in 1923. He was a Fellow of University College, Oxford, from 1871 to 1881, and Professor of Moral Philosophy in the University of St Andrews from 1903 to 1908. His *Philosophical Theory of the State* was published in 1899.

Green's *Principles of Political Obligation* represents the most important contribution of this school to political theory till the publication of Bosanquet's great work, but Caird and Wallace, who were men immediately concerned with metaphysics and the history of philosophy, also interested themselves in political theory on the same lines as Green. Ritchie's writings are of great interest, but may be considered as applying Green's principles to more specific political problems.

Green and his fellow-idealists represent the renewed liberalism of the last quarter of the nineteenth century. They are all of them, for all their Platonism and Hegelianism, in the succession of the Utilitarians. They were all fundamentally individualists and democrats. But they were convinced that Utilitarianism had become barren as a political creed because of the inadequate philosophy upon which it was based, and that no further progress could be made in an understanding of politics till a new philosophic basis was found for liberalism. Utilitarianism had equated human purposes with happiness. That had meant not simply that the State should take men as it found them—a doctrine for which much is to be said—but that men should take themselves as they found themselves—a very different doctrine, and one for which there is almost nothing to be said. The individual in Benthamite philosophy was reduced to a bundle of pleasures or desires, and the State to a collection of independent atoms. When the progress of the Industrial Revolution disappointed the facile optimism of the earlier Utilitarians their individualistic creed, which had in the early part of the century been a doctrine of reform and liberty, became largely a bulwark of reaction and privilege.

It demanded reform in the early days on the ground that if unwise State restrictions and interference were removed the natural harmony of economic interests would ensure that all would be well. When these restrictions had been removed and *laissez-faire* largely realised the doctrine was used to oppose any attempt to deal with the disharmonies of economic interests. Utilitarianism had done all that it could, but democracy was more alive than ever and faced with any number of new and unexpected problems. If democracy was to grapple with these new problems with any success some way had to be found of reconciling a true individualism with the new functions which were being thrust upon the State.

Green and his fellow-idealists had been profoundly influenced by Carlyle and his bitter criticism of the creed of "each for himself and the devil take the hindmost." They were far removed from either the facile optimism of the early Utilitarians or the rather cynical pessimism which succeeded it. They were concerned for the sufferings of the poor, and were abundantly conscious of the inequalities of the existing economic system. But, unlike Carlyle and Ruskin, they remained convinced democrats, and thought of social reform as the task of the new democratic State. They did not share Carlyle's contempt for the ordinary man and his leanings towards aristocracy. For they had got from Kant what Kant got from Rousseau, a profound belief in the worth and dignity of the ordinary man. They were political democrats because they were first of all spiritual democrats. They were convinced that the theoretical basis of democracy laid down by the Utilitarians was fundamentally unsound. Its foundations were not nearly deep enough; its conception of human nature too shallow. They felt that a new start had to be made and a proper conception of human nature and action acquired before an adequate political theory could be constructed. That is why none of them were concerned only with political theory. Their politics were to be the outcome of a view of human nature and of the world—of moral philosophy and of metaphysics.

In making their new start they went back beyond the French writers, who had, on the whole, inspired the Utilitarians—back to the real founders of modern democracy, the seventeenth-century Puritans, whose ideas the French writers of the eighteenth century had clarified, popularised, and cheapened. A recent writer on democracy, Mr Leonard

Woolf, has argued that democracy and Christianity are incompatible. Green and his school would have argued that such a judgment is profoundly mistaken, that democracy was, and must be, based on religion, that the doctrine of human equality is a religious doctrine or it is nothing. The fate of Utilitarianism, they would have said, shows how entirely insufficient, because how shallow, is a theory of democracy which seeks to-day to minimise the importance of religion. The Utilitarian doctrine of man, because it was essentially irreligious, had proved far too narrow to stand the strains and stresses of social and political life.

They were growing up when the reigning philosophy in the universities was that of John Stuart Mill. His fine and noble character had struggled in vain with the creed he had inherited, and his philosophy was really an eclecticism which had inspiring elements in it, but was incapable of producing fruitful social or political principles. A comprehensive philosophical system had to be put in its place. Utilitarianism or Associationism or Empiricism had to be fought all along the line. And so these liberals went for their philosophical inspiration to some very undemocratic sources, to Plato and to Hegel, as well as to Kant and the seventeenth-century Puritans; but their purpose in so doing was to carry out better and more thoroughly what the Utilitarians had begun.

We may perhaps elucidate the relation between the Utilitarians and the idealists by asking ourselves how, if the Utilitarian view of human nature is as fundamentally erroneous as the idealists maintained it to be, the Utilitarians accomplished as much as they did. Utilitarian psychology and Utilitarian ethics are really indefensible. A very little examination must show that it is just not the case that all men seek happiness in the sense in which the Utilitarians define happiness, and that the famous Utilitarian passage from each seeking his own pleasure to each seeking the greatest happiness of the greatest number is an obvious fallacy, and that the psychological Hedonism which the Utilitarians taught with such confidence is incompatible with the principles of justice which they so nobly defended in practice. "Each to count as one and none to count as more than one," so far from being derived from Hedonism, is flatly incompatible with it. There can seldom have been a doctrine which accomplished so much, and that on the basis of being scientific and systematic, which would so little bear criticism. If Utilitarianism was so fundamentally unsound, how did it accomplish such great things?

The answer may be partly that the practical success of a doctrine is no witness to its intellectual consistency: witness the extraordinary power of the Marxian theory of value. But it is also that the Utilitarians looked at politics from the point of view of the legislator, and they were largely concerned with saying what the State ought not to do. When Bentham said that pushpin was as good as poetry, what he meant practically by that absurd statement was not that it was as good for a man to like pushpin as to like poetry, but that the State should not use its power to encourage people to find pleasure in poetry rather than in pushpin. For the purpose of the State was to promote liberty, to take for granted man's free activities and use its power to promote and not to hinder freedom—a view which found eloquent and noble expression in John Stuart Mill's *Liberty*. The Utilitarians had found prevailing a view that it was the State's business to make men moral—a view which they rightly repudiated. They were convinced that the compulsory activities of the State must have strict limitations, because they believed in the beneficent effect of the men's voluntary non-political activities. These voluntary activities the State must take for granted. At the most they admitted that there might arise from such activities disharmonies and inequalities which the State, with due precautions taken, might correct. Its purpose in such action should always be to promote more harmoniously men's voluntary activities.

Now in this matter up to a point both Utilitarians and idealists are in agreement. For while the Utilitarians hold that you cannot by compulsion make men happy, but only, by removing hindrances, give men scope to find their own happiness, the idealists hold that you cannot by compulsion make men moral, but only, by removing hindrances, give men scope to live the good life. And up to a point the liberty which each school seeks to attain is the same, or rather, perhaps, certain kinds of State interference are equally condemned by both doctrines. Green says:

> Any direct enforcement of the outward conduct, which ought to flow from social interests, by means of threatened penalties—and a law requiring such conduct necessarily implies penalties for disobedience to it—does interfere with the spontaneous action of those interests, and consequently checks the growth of the capacity which is the condition of the beneficial exercise of rights.

Here Green is saying something the practical implication of which is the same as Utilitarian doctrine, at least up to a point. So long, therefore, as the Utilitarians were concerned with attacking State interference which was directed towards making men moral, it did not matter that they misconceived the way in which men make themselves moral. The work of freeing the individual from wrong kinds of State-compulsion had to be done in any case. There is a sense in which legislation has to take the individual and his possibilities for granted. It is the aim of legislation to set free the possibilities of the individual, and some setting free can be done regardless of what these possibilities are.

But sooner or later the limits of such action were bound to be reached, and a consideration of what the State should or should not do had to take account of what could and what could not be expected of individuals. Thus the inadequacy of Utilitarian psychology proved fatal. For Utilitarianism had taken the individual for granted, not in the sense that when the State has done all that it can the success of all social and political effort depends on individual effort and faith and vigour, but too much in the sense that individuals left to themselves work in natural harmony. Each seeking unhindered his individual happiness will produce the happiness of all. The Utilitarians had approached the problems of democracy as superior persons, calculating, from the calm height of the scientific legislator, like Bentham, or of the civil servant at the India House, like James Mill, the efforts of the masses whom their wisdom was to guide. They wanted to make politics as much as possible an exact science; and the scientist, when he approaches social questions, is always apt to regard human nature other than his own as being atomistic and homogeneous. The more it is so the more is it ready for the impress of his experimenting genius. The idealists, on the other hand, were real democrats. They approached the problem of democracy from the standpoint of the ordinary citizen. T. H. Green, though a college tutor and a university professor, was intensely interested in the affairs of his own city of Oxford. He was a member of the Oxford School Board and a hard-working member of the Oxford City Council. It was characteristic of him that he was not appointed to the City Council as one of the University members, but stood in the ordinary way as a candidate for the north ward of the city. He did his share in the dull, day-to-day committee work of party organisation. He both served on the School Board and was the chief agent in founding the City of Oxford School for Boys. He took an active part in the agitation for temperance reform, and characteristically at the same time set up a coffee tavern in St Clement's. He saw more than most people what an amount of steady, disinterested devotion from ordinary men and women it takes to run a modern democracy. He understood that because he had taken part in the running of politics himself. He knew what being an active citizen meant. Something of the same could be said of Edward Caird's life in Glasgow and Bosanquet's in London. Their understanding of the State came from their serving it as ordinary citizens.

Such a standpoint was bound to make all the difference to their democratic philosophy. They knew well how much democracy asks of the ordinary man, and therefore how entirely inadequate Hedonism is as a foundation of democratic theory. They knew, as all do who take an active part in the citizens' side of politics, the active and inspiring work done in that kind of political effort by those who get their inspiration from religion. They started with an active participation in social life and social work, and then asked what could the State and the State's activities do to help them in their problems. The only way in which democracy can be understood is by being one of the ordinary people who have to work it. It cannot be understood from the top, from the standpoint of the professional legislator or the professional civil servant. In talking of these men as idealists we are apt to imply that idealists are remote from practical affairs, men speculating abstractly in the State without knowing anything of the ordinary difficulties of politics. But it is only men and women who have taken part in the dull spadework of politics and social effort, grappling along with other ordinary men with difficulties arising from incompetence and complacence and fatalism, who know what an unusual amount of idealism goes to the running of a practical democracy. T. H. Green and his school were idealists, but they were under no illusions about human nature—no illusions either way. Their idealism consisted in regarding the State from the point of view of what could be made out of it. They had learned from Plato that the nature of any social institution which has had an historical development is best understood by looking at it from its highest realisation downward rather than from its rudimentary beginnings upward. The justification of the State, and, indeed, of any institution, depended for them on the opportunities which it awarded men for their good use of it. Such an attitude is entirely compatible with recognising how far institutions fall short of what they might be, or what perverted use men may make of them. There is a great chapter in Green's *Principles of Political Obligation* entitled "Will, not Force, the Basis of the State." The very title is taken by some critics to show a hopelessly idealistic outlook. But how sane is the temper of this paragraph!

> The idea of a common good which the State fulfils has never been the sole influence actuating those who have been agents in the historical process by which States have come to be formed; and even so far as it has actuated them, it has been only as conceived in some very imperfect form that it has done so. This is equally true of those who contribute to the formation and maintenance of States rather as agents and of those who do so rather as patients. No one could pretend that even the most thoughtful and dispassionate publicist is capable of the idea of the good served by the State to which he belongs in its fulness. He apprehends it only in some of its bearings; but it is as a common good that he apprehends it, *i.e.*, not as a good for himself or for this man or that more than for another, but for all members equally, in virtue of their relation to each other and their common nature. The idea which the ordinary citizen has of the common good served by the State is much more limited in content. Very likely he does not think of it at all in connection with anything which the State represents to him. But he has a clear understanding

of certain interests and rights common to himself with his neighbours, if only such as consist in getting his wages paid at the end of the week, in getting his money's worth at the shop, in the inviolability of his own person and that of his wife. Habitually and instinctively, *i.e.*, without asking the reason why, he regards the claim which in these respects he makes for himself as conditional upon his recognising a like claim in others, and thus as in the proper sense a right—a claim of which the essence lies in its being common to himself with others. Without this distinctive recognition he is one of the "dangerous classes," virtually outlawed by himself. With it, though he have no reverence for the State under that name, no sense of an interest shared by others in maintaining it, he has the needful elementary conception of a common good maintained by law. It is the fault of the State if this conception fails to make him a loyal subject, if not an intelligent patriot. It is a sign that the State is not a true State, that it is not fulfilling its primary function of maintaining law equally in the interest of all, but is being administered in the interest of classes; whence it follows that the obedience which, if not rendered willingly, the State compels the citizen to render is not one that he feels any spontaneous interest in rendering, because it does not present itself to him as the condition of the maintenance of those rights and interests, common to himself with his neighbours, which he understands.[1]

T. H. Green and his school are also idealists in that they are concerned with the moral questions involved in politics. They are not simply trying to describe what the State actually is or does, but to deal with the principle of political obligation. That is regarded by them first and foremost from the point of view of the individual—"Why should I obey the State?" but the answer to that question depends for them on what the State contributes or is capable of contributing towards the moral life. In the first paragraph of his lectures Green says:

My purpose is to consider the moral function or object served by law or by the system of rights and obligations which the State enforces, and in so doing to discover the true ground or justification for obedience to law. My plan will be (1) to state in outline what I consider the true function of law to be, this being at the same time the true ground of our moral duty to obey the law, and throughout I distinguish moral duty from legal obligations; (2) to examine the chief doctrines of political obligation that have been current in modern Europe and by criticising them to bring out more clearly the main points of a truer

[1] *Principles of Political Obligation*, § 121.

doctrine; (3) to consider in detail the chief rights and obligations enforced in civilised States, inquiring what is their justification, and what is the ground for respecting them on the principle stated.[1]

Green then argues that

the value of the institutions of civil life lies in their operation as giving reality to the capacities of will and reason and enabling them to be freely exercised. In their general effect, apart from particular aberrations, they render it possible for a man to be freely determined by the idea of a possible satisfaction of himself instead of being driven this way and that by external forces, and thus they give reality to the capacity called will; and they enable him to realise his reason, *i.e.*, his idea of self-perfection, by acting as a member of a social organisation in which each contributes to the better being of all the rest.[2]

This is the moral justification of social institutions in general. But law and the State need a special justification in that, as distinguished from the other institutions of social life, they imply force, and the relation of force to the moral life is a peculiar one.

The *jus naturæ* is distinguished from the sphere of moral duty because admitting of enforcement by law. Moral duties do not admit of being so enforced. The question sometimes put, whether moral duties should be enforced by law, is really an unmeaning one; for they simply cannot be enforced. Nay, the enforcement of an outward act, the moral character of which depends on a certain motive and disposition, may often contribute to render that motive and disposition impossible; and from this arises a limitation to the proper province of law in enforcing acts. . . . Thus the *jus naturæ*, the system of rights and obligations, as it should become no less than as it actually is maintained, is distinct from morality in the proper sense. But it is related to it. . . .[3]

Thus we begin the ethical criticism of law with two principles: (1) that nothing but external acts can be matter of 'obligation' (in the restricted sense); and (2) that, in regard to that which can be made matter of obligation, the question of what should be made matter of obligation—the question of how far rights and obligations as actually established by law correspond to the true *jus naturæ*—must be considered with reference to the moral end, as serving which alone law and the

[1] *Op. cit.*, § 1. [2] *Op. cit.*, § 7. [3] *Op. cit.*, § 10.

obligations imposed by law have their value. In a later paragraph he says:

> The business of law is to maintain certain conditions of life—to see that certain actions are done which are necessary to the maintenance of those conditions, others omitted which would interfere with them.[1]

This is, then, Green's fundamental position as regards the moral function of law—that compulsory morality is a contradiction in terms, and yet that law serves a moral end because it helps to maintain certain conditions of life. Because its relation to morality is ancillary, not creative, the State on this view must be distinguished from society. It acts as a framework within which social institutions, which have a real life of their own, may flourish. "A State presupposes other forms of community, with the rights that arise out of them, and only exists as sustaining, securing, and completing them." From this general position there follows Green's account of the nature of rights and the new and significant meaning he gives to "natural rights."

The end of the State is

> to render it possible for a man to be freely determined, and therefore rights—the separate purpose of the State—are aids to liberty or liberties. But liberties are of no use or have no meaning except in relation to a good for which they are to be used. 'Should be' implies on the part of whoever is capable of it the conception of an ideal, unattained condition of himself, as an absolute end. Without this conception the recognition of a power as a right would be impossible. A power on the part of anyone is so recognised by others, as one which should be exercised, when these others regard it as in some way a means to that ideal good of themselves which they alike conceive; and the possessor of the power comes to regard it as a right through consciousness of its being thus recognised as contributory to a good in which he too is interested. No one, therefore, can have a right except (1) as a member of a society; and (2) of a society in which some common good is recognised by the members of the society as their own ideal good, as that which should be for each of them.[2]

Granted, then, that in any given society there is some kind of recognition of a common good, there are certain powers of action which ought to be safeguarded and recognised, because they contribute to the maintenance and furtherance

[1] *Op. cit.*, §§ 10 and 11.

[2] *Op. cit.*, § 25.

of that common good. It does not follow that they will be so recognised, and therefore a distinction must be made between rights which are actually recognised, legal rights, and rights which ought to be recognised. This obviously corresponds to the old distinction of positive and natural law; but natural law is given an entirely new nature by Green. It remains an ideal to which actual law ought to conform, but it is not an immutable ideal, the same at all times and places. It is itself dependent on the moral conditions of society at any given time. The rights which ought to be recognised depend on the common good actually recognised by that society at that time. In that sense politics must always take ethics for granted.

When we, therefore, as active citizens, are considering how far we should call on the resources of the State to maintain a certain system of rights and obligations, not only are we to remember that any system of rights and obligations can only maintain favourable circumstances for the exercise of the good life, not create the good life, but we are also to remember that our conception of what is the good life which is to be furthered and assisted by law must depend not on an abstract good, not on our own conception of good, but on what we believe members of society in general will recognise to be for the common good. When we appeal from the law as it is to the law as it ought to be our appeal is to be based on a reasoned faith in the capacities and decencies of the ordinary man of our own time and society. Our appeal is to be from the State as it is to the State as it reasonably might be, considering what its citizens are.

This has none of the definite and decisive character of the old appeals to natural and inalienable rights. It assumes a democracy which has got beyond slogans and formulæ and is able to consider political questions on their merits. But there is no question that it does presuppose that the State is being asked continually to justify itself before its citizens. The doctrine that the justification of the State's force depends on the services which that force renders ought to imply that when these services are not rendered the State's force is not justified, and political obligation disappears. It is one of the merits of Green that he both recognised that the State should and might render immense services to morality, and was also perfectly clear that it did not always render that service,—might, indeed, do the opposite; that the citizen had therefore rights against the State. If the State normally merits the citizen's obedience there are times when it is the citizen's duty to disobey the State.

> If we regard the State as the sustainer and harmoniser of social relations it would follow that the individual can have no right against the State; that its law must be to him of absolute authority. But in fact, as actual States at best fulfil but partially their ideal function, we cannot apply this rule to practice. The general principle that the citizen must never act otherwise than as a citizen does not carry with it an obligation under all conditions to conform to the law of his State, since those laws may be inconsistent with the true end of the State as the sustainer and harmoniser of social relations. . . . Thus to the question: Has the individual no rights against enactments founded on imperfect views of social well-being? we may answer: He has no rights against those founded on any right to do as he likes. Whatever counter-rights he has must be founded on a relation to the social well-being and that a relation of which his fellow citizens are aware. He must be able to point to some public interest, generally recognised as such, which is involved in the exercise of the power claimed by him as a right; to show that it is not the general well-being, even as conceived by his fellow-citizens, but some special interest of a class that is concerned in promoting the exercise of the power claimed.[1]

But though Green is careful to state all the conditions which must exist before a citizen can have rights against the State, he does yet agree that

> there may be cases in which the public interest—not merely according to some remote philosopher's view of it, but according to conceptions which the people are able to assimilate—is best served by a violation of some actual law.

We get from Green, therefore, a far higher conception of the State's function than we do from the Utilitarians. The good life is the end of all social activity. It cannot exist without freedom. The State can only further it indirectly, and may, by mistaking its sphere and capacities, do harm. But the State's compulsions are not the only hindrances to

[1] *Op. cit.*, §§ 143 and 144.

liberty, and the good citizen will consider what in social and economic conditions are harming the conditions necessary to the living of the good life, and ask whether the State's compulsion may not be so used in the removal of these harmful conditions as to produce an addition of real liberty. So the social legislation of the last half of the nineteenth century could be defended on the principle that such State action, by hindering economic or social inequality or lack of freedom, increased men's freedom. This is the line, for example, taken by Ritchie in his *Principles of State Interference*. This political theory is in practice far more empirical than was Utilitarianism. For it implies that when we ask what the State ought or ought not to do we have to consider the capacities of the social institutions of the time and of the citizens, and our answer will probably only be that the balance of advantages are in one direction or another. This idealism does not pretend to relieve men of their responsibilities as citizens, of studying the facts as thoroughly and carefully as they can, and thus acting on what is a reasoned faith. To those, therefore, who think that a political theory should give definite and clear-cut answers to practical political questions, and explain just what the State ought and just what it ought not to do, or exactly when the citizen is justified in disobeying the law, Green's teaching may seem indefinite and inconclusive.

> In such a state of things, the citizen has no rule of 'right' (in the strict sense of the word) to guide him. . . . Was there then nothing to direct him either way? Simply, I should answer, the general rule of looking to the moral good of mankind, to which a necessary means is the organisation of the State, which again requires unity of control in the common interest, over the outward actions of men. . . . It must be admitted that without more knowledge and foresight than the individual can be expected to possess, this rule, if he had recognised it, could have afforded him no sure guidance; but this is only to say that there are times of political difficulty in which the line of conduct adopted may have the most important effect, but in which it is very hard to know what is the proper line to take.[1]

There are, no doubt, times when to be told that circumstances alter cases and principles need knowledge and judgment

[1] *Op. cit.*, § 106.

for their application may only paralyse men's actions, when the clear-cut if erroneous pronouncements of dogmatic schools are actually more effective. Green's principles imply for their proper application an educated democracy.

> Yet they have writ no rule
> nor rubric whereby conduct can in lesser affairs
> accommodate these principles, when they conflict
> in upright personalities, nor square their use
> with the intricate contingencies that knit our lives,
> and the interaction of unrelated sequencies.
> In that uncharted jungle a good man will do right,
> while an ill-disposition will miss and go wrong.[1]

A. D. LINDSAY

[1] Robert Bridges, *The Testament of Beauty.*

BOOK LIST

A. PRIMARY AUTHORITIES

GREEN, T. H.:

1. *Prolegomena to Ethics.* 1883.
2. Works, edited by R. L. Nettleship. 3 vols. 1885–88.
3. *Lectures on the Principles of Political Obligation.* 1895.

B. SECONDARY AUTHORITIES

FAIRBROTHER, W. H.: *The Philosophy of T. H. Green.* 1896.
MUIRHEAD, J. H.: *The Service of the State.* 1908.
NETTLESHIP, R. L.: *Memoir of T. H. Green.* 1906.
RITCHIE, D. G.: *The Principles of State Interference.* 1891.
SIDGWICK, H.: *Lectures on the Ethics of T. H. Green.* 1902.

VIII

MATTHEW ARNOLD AND THE EDUCATIONISTS

MATTHEW ARNOLD is an eminent Victorian about whom Lytton Strachey did not enlighten us, though he has not escaped attacks from the post-War generation, one of which I shall refer to at the end of this essay. He was almost as eminent in prose as in poetry, and more than half his prose writings are concerned with political and social ideas, mainly, of course, in their relation to the educational problems of his day. Yet, while Carlyle, Ruskin, and William Morris receive full recognition as political thinkers from students of modern political theory, Arnold's political ideas have been generally passed over or misunderstood.

It is to some extent, perhaps, a case of *embarras de richesses.* There were so many Matthew Arnolds. There were the Arnolds that the public knew. First of all, of course, there was Arnold the poet, the third of the great mid-Victorian trio, who, as he himself says justly enough, possessed " less poetic sentiment than Tennyson, less intellectual vigour and abundance than Browning, but more of a fusion of the two than either." Then there was Arnold the literary critic, and the publication of the brilliant *Essays in Criticism* (1865) is one of the major events in the history of nineteenth-century English literature. Even more conspicuous in the public eye was Arnold the prophet of culture, " the elegant Jeremiah " of that popular mythology which the journalists of every age formulate about great men they cannot understand. In this Arnold was in some sense a precursor of the " Gloomy Dean " ; and, indeed, he had not a little in common with Dr Inge, though his " vivacities " remind us more often of Mr Bernard Shaw. Later, too, he became famous as an unorthodox theologian ; yet his books, like *Literature and Dogma* and *God and the Bible*, which seemed flippant and almost blasphemous to most religious people of his day, and were read surreptitiously and with glee by hosts of young persons, contain nothing which would shock a mild modernist of our own time. Lastly, there was revealed to an astonished generation, by the *Notebooks* published after his death, a devotional Arnold, an Arnold who lived in daily communion with God as a sincere, passionate, and humble Christian.

So much for the Arnolds known to the world. The professional Arnold was more obscure. As H.M.I. of elementary education he tramped the schools for thirty-five years (1851–86) and wrote reports which are still read by the curious in such matters. And twice he acted as Assistant Commissioner to Royal Commissions on education, producing reports at their behest upon education in foreign countries. These reports make excellent reading and are full of political ideas. But Blue Books! Who read them then or reads them now? And so the political ideas they contain have lain buried, while Arnold's later political essays, with the exception of *Culture and Anarchy* and *Friendship's Garland*, have been almost equally neglected. Arnold is so renowned, so prolific, and so versatile a writer in other fields that he has himself obscured his own reputation as a political thinker.

Every one, of course, knows *Culture and Anarchy*, in some ways his greatest, certainly his most characteristic, prose work. But *Culture and Anarchy* is not a safe guide to his political ideas, despite its sub-title, "An Essay in Political and Social Criticism." For one thing, it was essentially a popular book, in which he attempted to gain the ear of the general public, especially the Nonconformist public, for principles already expounded in more serious educational and political essays. Further, it was written at a time of great political excitement, immediately after the passing of the Reform Act of 1867, when many felt that England was drifting towards anarchy. 'Cool' is, as Sir Edmund Chambers has recently pointed out,[1] a favourite epithet with Arnold the poet, and coolness was an essential quality of Arnold the thinker. Arnold kept his head, and that is one of his outstanding qualities among his contemporaries. But the political excitement of 1866–69 was

[1] *Matthew Arnold* (Warton Lecture on English Poetry, 1931) (1932).

too much even for him. His temperature rose, not very high, but sufficiently to deflect him from the usual tenour of his way. Thus he expresses himself far more strongly in *Culture and Anarchy* on the State as a centre of authority and on the necessity of a firm executive than in any other of his political writings before or after; and he toned down some passages in the second edition of the book (1875) when the excitement had evaporated. I may quote one amusing example of this which throws light on Thomas Arnold as well as Matthew. After dwelling upon the importance of supporting the executive " in repressing anarchy and disorder " Thomas Arnold's son continues, in a disorderly sentence of anarchical structure:

> With me, indeed, this rule of conduct is hereditary. I remember my father, in one of his unpublished letters written more than forty years ago, when the political and social state of the country was gloomy and troubled, and there were riots in many places, goes on, after strongly insisting on the badness and foolishness of the Government, and on the harm and dangerousness of our feudal and aristocratical constitution of society, and ends thus: "As for rioting, the old Roman way of dealing with *that* is always the right one; flog the rank and file, and fling the ringleaders from the Tarpeian Rock!" [1]

This was cut out in 1875, probably because Arnold had ceased to feel comfortable about it. Another reason for caution in relying too much upon *Culture and Anarchy* as an expression of his political views is that the whole book is steeped in irony. He was writing *Friendship's Garland* at the same time, and the high spirits of that brilliant piece of political satire overflow into the twin volume. Readers without a sense of humour, or even readers who are not acquainted with Arnold's special type of humour and what he himself called his " vivacity," may easily misunderstand points in the argument, points which are quite plain in his more serious essays on politics.

The best book I know on English political thought at the time of Arnold is a little volume in the Home University Library by Professor Ernest Barker.[2] I am sure that Professor

[1] *Culture and Anarchy*, p. 203 (Cambridge Press, 1932).

[2] *Political Thought in England, 1848–1914: From Herbert Spencer to the Present Day*.

Barker enjoys Arnold's wit as much as any man, but it is clear that he has relied too much on *Culture and Anarchy*, and has seriously misrepresented Arnold in consequence. His bibliography mentions no other writing by Arnold, and in the text he classes Arnold with Carlyle and Ruskin as an "authoritarian." Had Dr Barker studied Arnold's essays on "Democracy" and on "Equality" he must have written differently about him, for Arnold is not of the school of Ruskin and Carlyle at all, despite some likenesses, and derived his ideas from quite other sources, while "authoritarian" is a very misleading label. A larger book on the same period, Dr Murray's *The English Social and Political Thinkers of the Nineteenth Century*, is even more at sea, and for much the same reason. When, for instance, I find him saying that Arnold possessed "an unbounded admiration" for the English aristocracy; that "the pillar of his politics is liberty"; and that he "summarily dismisses" (among other contemporary topics of interest) the extension of the franchise, the question of the relation between Church and State, and the problem of national unity, I can only suppose that Dr Murray is totally unacquainted with the writings he professes to be discussing.

The purpose of the ensuing essay is not to defend or to criticise Arnold, though I may, perhaps, be allowed to praise him a little; but to expound him, to give some account of his political and social ideas, in the hope that this exposition may incite some more competent student of politics to assign Arnold his true place in the roll of English political thinkers, a place which I suspect should be no mean one. Before attempting this, however, I wish to say something on what I may call his political education. It must be a brief sketch of a large subject. But without some reference to the sources of Arnold's thought his ideas cannot be readily appreciated. Five main influences may be distinguished. First and perhaps paramount is that of Thomas Arnold.

As Matthew Arnold himself quaintly puts it, he was "papa's continuator." Thomas Arnold died at the age of forty, just after his eldest son had gone to Oxford, but his influence was an abiding one, perhaps all the more abiding for the premature break of the material link. Matthew never found Thomas out, as most sons do who live to be their father's elders. And it was from Thomas that young Matthew learned to reverence Aristotle, a writer whom the Doctor never tired of talking about, quoting, discussing; so that by the time Matthew left Rugby he must have had Aristotle in the blood. Indeed, the main reason why Thomas Arnold sent his son to Oxford, so he tells us, was that he might study Aristotle the better.[1] This passion was prompted by no ideal of pure scholarship. To the elder Arnold Aristotle was not a classic so much as a modern author whose principles were of vital importance to England of the thirties and forties. "Aristotle and Plato," he says,

> and Thucydides and Cicero and Tacitus are most untruly called ancient writers. They are virtually our own countrymen and contemporaries, but have the advantage which is enjoyed by intelligent travellers, that their observation has been exercised in a field out of the reach of common men, and that, having thus seen in a manner with our eyes what we cannot see for ourselves, their conclusions are such as bear upon our own circumstances.[2]

In the same way he regarded much of ancient history as essentially modern. When Matthew, then, appeals to "culture" as the real key of political wisdom he is thinking chiefly of the classics, and especially the classical philosophers, as interpreted by his father.

Thomas Arnold's liberalism was of a brand peculiar to himself; and though his son did not politically see eye to eye with him his liberalism also was of the cross-bench order, and both were far more sympathetic with working-class movements, then very much in their infancy, than with the current philosophical radicalism of the day. Moreover, there was the life at Rugby itself—the republic of Plato interpreted in school terms, the influence of which upon Matthew must have been profound; and, just as Robert Owen, having fashioned and seen the New Lanark experiment, could never understand why his principles were not adopted wholesale and the millennium ushered in without further ado, so the younger Arnold, having been a boy at Rugby in the great days of its transformation, dreamed for the rest of his life of an indefinite multiplication of Rugby day schools promoted by the State.

Yet even more profound than the influence of Rugby was

[1] A. P. Stanley, *Life of Arnold*, vol. i, p. 14.

[2] Quoted by Joshua Fitch, *Thomas and Matthew Arnold*, p. 35.

that of Oxford, the beauty of which took the poet's eye and inspired him with a lifelong passion, so that he always turned to it as the spiritual capital of England. When he reached the university the "Oxford Movement" was in full swing, and that, too, influenced him, though he was never interested in ecclesiasticism. What he picked out was not dogma or ceremony, but the idea of the Church as an institution—in short, the political idea of the movement, the idea which is still prominent in the Modernism of our day. And of the Tractarians, though he refers to Pusey and others with respect, Newman, above all, was his hero. After his father Newman was the man who influenced him most, and anyone who compares *Culture and Anarchy* with *The Idea of a University* must see how great was the debt.

Our knowledge of Arnold's life at Oxford is meagre at present, though we shall no doubt learn more when his letters to Clough are published,[1] and though, of course, there are always *The Scholar Gipsy* and *Thyrsis* to delight us. It is clear, however, that his reading there was not restricted to Aristotle. Goethe and the French began to interest him. The spell of France, indeed, became a dominating influence in his life,[2] and the three main departments of his thought may each be traced back to a great Frenchman: in literary criticism to Sainte-Beuve, in moral ideas to Renan, in politics to de Tocqueville. The last-named published his *Democracy in America* in 1835, and the book was probably read by Arnold at Oxford. In any case it left an indelible impression upon his mind, with its spectacle of a society without culture, without traditions, without anything that could rightly be called State institutions; and it was probably de Tocqueville who sent him back with renewed zest to Burke, "of whom we can never read too much." One thing is clear: he rose from his perusal of the *Democracy in America* determined to dedicate his life to prevent England becoming Americanised; and the earliest of the *Letters*, dated 1848, contains the sentence: "I see a wave

[1] H. F. Lowry, *The Letters of Matthew Arnold to Arthur Hugh Clough* (Oxford, 1932) appeared after this article was written.

[2] Too much so, as he himself seems to admit in one of his later essays ("Numbers," in *Discourses in America*). It is curious to speculate what Arnold would have thought (and said!) about France in 1932.

of more than American vulgarity, moral, intellectual, and social, preparing to break over us."

A further instalment of his political education was provided by his appointment in 1851 as His Majesty's Inspector of Schools. Thus he was ten years studying England—and an inspectorship of schools gives one unique opportunities of such study—before he wrote his first essay in politics. His official work necessitated constant travel up and down the country, and of all Victorian prophets he knew his England best. Moreover, it was the cities and coasts of Philistia in which his duties lay, for at first the organisation of the Education Department assigned Church of England schools to clerical inspectors, which meant that Arnold, the layman, for some years visited the schools of Nonconformists alone. In these travels he discovered an England as crude, as formless, as uncultivated as the America of de Tocqueville, and wherever he moved he noted on the one hand the smug self-complacency of the middle classes, and on the other the abject misery and brutality of the poor. Arnold saw that the real hope for the poor, and for England as a whole, lay with the middle classes, for the simple reason that the immediate future of the country was theirs. Since Wesley the majority of the middle classes had become nonconformist, and after 1867 the majority of the electors were nonconformist also. But nothing could be done for these middle classes until they were educated, and they could not be educated, as he also saw, until the State provided schools for them. Arnold was not indifferent to popular education, as some have imagined—far from it!—but he felt that England had begun at the wrong end. It was the industrialised middle classes whose ideas would rule England for the next half-century or more, and they were "nearly the worst educated people in the world." Furthermore, State schools could not be provided until appropriate organs of the State had been created for that purpose, and the County Councils Act, which, for the first time, gave us those organs, was not passed until 1888, the year of Arnold's death.

Arnold accepted the inspectorship unwillingly, and complained of its drudgery, but it was not long before he came to perceive that his father's work could best be carried on in the field of State education. Thomas Arnold had begun to civilise the Barbarians. Matthew's mission was to civilise the Philistines. Somehow he must awaken the country to the need of secondary education and the need of State action to that end. His chance came with the setting up of three Royal Commissions on education in the decade of 1858–68: (1) the Newcastle Commission of 1858 on elementary education, which reported in 1861; (2) the Clarendon Commission of 1861 on the nine great public schools, which reported in 1864; and (3) the Taunton, or Schools Inquiry, Commission of 1864 on the other endowed schools of the country, which reported in 1867. He was appointed Assistant Commissioner for the first and third, with a special duty to investigate and report on foreign education. He did no official work for the second, but nevertheless he published a book on the subject of its inquiry. Thus we have three publications from him in connection with these three Commissions: (1) *Popular Education on the Continent* (1861), his report for the Newcastle Commission, to which he added a special introduction, of great importance for our present purpose, on "Democracy and the Modern State," afterwards republished in the volume of *Mixed Essays* (1879) under the title of "Democracy"; (2) *A French Eton: or Middle-class Education and the State* (1864), which was a kind of retort to the Clarendon Commission, a charming and characteristic book describing two typical French schools and making an eloquent appeal for State secondary education in England; (3) *Schools and Universities on the Continent* (1868), his report for the Taunton Commission, the last two chapters of which continue and reinforce the argument of *A French Eton*, with the added experience of a second visit to the Continent.

The first of the two chapters just mentioned begins with the following passage:

> I have now on two occasions, first in 1859 and again in 1865, had to make a close study, on the spot, and for many months together, of one of the most important branches of the civil organisation of the most civilised States of the Continent. Few Englishmen have had such an experience. If the convictions with which it leaves me seem strange to many Englishmen, it is not that I am differently constituted from the rest of my countrymen, but that I have seen what would certainly give them too, if they had seen it with their own eyes as I

have, reflections which they have never had before. No one of open mind, and not hardened in routine and prejudice, could observe for so long and from so near as I observed it the civil organisation of France, Germany, Italy, Switzerland, Holland, without having the conviction forced upon him that these countries have a civil organisation which has been framed with forethought and design to meet the wants of modern society; while our civil organisation in England still remains what time and chance have made it.

The only Continental states that reminded him of England were Austria and the Papal state of Rome. He continues:

> Modern States cannot either do without free institutions, or do without a rationally planned and effective civil organisation. Unlike in other things, Austria, Rome, and England are alike in this, that the civil organisation of each implies, at the present day, a denial or an ignorance of the right of mind and reason to rule human affairs. At Rome this right is sacrificed in the name of religion; in Austria, in the name of loyalty; in England, in the name of liberty. All respectable names; but none of them will in the long run save its invoker, if he persists in disregarding the inevitable laws which govern the life of modern society.

By 1868 the political education of Matthew Arnold was complete. Inspired by the teaching of a father with a passion to set up the Kingdom of God in England, steeped in Aristotle, Plato, Burke, and de Tocqueville, better acquainted than any of his contemporaries with the realities of English social life, especially of that "core of English society, Protestant Dissent," and all this crowned with an unexampled study of Continental State service in action, he was ready to speak out, and he did.

The Taunton Commission had been much impressed with Arnold's views. Their report advocated elaborate reforms in secondary education, together with the establishment of a State education service to carry them out. But Royal Commissions at this time were not usually set up to recommend anything constructive, any new step forward, still less any State action. All they were expected to effect was the removal of medieval restrictions to the freedom of existing institutions. In other words, those who set them up were inspired by Benthamite ideals. The upshot of the Taunton Commission was very disappointing. The mouse that emerged from a mountainous report was the Endowed Schools Act of 1869, which gave the State power to redistribute existing endowments—a very useful measure as far as it went, but falling far short of what Arnold and the Commissioners had hoped for.

Meanwhile he had already begun to attack the whole problem of national culture and the " civil organisation " of England in a series of articles in the *Cornhill Magazine*, beginning in July 1867 and continuing into September 1868, articles reprinted early in 1869, with a special preface, as *Culture and Anarchy*. The book, as I have said, reflects the tense political excitement of the period 1866–69, which saw riots in London, Bright's campaign in the country, the passing of the Second Reform Act, and threatened a spate of liberal, not to say radical, legislation. Arnold's calm was undoubtedly somewhat ruffled by these events, but he certainly did not believe with Carlyle that England was about to shoot Niagara into the whirlpool of anarchy. As I have expressed it elsewhere, what he did was to use certain anarchical tendencies and lawless incidents of his own day, due to a temporary phase of intense political excitement, as illustrations of the deep-seated spiritual anarchy of the English people, an anarchy which expressed itself in its hideous, sprawling industrial cities, its loud-voiced assertion of personal liberty, its dismal, stuffy, and cantankerous forms of Christianity, its worship of size and numbers and wealth and machinery generally, its State-blindness, and its belief in collision—collision of parties, of sects, of firms—as the only way of salvation.[1]

Of the other book of this period, *Friendship's Garland*, I can say nothing here, beyond observing that, pretending to be letters expressing the views of an outspoken young Prussian *savant*, whom Arnold invents as the mouthpiece of his entertaining sallies upon British self-complacency, it is one of the most delightful political satires in the English language.

Arnold was a sincere patriot who never shrank from criticising his own country. He was a member of the middle classes who spent a large portion of his life castigating middle-class vulgarity and narrow-mindedness. He was a Liberal in politics ; he believed that the future of England and of the world lay with some form of Liberalism ; yet he showed himself an untiring and uncompromising opponent of almost every

[1] *Culture and Anarchy*, p. xxxiii.

Liberal measure of the age. During his life the Liberal Party won two great victories at the polls, one in 1868, following on the Second Reform Act, and the other in 1880, preceding the Third Reform Act. The bouquets Arnold threw the conquerors of 1868 were *Culture and Anarchy* and *Friendship's Garland*. His tribute to the crowning mercy of 1880, an essay called "The Future of Liberalism," was in style more sober, but not a whit less hostile. In this he describes himself as a "Liberal of the future"—that is to say, "a politician of that commonwealth of which the pattern, as the philosopher says, exists perhaps somewhere in heaven, but certainly is at present found nowhere on earth."[1] The true politics, in his view, as in Plato's and Aristotle's, were concerned with the question 'how to live.' But let me quote his own words:

> The true and noble science of politics is even the very chief of the sciences, because it deals with this question [the question 'how to live'] for the benefit of man, not as an isolated creature, but in that state "without which," as Burke says, "man could not by any possibility arrive at the perfection of which his nature is capable"—for the benefit of man in society. Now of man in society the capital need is, that the whole body of society should come to live with a life worthy to be called *human*, and corresponding to man's aspirations and powers. This, the humanisation of man in society, is civilisation. The aim for all of us is to promote it, and to promote it is above all the aim for the true politician.[2]

In an address delivered to working men a year or two earlier he declared:

> I have no very ardent interest . . . in politics in their present state in this country. What interests me is English civilisation; and our politics in their present state do not seem to me to have much bearing upon that. English civilisation—the humanising, the bringing into a harmonious and truly humane life, of the whole body of English society—that is what interests me. I try to be a disinterested observer of all that really helps and hinders that.[3]

In the operations of the "Liberal practitioners" of his time he could see little enough to help and much to hinder this humanising process. What the nation needed above all things was building up; they were all for pulling down. They

[1] *Irish Essays*, p. 144. [2] *Ibid.*, p. 149. [3] *Ibid.*, p. 118.

were sworn to "the politics of Dissent," which seemed to him "quite played out."[1] The kind of measures that excited them were the Deceased Wife's Sister Bill, which ministered to "that double craving so characteristic of our Philistine, and so eminently exemplified in that crowned Philistine, Henry the Eighth—the craving for forbidden fruit and the craving for legality,"[2] or the Burials Act of 1880 for enabling Nonconformists to use their own form of service in the parish churchyard, which meant substituting a liturgy in the style of Eliza Cook for a liturgy in the style of Milton,[3] or the Bill "for granting Local Option, as it is called, for doing away with the addiction of our lower classes to their porter and their gin."[4] And all the while they looked with delight upon the spread of great centres of manufacture, such as St Helens or Bolton or Wigan, which Cobbett rudely but justly called "hell-holes," and expressed their own vision of the good life in the mean and unlovely suburbs that disfigured the hills to the north and south of London. And even their more important measures were conceived in so mechanical and doctrinaire a fashion that they caused as much harm as good. Free Trade, for instance, had been introduced in order, he declared, not to promote "the humanisation of man in society," but in order that cheap food might act as a stimulus to the production of wealth and to the growth of population. Arnold ironically confesses to doubts "whether the indefinite multiplication of manufactories and small houses . . . and poor people can be an absolute good in itself," and he notes that in times of bad trade an overplus of these commodities may prove an embarrassment. But *The Times* is always with us, and *The Times* is there to clear these doubts with its "firm philosophy" and to fortify him against the depressing sights which assail him in the east of London, "whither my avocations often lead me." Indeed, he finds it helpful, he says, to carry about with him one particular passage from that journal, a passage "full of the finest economical doctrine." The cutting runs as follows:

> The East End is the most commercial, the most industrial, the most fluctuating region of the metropolis. It is always the first to suffer;

[1] *Irish Essays*, pp. 137–138.
[2] *Culture and Anarchy*, p. 181.
[3] *Irish Essays*, p. 175.
[4] *Ibid.*, p. 174.

> for it is the creature of prosperity, and falls to the ground the instant there is no wind to bear it up. The whole of that region is covered with huge docks, shipyards, manufactories, and a wilderness of small houses, all full of life and happiness in brisk times, but in dull times withered and lifeless, like the deserts we read of in the East. Now their brief spring is over. There is no one to blame for this, it is the result of Nature's simplest laws! [1]

The Times, thus quoted by Arnold in 1868, makes grim reading in 1933, when the winds of prosperity have been followed by an economic blizzard, and half the industrial life of Britain lies "withered and lifeless."

As for the Irish question, which overshadowed the politics of Arnold's time as the desperate plight of finance and trade does those of ours, he attacked Gladstone's whole policy as being disintegrating just where it should have been constructive, and based upon the prejudices of English Nonconformists instead of the real needs of Irish Roman Catholics. The Irish Church, for example, had, he declared, been disestablished in 1869 not in the interests of reason and justice, but by "the power of the Nonconformists' antipathy to Church establishments." Had reason and justice been pursued, to say nothing of the policy of trying to win the affection of the people of Ireland, the Church property of Ireland would have been distributed among the three main Churches of Ireland, the Roman Catholic, the Anglican, and the Presbyterian.[2] The Home Rule scheme, again, seemed to him a proposal for surgical amputation when what the body politic needed was strengthening and consolidating from within. Set up an efficient system of local government; let the executive defend the tenant from the landlord's tyranny; fill the country with good schools and give her Catholic universities; make the Roman Catholic Church one of the established Churches of the country—such was his solution of the Irish problem. It was a statesman's solution, and, had it been then tried, who will say that it might not have succeeded? But the way was barred: "No road," by order of Mr Spurgeon.

> "Go to the Surrey Tabernacle," say my liberal friends to me, "regard that forest of firm, serious, unintelligent faces uplifted towards Mr Spurgeon, and then ask yourself what would be the effect

[1] *Culture and Anarchy*, pp. 189–190. [2] *Ibid.*, p. 33.

produced on all that force of hard and narrow prejudice by a proposal of Mr Gladstone to pay the Catholic priests in Ireland, or to give them money for their houses and churches, or to establish schools and universities suited to Catholics, as England has public schools and universities suited to Anglicans, and Scotland such as are suited to Presbyterians. What would be Mr Gladstone's chance of carrying such a measure?"[1]

Arnold was as deeply interested and concerned with Irish affairs as Burke had been in his day and from very much the same point of view. "You do not suppose," he quotes Bright as saying in 1881, "that the fourteen members of the Government spend days and weeks in the consideration of a measure such as the Irish Land Bill without ascertaining in connection with it everything everybody else can know"; upon which his comment is that to know everything is not enough; what is chiefly required in Irish affairs is that some one should *think* about them. And he took the trouble to collect and reprint Burke's *Letters, Speeches, and Tracts on Irish Affairs* in the hope that they might set some one thinking.

All these things being so, to what purpose was party politics? The wise should keep out of them, should keep off the public stage altogether.

> Plenty of people there will be without us—country gentlemen in search of a club, demagogues in search of a tub, lawyers in search of a place, industrialists in search of gentility—who will come from the east and from the west, and will sit down at that Thyestean banquet of claptrap which English public life for these many years past has been.[2]

Parliament was hopeless for long to come:

> Parliamentary Conservatism will and must long mean this, that the Barbarians should keep their heritage; and parliamentary Liberalism, that the Barbarians should pass away, as they will pass away, and that into their heritage the Philistines should enter. . . . Presently perhaps, Mr Odger and Mr Bradlaugh will be there with their mission to oust both Barbarians and Philistines, and to get the heritage for the Populace.[3]

It is a succinct history of Parliament from 1870 to 1932! and beyond 1932, for the end is not yet. But if Parliament

[1] *Irish Essays*, p. 38.
[2] *Culture and Anarchy*, pp. 209–210. [3] *Ibid.*, p. 210.

be no remedy, whither is one to look? Arnold turned to the schools, and especially to the schools of the middle classes, and, lo! they were not to be found.

This kind of thing, of course, gave immense pleasure to the Tories, and irritated the Liberal politicians past bearing. Yet neither of them understood Arnold in the least. He was a genuine Liberal, a far better Liberal than the professional party hacks; and when Gladstone brought in the Third Reform Bill, to enfranchise the agricultural labourer, a really Liberal measure which seemed even revolutionary to many of his followers, Arnold approved without qualification. "Not," he writes,

> that there is either any natural right in every man to the possession of a vote, or any gift of wisdom and virtue conferred by such possession. But if experience has established any one thing in this world, it has established this: that it is well for any great class and description of men in society to be able to say for itself what it wants, and not to have other classes, the so-called educated and intelligent classes, acting for it as its proctors, and supposed to understand its wants and to provide for them. They do not really understand its wants, they do not really provide for them.[1]

For all its quietness of utterance this is a profoundly democratic profession of faith, though, as a disciple of Burke, Arnold will have nothing, it will be noted, to do with "natural rights." He disliked and distrusted political mysticism, together with abstract political notions generally. Elsewhere he declares:

> So far as I can sound human consciousness, I cannot perceive that man is really conscious of any abstract natural rights at all. The natural right to have work found for one to do, the natural right to have food found for one to eat, rights sometimes so confidently and so indignantly asserted, seem to me quite baseless. It cannot be too often repeated: peasants and workmen have no natural rights, not one. Only we ought instantly to add, that kings and nobles have none either. If it is the sound English doctrine that all rights are created by law and are based upon expediency, and are alterable as the public advantage may require, certainly that orthodox doctrine is mine.[2]

I do not think that Arnold liked the word "progress" either. Certainly he does not appear to use it. At the same

[1] *Irish Essays*, p. 147. [2] *Mixed Essays*, pp. 61–62.

time he was deeply conscious that England, and European nations generally, were, in the mid-nineteenth century, at the beginning of a great period of what he calls " expansion " or, sometimes, " transformation," which he contrasts with periods of " concentration," such as the eighteenth century, or the age of Imperial Rome. Whether such expansion meant progress depended, of course, on how it was directed. He had a great contempt for the Benthamite notion that all we need do was to remove individual shackles upon freedom and leave human nature to do the rest. He was no Prussian, no believer in the authoritarian State, as Professor Barker suggests, but still less is Dr Murray right when he suggests that " liberty is the pillar of his politics." Not that he was opposed to political liberty; he insisted that in France and in Prussia there was not enough political liberty; but he saw very plainly that there was no danger at all of political liberty being crushed in England—his Nonconformist friends and fellow-Liberals would see to that.

It seemed, therefore, to him all the more necessary that the other aspects of modern democracy should be emphasised, aspects which would be likely to be overlooked in England; and among these he distinguished three as of special importance: (1) social equality; (2) the education of the middle classes; (3) the necessity of extending both the structure and activity of the State. It will be convenient to consider his views under these three heads.

To Arnold, as to de Tocqueville, the real significance of the democratic movement of this era of expansion was not political liberty but social liberty, or Equality, and if we are to seek for a central pillar to his politics it is in Equality we shall find it. For Arnold not only perceived this tendency, but applauded it. It may seem surprising to find that the fastidious professor of poetry at Oxford, the " elegant Jeremiah," the prophet of culture, whom Frederic Harrison compared with Hotspur's popinjay offering parmacety for the inward bruises of society,[1] was a leveller and egalitarian; but so he was, indeed, from first to last.

The essay on " Equality " of 1878, with Menander's " choose equality and flee greed " as its text, is simply an

[1] *Culture: a Dialogue* (*Fortnightly Review*, November 1867).

expansion of principles already laid down in the essay on "Democracy" of 1861, and the burden of both is that the inequalities of class and property in modern England have the inevitable effect of "materialising our upper class, vulgarising our middle class, and brutalising our lower class."[1] So he puts it in "Equality," and in "Democracy" he says:

> Can it be denied that to live in a society of equals tends in general to make a man's spirits expand and his faculties work easily and actively; while to live in a society of superiors, although it may occasionally be very good discipline, yet in general tends to tame the spirits and to make the play of the faculties less secure and active? Can it be denied that to be heavily overshadowed, to be profoundly insignificant, has, on the whole, a depressing and benumbing effect on the character?

And he continues:

> The question is about the common bulk of mankind, persons without extraordinary gifts or exceptional energy, and who will ever require, in order to make the best of themselves, encouragement and directly favouring circumstances. Can any one deny that for these, the spectacle, when they would rise, of a condition of splendour, grandeur, and culture, which they cannot possibly reach, has the effect of making them flag in spirit, and of disposing them to sink despondingly back into their own condition? Can any one deny that the knowledge how poor and insignificant the best condition of improvement and culture attainable by them must be esteemed by a class incomparably richer-endowed tends to cheapen this modest possible amelioration in the account of those classes also for whom it would be relatively a real progress, and to disenchant their imaginations with it?[2]

At the same time he notes and detests the "hideous English Toadyism" with which "lords and great people" are treated by the middle class, with its "immense vulgar-mindedness."[3] He notes, too, that the upper classes in England, "with no necessary function to fulfil, never conversant with life as it really is, tempted, flattered, spoilt from childhood to old age . . . is inevitably materialised, and the more so the more the development of industry and ingenuity augments the means of luxury."[4]

Lastly, the lower classes, sunk at the bottom of the social well, what hope or light for them? In answer, he

[1] *Mixed Essays*, p. 87.
[2] *Ibid.*, pp. 10–11.
[3] *Letters*, November 21, 1859.
[4] *Mixed Essays*, p. 88.

quotes from a contemporary French journalist, who writes of the English poor: "I consider this multitude to be absolutely devoid, not only of political principles, but even of the most simple notions of good and evil." [1] And elsewhere, speaking of France, he points to "the intelligence of their idea-moved masses which makes them politically as far superior to the insensible masses of England as to the Russian serfs." [2]

And so with the populace in Arnold's day it did not seem possible to do much. The task of popular education had been undertaken; he was himself an agent of it; and popular education in the long run would leaven the whole lump. But at the moment what was far more urgent was the education of the middle class, for this class was the heir of the aristocracy, and the future of England lay in its hands.

Arnold's views on the middle classes, or, as he called them, the Philistines, are too well known to be discussed in detail here. Most of *Culture and Anarchy* is about them—indeed, nearly everything he wrote in prose, literary criticism and his theological books included, is more or less concerned with them and their state of mind. This preoccupation was a tribute to their importance, not a mark of inveterate hostility. Indeed, he might laugh at them, he might scold them, he might preach at them, but he had a very real regard for them, and even some respect for them on certain sides of their character. In one of his later essays he wrote:

> The Puritan middle class, with all its faults, is still the best stuff in this nation. Some have hated and persecuted it, many have flattered and derided it—flattered it that while they deride it they may use it; I have believed in it. It is the best stuff in this nation, and its success is our best hope for the future. But to succeed it must be transformed.[3]

In the past the aristocracy had deserved well of England; they had made a great nation of her, and they had set a high standard of manners and integrity—they had, in a word, been the upholders of English civilisation. But their day was over; they were deteriorating, and with their constitutional stiffness of mind and impenetrability to ideas they were ill-suited to an era of change and expansion. It was necessary,

[1] *Mixed Essays*, p. 84. [2] *Letters*, March 10, 1848.
[3] *Mixed Essays*, p. 142.

therefore, to turn for leadership to the middle classes—and "the middle classes were the worst educated in the world"! They were self-complacent, crude, energetic; but they had no culture, dignity, or social manners, while their only ideas were liberty and industry—and "all the liberty and industry in the world" could not make England a *great* nation: what alone could do that were ideas and "a fine culture." Unless, then, the middle classes were transformed England was bound to become like America, the America de Tocqueville describes in such penetrating and depressing fashion; for America stood as a warning of what happened to a nation which acquired social equality before any high standard of social life and manners had been formed.[1]

This was the fear, the fear of Americanisation, which haunted Arnold and inspired everything he wrote upon the need for efficient schools for middle-class children. "Regard the necessities of a not distant future, and organise your secondary education," he begged the Newcastle Commission to say boldly to the Government. Two other commissions followed, both upon secondary education, but nothing came of them. Meanwhile the middle classes continued to be the worst educated in the world, continued to send their boys to be educated with Mr Creakle at Salem House.[2] And the reason, as Arnold very well knew, was that middle-class education, if it was to be efficient and organised, must be State education.

It was therefore as the provider of schools that Arnold first came to consider the nature and function of the State. In his day the English State was still the old police State, very much discredited. He points out that neither the aristocracy nor the middle class were believers in State action. The aristocracy were jealous of the executive in the interests of their own order. The middle classes profoundly distrusted State action, which had meant religious intolerance in the past, and at the same time despised it because they had successfully resisted it. But now the middle class had everything to gain from the State, for the State, owing to its great resources and power, was in a position "to bestow certain broad collective benefits upon the nation incomparably better than anything

[1] *Mixed Essays*, p. 68. [2] *Irish Essays*, pp. 62–63.

the middle classes could furnish by themselves."[1] These words, written in 1861, are, I fancy, the earliest clear anticipation of what Dicey calls the "collectivistic period," and which he dates from 1865. The first thing, then, that Arnold looked to from the State was public service. He wished to see the police State superseded by the service State.

His second hope was that the State would provide an unsectarian centre to the national life, would act as an example of civil unity, transcending all religious divisions. Such a centre and example were undoubtedly the supreme need of Arnold's time, the miserable squabbles of which are summed up in the concluding lines of his *Dover Beach*:

> And we are here as on a darkling plain
> Swept with confused alarms of struggle and flight,
> Where ignorant armies clash by night.

The state of affairs is well illustrated by a passage from *Popular Education on the Continent*:

> I heard the other day of an English National school aided by public money, the only school in the place, which had for one of its regulations that no child of dissenting parents should be admitted unless he consented to be baptised. I saw with my own eyes, the other day, in a British school aided by public money, a printed placard stuck up in a conspicuous place in the schoolroom, offering a reward of £10 to any Roman Catholic who could prove, by text, ten propositions; such as, that we ought to adore the Virgin Mary, that we ought to pray for the dead, etc. . . . Is it tolerable that such antics should be played in schools on which the grant of public money confers a public character? Would it be possible that they should be played in a public school in France, where the State permits liberty of conscience, but not liberty of persecution? In England the State makes itself denominational with the denominations,

and so "has been betrayed into a thousand anomalies."[2]

And he quotes Guizot:

> It is, in general, desirable that children whose families do not profess the same creed should early contract, by frequenting the same schools, those habits of reciprocal friendship and mutual tolerance which may ripen later, when they live together as grown-up citizens, into justice and harmony.[3]

[1] *Mixed Essays*, p. 28. [2] *Popular Education*, p. 148. [3] *Ibid.*, p. 69.

The growth of religious tolerance since the Education Act of 1902 is a striking testimony to the truth of Guizot's words, for that Act, which brought the denominational and undenominational elementary schools so close together that they became hardly distinguishable from each other, and promoted the great developments in municipal non-sectarian secondary education, has probably done more for the decline in religious asperity than anything else in the history of modern England.

But Arnold hoped for more than this. He would have liked to see all the great religious denominations of the country established, as the Church of England is established, convinced that only by nationalising the Churches and subordinating them to the State, which transcends them all, would they come to respect each other and work together, and that by this means, too, the sectary might be lost in the citizen. But here he is out of touch with modern notions, or modern notions have not yet caught him up. I sometimes wonder what Arnold would have made of *Churches in the Modern State*, by Neville Figgis, who was himself a great admirer of Arnold, and to whom, as a matter of fact, I owe my introduction, as an undergraduate, to *Friendship's Garland*.

But, above all, Arnold looked to the State to become the centre of national life, transcending all *classes*. He is fond of quoting Burke's famous apostrophe to the State as "a partnership in all science, a partnership in all art, a partnership in every virtue and in all perfection." He thought of it as a framework of the national community through which the best of the nation might find expression, the organ by which those choice spirits scattered throughout all classes, those "generous and humane souls, lovers of man's perfection, detached from the prepossessions of the class to which they might naturally belong, and desirous that he who speaks to them should, as Plato says, not try to please his fellow-servants, but his true and legitimate masters the heavenly Gods,"[1] would be able to work through and upon the whole body politic. He thought of the State as the focus of national culture and the promoter of its development. It is in the light of these notions that his advocacy of a literary academy should be viewed, an advocacy which his contemporaries misunderstood and freely ridiculed.

[1] *Mixed Essays*, p. 59.

All this is not socialism, which Arnold distrusted as too rigid, and inclined to level down, when he wished to level up. In " Equality " he writes:

> Socialistic and communistic schemes have generally, however, a fatal defect; they are content with too low and material a standard of well-being. That instinct of perfection which is the master-power in humanity always rebels at this, and frustrates the work. Many are to be made partakers of well-being, true; but the ideal of well-being is not to be, on that account, lowered and coarsened.[1]

Nor is it Prussianism, for Arnold had no leanings whatever towards the absolute State. His ideal was the service State in a democratical society, functioning through a bureaucracy which attracted the best brains and spirits of the country.

Arnold probably used the word ' state ' in too wide a sense. Had he, for instance, lived to read the writings of Professor McIver he might have distinguished between the ' community '—to which Burke's apostrophe will apply—and the ' State ' as the organ or machine of government. Then, again, since his day the notion of the State has gone up like a rocket with the Hegelians and come down like a stick with the followers of Treitschke. It is, indeed, sadly discredited. It is more than discredited. Like Lear's wit, it has been " pared o' both sides " by the claims of national associations and corporations on the one hand and those of international law and amity on the other.

And yet, despite all this, is not Arnold's ideal being realised? Has it not, in part at least, become an actuality? Could he have watched the development of secondary education in England since 1902, and especially the work of his old department under that truly great prophet of culture, Robert Morant, he would have been filled with delight, although, no doubt, critical in detail and not losing his head. Surely, too, in the reconstituted Board of Education, together with the new local education authorities, he would have seen the beginnings of that " civil organisation " for which he pleaded. Nor would he fail to note that government in this country, which nowadays means service, is improving every year,

[1] *Mixed Essays*, p. 70.

because the Civil Service, central and local, is attracting to it more and more the best spirits in England. And if this be so it follows that the honour and dignity of the public service is year by year increasing, since it is only noble souls that ennoble a service. When Arnold wrote so eloquently of the State he was pleading with the English people ; asking them, a little pathetically, as it seems to us now, to show some respect for the public work to which he devoted his life.

Here we touch upon a very interesting feature of Arnold's political writings: he was one of the few civil servants of modern times who have attempted to work out the philosophy of public service in a democratic community. The men of theory in universities and elsewhere have been debating the nature of the 'State' since the time of Plato and Aristotle, until it has assumed the proportions of the supernatural, divine, or diabolical according to the prejudices of the debater. And yet to a civil servant who has sat in the machine, had his hands on the levers, and helped to guide it aright the State is not a juggernaut, but a simple, human, and practical affair. In some countries, of course, where the machine has been seized by a single class, party, or sect, by a usurping minority, calling itself Bolshevik or Fascist, the State may wear to Englishmen a very forbidding appearance, reminding them of the bad old days of the police State in England. But in a country which is truly democratic, as England is gradually coming to be, though she has not yet reached the goal, the State is seen to be simply the community organised for the purpose of supplying public services. And those who are or have been civil servants, whether their work lies in the sphere of public health, or education, or the newly created B.B.C., whether they are directed from Whitehall or from some department of local government, realise this well enough. A distinguished dignitary of the law has recently tried to make our flesh creep with talk of a "new despotism" enthroned in Whitehall. To anyone who has taken his orders as an official from Whitehall such talk is ludicrous. The real danger there is not tyranny, but timidity. The English state machine is never likely to get out of hand, for those who compose it are only too well aware that they are the servants of public opinion, only too ready to withdraw a suggestion or project, however valuable, at the slightest hint of opposition, and only too conscious of the sword of Damocles perpetually hanging above their heads in the shape of "questions in Parliament." One of the greatest and most pregnant proposals for social benefit ever placed, in my opinion, before Parliament was Clause 10 of the Education Act of 1918, which, had it come into operation, would have instituted part-time education of a very broad and practical kind for all young persons in the country up to the age of eighteen. The expenditure involved would have been repaid a thousand times in the increased health and heightened morale of the people as a whole. Indeed, it is likely enough that in these days of unemployment it might have proved a real economic boon, while it would certainly have decreased our present police costs by diminishing the number of young criminals we now have upon our hands. Day continuation schools would have been a forward step in English civilisation. The clause to found them actually reached the Statute Book, but never got any farther. A little more courage, a little more willingness to take risks among the official advisers of the Minister of that time—and how great would have been our gain!

Nor was Arnold in the least blind to the weaknesses and timidities of Government departments. He was himself a servant of one for over thirty years, had watched an even greater betrayal than that of 1918, and never wearied of denouncing it in his official reports. The great educational tragedy of the second half of the nineteenth century was the institution of "payment by results," which, in the interests of economy, shackled the elementary schools for a generation, and even still, to some extent, influences them. The system was contrary to all traditions of the Education Department, and had there been a courageous official at the head, like its first chief, Kay-Shuttleworth, it would never have been consented to. But it was convenient from the administrative point of view; it meant a quiet life at Whitehall; and Kay-Shuttleworth's successor was not the man for a fight. When, therefore, Arnold advocated an extension of State service in England he had no illusions. He knew that civil servants were human, all too human, that they loved easy paths, that it was only the exceptional ones among them, a Kay-Shuttleworth or a Morant, who would strike out for themselves and carry their department along with them. Yet he saw that, for all its inevitable faults, the Civil Service was an essential instrument in that " progress towards man's best perfection—the adorning and ennobling of his spirit," that a truly national education could only be effected by such means, and that the Civil Service would itself be transformed and ennobled by the educational system it was called upon to build. His vision of the future, and of the part the State would play therein, was at once lofty and cool-headed; it is a vision which I think anyone who has worked in the ranks of the public education service of our time can share.

The foregoing comments are prompted in part by the reading of a recent book by Mr Leonard Woolf, in which he goes out of his way to attack Arnold as a political mystic. *After the Deluge: a Study of Communal Psychology*, a treatise on the political notions preceding and causing the Great War, is full of acute observations, with the general tenour of which I find myself in considerable agreement. If, however, an amateur in political science may venture so far, I cannot help feeling that the discussion is in places superficial and the positions taken up inconsistent at times one with another. Certainly Mr Woolf goes seriously wrong about Arnold, partly through laying overmuch stress, like Professor Barker and Dr Murray, on *Culture and Anarchy*, though he has clearly read, and to some extent admired, the essays on " Democracy " and " Equality," partly because he mistakes Arnold's moderation and refusal to commit himself to any doctrinaire view for muddleheadedness, partly because of his own intense prejudice against State action, but chiefly, I think, because he fails to catch the twinkle in Arnold's eye or to appreciate in the very slightest his comic muse. In anyone who has enjoyed the high spirits, the delicious irony, and the urbane malice of *Culture and Anarchy* the following passage in Mr Woolf's book can only raise a smile:

> He sees himself as a crusader in the cause of culture or " sweetness and light " against Philistinism and English Liberalism. It was the *Zeitgeist*, breathing heavily over Britain, which embodied itself in the Philistine and the Puritan or Nonconformist, so hateful to him; yet he is completely unaware that the priggery of his own mind and the

nasal sermonizing of his essays, so hateful to us, are products of the same unholy spirit breathing through him. The Pharisee is full brother to the Philistine, and not even a fig-leaf divides the Phariseeism of Matthew Arnold from the Philistinism of his contemporaries. That is why the tone and rhythm, even the style, of his essay on " Sweetness and Light " are so like those of a good Nonconformist sermon.

To this there is only one retort possible: Go and take a course in *Friendship's Garland*, study the effects of the most delicate ironist of Victorian England, and try again!

Arnold, as I have pointed out, distrusted abstract political notions and disliked political mysticism. Mr Woolf, strangely ignoring Carlyle, Ruskin, and even Hegel, attempts to find in Arnold the first prophet of the " authoritarian democratic great State," and to justify his contention by stamping Arnold as a political mystic. The only passage he quotes in support of this is one from *Culture and Anarchy*, in which, after claiming that men are led by the worst part of their natures into dissensions, disputes, and disunion, and by their better selves towards social harmony, peace, and the good of the commonweal—a claim which one would have thought to be a truism —Arnold goes on to declare, as Aristotle did before him, that the State—by which, be it remembered, he understood all communal activity, religious, artistic, intellectual, as well as political—existing, as it should, to promote the good life, is that in which our best selves will naturally find their expression.[1] To interpret this as mysticism is to take as imperative what was merely the optative mood in Arnold's thought. He had, indeed, no reverence for the State in the abstract; he had no illusions about the State as it existed in France under Napoleon III, or in Germany under Bismarck. On the contrary, he maintained that the State in France and in Prussia was over-centralised and tyrannical. All he really contended was that more State activity was essential to a developing civilisation in England, as, indeed, has been abundantly proved, and that in an ideal community the best thought and aspiration would find their expression in communal action; in other words, he was translating Plato's *Republic* into Victorian terms. As for " authoritarianism," he believed, of course,

[1] *Culture and Anarchy*, pp. 95–96.

that the first duty of a Government in power was to keep order in times of crisis—as what political thinker does not?—but, for the rest, the authority he speaks of as belonging to the State in a community governed by right reason is simply the authority which is accorded by the best in us to our guiding ideals and principles.

But Mr Woolf will allow nothing good or noble about the State or its authority. He writes:

> The State should be regarded, from the point of view of civilisation, as on the same level as a drainage system or a power-station. It has no more connection with our best selves than has a sewage farm, and it is reasonable to expect just as little and just as much sweetness and light in the State as in a water-closet.

There speaks the outsider and the doctrinaire. Mr Woolf forgets that the 'machinery' of the State consists of the Civil Service, and that the Civil Service is composed of men and women. Does he deny the desirability of recruiting good brains and ardent spirits for that service? Yet, if the Board of Education and Ministry of Health be thought of as mere sanitary arrangements, how can those brains and spirits be attracted into them? In truth, the estimation in which a profession is held by the ordinary citizen is a matter of the utmost moment to its morale and its future. The chief crime about the poisonous system of "payment by results," already referred to, was not the ridiculous and futile examinations which it imposed upon the children, but the assumption underlying it that the only motives which could be trusted to keep the teaching profession efficient were motives of self-interest. Kay-Shuttleworth, the founder of our public teaching service, conceived of it as a band of missionaries. Robert Lowe, in the name of the people of England, branded the teachers as educational wage-slaves doing piece-work, and so degraded the whole profession. Think ignobly of the State and the same degradation will inevitably overtake the Civil Service.

It is symptomatic of the way in which Matthew Arnold is misunderstood by the present generation that two well-known writers of the political left should entertain diametrically opposite views of his political ideas. While Mr Woolf condemns him as a protagonist of the modern absolute State

Mr Tawney takes the essay on "Equality" as the text for a trenchant volume of his own, also entitled *Equality*, the burden of which is an onslaught upon snobbery in English education as exemplified by the existence of different types of schools for different social classes, an onslaught which I think Arnold would have unhesitatingly endorsed. Indeed, Arnold's true political heirs in our time are not the Treitschkes and Mussolinis and Lenins, as Mr Woolf seems to imagine, but rather men like Mr Tawney, who combine a passion for education, to which they devote their lives and their best thought, with that profound belief in the possibilities of human nature and the value of human personality which is the heart of the democratic creed, as Mr Woolf himself attests; and yet look to the machinery of the modern State for the realisation of their ideals. To such men education and the public service, both growing more liberal with each generation, and embracing a larger and larger proportion of the best and brightest spirits of the time within their ranks, are the two chariot-wheels of civilisation, the meaning of which is not power or wealth, or even the conquest of nature, but simply "the adorning and ennobling" of the spirit of man. But on this I cannot do better than quote from Arnold himself, and I will conclude, therefore, with a well-known passage from that essay on "Sweetness and Light" which seems to Mr Woolf so full of priggery and nasal sermonising.

> Again and again I have insisted how those are the happy moments of humanity, how those are the marking epochs of a people's life, how those are the flowering times for literature and art and all the creative power of genius, when there is a national glow of life and thought, when the whole of society is in the fullest measure permeated by thought, sensible to beauty, intelligent, and alive. Only it must be *real* thought and *real* beauty; *real* sweetness and *real* light. Plenty of people will try to give the masses, as they call them, an intellectual food prepared and adapted in the way they think proper for the actual condition of the masses. The ordinary popular literature is an example of this way of working on the masses. Plenty of people will try to indoctrinate the masses with the set ideas and judgments constituting the creed of their own profession or party. Our religious and political organisations give an example of this way of working on the masses. I condemn neither way; but culture works differently. It does not try to teach down to the level of inferior classes; it does not try to

win them for this or that sect of its own, with ready-made judgments and watchwords. It seeks to do away with classes; to make the best that has been thought and known in the world current everywhere; to make all men live in an atmosphere of sweetness and light, where they may use ideas, as it uses them itself, freely—nourished and not bound by them.

This is the *social idea*; and the men of culture are the true apostles of equality. The great men of culture are those who have had a passion for diffusing, for making prevail, for carrying from one end of society to the other, the best knowledge, the best ideas, of their time; who have laboured to divest knowledge of all that was harsh, uncouth, difficult, abstract, professional, exclusive; to humanise it, to make it efficient outside the *clique* of the cultivated and learned, yet still remaining the *best* knowledge and thought of the time, and a true source, therefore, of sweetness and light.

Such a man was Arnold himself. Such a man is Mr Tawney, and all those, of whatever political colour, who believe in education and work for it. Such a man is the humblest official of the Board of Education, the local education authorities, the B.B.C., or the public library service, who thinks nobly of his profession and strives to make himself worthy of it.

J. Dover Wilson

BOOK LIST

Works by Matthew Arnold:

Popular Education on the Continent (with an introduction on "Democracy and the Modern State"). 1861.

A French Eton: or Middle-class Education and the State. 1864.

Schools and Universities on the Continent. 1868. A special preface was written for the second edition in 1874.

Culture and Anarchy: an Essay in Political and Social Criticism. 1869.

Friendship's Garland. 1871. A reprint of letters in the *Pall Mall Gazette*, 1866–67, 1869–70.

Mixed Essays. 1879. Containing "Democracy," 1861; "Equality," 1878; "Irish Catholicism and British Liberalism," 1878; "*Porro Unum est Necessarium*," 1878.

Letters, Speeches, and Tracts on Irish Affairs by Edmund Burke. 1881. Edited, with an introduction.

Irish Essays. 1882. Containing "The Incompatibles," 1881; "An Unregarded Irish Grievance," 1881; "*Ecce, convertimur ad gentes*," 1879; "The Future of Liberalism," 1880.

IX

WALTER BAGEHOT AND THE SOCIAL PSYCHOLOGISTS

IT is significant that in the series of volumes on the history of social theory of which this volume is the eighth and last only one section should be assigned to the subject of social psychology. Yet there is some justice in the assignment, for that is one of the youngest of all the social sciences, being, as it is, mainly a product of the last sixty years. Indeed, it cannot yet be said finally to have determined the boundaries of its own discipline or its methods of investigation and treatment. Even now, as a separate study, it appears to be more popular on the Continent and in the United States than it is in this country. Yet, at the outset, one must guard against a misapprehension. It is true that social psychology has only recently acquired the status of a separate science and been acknowledged as such by the assignment to it of a separate paper in the degree examinations of the University of London. Nevertheless, that is not to say that social psychology of a kind has not previously existed. All social thinkers of the past make assumptions concerning the nature of man and of his social capacities. The previous volumes in this series make that quite apparent. What has happened in recent years—during and since the Victorian era—is that these assumptions have been *isolated* for study and analysis. Or, to be more precise, only lately has the tacit claim of political theorists to make their own assumptions been denied, and the counter-claim made that they must take over *data* as to human nature and its implied social processes from the psychologists.[1]

[1] Professor R. S. Woodworth's *Contemporary Schools of Psychology* has been published since this article was written. In addition to containing much material relevant to the general theme of this article, it develops at greater length the particular point made above. See especially p. 196 *et seq.* One passage is particularly apposite : " Before that time [*i.e.*, the publication of McDougall's *Introduction to Social Psychology* in 1908] psychology had made no serious attempt to be of service to the social sciences,

In other words, the Victorian, Edwardian, and Georgian eras have witnessed, to a steadily increasing extent, a critical questioning of past assumptions made by older thinkers; and a real attempt has been made during this period to determine scientifically the limits of hypothesis within which political theory may be constructed. Possibly this may account for the hostility with which social psychology is regarded in some quarters. The calling into question of dogmatic, and mainly unconscious, assumptions is not always at first likely to be welcomed. Too much political theory of the past (and perhaps of the present) has been mere rationalisation of the thinker's unconscious processes, and the erection of his wish-fulfilments into a completed system. To drag these processes into the light of analysis would be to destroy the system in many cases. Much that is most valuable in current speculation has been the performance of this very task by thinkers as diverse as Vilfredo Pareto in Italy, Ross, Wolf, Sorokin, and a score of others in the United States, and such scholars as J. A. Hobson and Graham Wallas in this country.

How, then, are we to define the scope of social psychology? No finally accepted definition has been put forward,[1] yet there is sufficient agreement for us to be able to limit the area of the subject to three main topics of investigation. The first concerns the science of human nature. With what endowments does man start his social life; which are acquired and which are inherited; and how does social organisation modify them? The second concerns social processes. What

but had left it to each sociologist or historian or economist to improvise a psychology for his own use. That these improvised psychologies were crude was really the fault of the scientific psychologists, who had taken no pains to consider how they themselves could provide a psychology that should throw light on social problems. Scientific psychology had been so immersed in the study of intellectual performances, and in the details of sensation, memory, and habit formation that it had scarcely touched the problems of motivation. Now the social sciences were not concerned with the details of mental or motor processes, but they would like to know the motives of human conduct. Did men live in groups, and submit to government, through fear of each other, or through calculation of the greatest good of the greatest number? . . . Those who needed an answer to these questions took the best answer that suggested itself, while psychology passed by on the other side." The older theories of motivation are briefly examined in the Appendix of the present volume. Perhaps Professor Woodworth ignores too completely these earlier discussions of the problem.

[1] For an extensive bibliography on the discussion of this subject, and of the province of social psychology, its data and methods, the student is referred to L. L. Bernard's *An Introduction to Social Psychology* (Allen and Unwin, 1927), pp. 591–594.

are the psychological factors involved in group activity; is there a group mind or a general will; what is the nature of tradition; and how are the conflicting forces making for stability and for change to be explained? The third concerns social beliefs. What processes and assumptions determine political belief, and what factors determine the formation of public opinion? Such, put very briefly, are the themes the social psychologists are trying to investigate. Not all, of course, are concerned with the same issues; nor has anything like a coherent system been developed. Yet the science has grown enormously in the last sixty years, and is certain to expand even more rapidly in our own age, with developing technique and more data.

The mere enumeration of the problems of this science brings to light one important fact for the historian of ideas. It is that they overlap other established disciplines, and, in particular, psychology, ethics, and politics. This is important, since it means that if one is to seek for the origins of social psychology one must look for them in these three departments of knowledge. The method of the growth of all sciences has been the same: the differentiation from an established body of knowledge of a separate set of issues to be separately investigated. Early social psychology is interwoven, so to speak, in works on ethics, psychology, politics, and even philosophy. If one analyses, for instance, such a work as Dugald Stewart's *Philosophy of the Active and Moral Powers of Man* one will not only find in it a treatment of ethical problems and a comprehensive system of individual psychology, but one will also discover many quite definite answers—either explicit or by implication—to the questions appertaining specially to social psychology. In one sense—in the sense of a separate study—it is true that social psychology is but the product of very recent years. But in the broader sense just indicated a much longer history may be claimed for it, though it is a history, curiously enough, which nobody has yet written. An attempt has been made in the Appendix [1] to sketch the development of some of the leading ideas pertaining to social psychology in England prior to the appearance of *Physics and Politics*, and to indicate something of the wider background against which

[1] See p. 251.

Bagehot's work should be read. The purpose of both this article and the Appendix is thus a very limited one: a mere footnote to the full story. It is to outline the main factors which were at work before and during the Victorian period to produce, in the fullness of time, the independent study, and without which it could never have come into separate being. That attainment of independence was not completed, so far as this country is concerned, until the present century. The Victorian period was but a prelude: an epoch during which psychology was undergoing a reorientation, both as to procedure and outlook, which was essential if it was to progress beyond the rationalism of the eighteenth century; and from that reorientation came social psychology.

II

It was the rapid development of the theory of organic evolution in the first half of the nineteenth century, culminating in the doctrine of 'natural selection' propounded by Darwin and Wallace in 1858, which was directly responsible for the beginning of a new phase in social and ethical speculation. So far as psychology in all its branches is concerned, the consequences of the evolutionary theory were vast, for it became the background against which all subsequent work had to be written. The term 'biological' became "the symbol for a new way of thinking," inasmuch as it stressed both the *genetic* approach to human problems and the idea of the relation of *function* to life. By giving primacy to the two conceptions of heredity and adaptation it destroyed the older associationism, not only by this emphasis on organic function in the life-process, but also by raising the problem (which emerged out of the emphasis on heredity) of the relation between inherited uniformity of mental structure and the existence of individual differences. Thus an impetus was given to the greater accumulation of data, and stress was put upon the comparative viewpoint. Nothing, perhaps, could illustrate this more vividly than two remarks made by the German anthropologist Burmeister shortly before the appearance of Darwin's book. "It is not worth while," he said, "to look into the soul of the negro. It is a judgment of God which is being executed that, at the approach of civilisation, the savage man must perish." And again: "I have often tried to obtain an insight into the mind of the negro, but it was never worth the trouble."[1] Obviously that attitude would now be swept away entirely, and comparative psychology could be given a unifying principle it had hitherto lacked. Moreover, the new doctrine eventually involved a totally fresh reinterpretation of the theory of instinct, and a deeper and more fundamental explanation could be given to it than had formerly been possible, for man's position in the animal world was better appreciated. Hence animal psychology found an increasingly important place in psychological studies from then onward. Lastly, a fresh basis was given for the study of the unconscious. Such glimpses as had hitherto been obtained of unconscious forces in the human mind and in social life were rather occasional and empirical guesses, for they lacked the significance derived from a biological interpretation. Thus the beginning of that movement which has produced Freud, Jung, and Adler and the vast literature of exegesis upon them.

The fifteen years immediately preceding Bagehot's writing of *Physics and Politics* were years of immense speculative activity in this country. A general sense of intellectual achievement can be discerned in all the writers of that period, a feeling almost of exuberance, and the sense that what had previously been hidden was at last being made manifest. The scientific method seemed to open up illimitable possibilities in the study of man; and Bagehot's own work is a monument to that general and pervasive feeling. "It is our happiness," wrote Tylor, the anthropologist, in 1870, "to live in one of those eventful periods of intellectual and moral history when the fast-closed gates of discovery and reform stand open at their widest."

Physics and Politics opens with a statement of the same prevailing feeling:

> One peculiarity of this age is the sudden acquisition of much physical knowledge. There is scarcely a department of science or art which is the same, or at all the same, as it was fifty years ago. A new

[1] *Der Schwarze Mensch*, quoted by A. C. Haddon in *The History of Anthropology*, p. 82.

world of inventions . . . has grown up around us which we cannot help seeing; a new world of ideas is in the air, and affects us though we do not see it.

This feeling was largely due to a vivid sense of the idea of *development.* It seemed to imply that man himself was part of a vast developmental process of which he had not hitherto been fully aware, and to which he was at last awakening. Or, as Bagehot put it:

Perhaps the most marked result of late thought [is] that by it everything is made an 'antiquity.' . . . Man himself has, to the eye of science, become 'an antiquity.' She tries to read, is beginning to read, knows she ought to read, in the frame of each man the result of a whole history of all his life, of what he is, and what makes him so —of all his forefathers, of what they were and what made them so.

Geology, palæontology, anthropology, and a dozen other sciences all seemed to teach this same lesson—that man was the product of the ages; and the theory of evolution crystallised the sentiment into a formula.

Even the briefest survey of the works of this period will suffice to show the nature of this intellectual ferment. Carpenter rewrote his *Principles of Human Physiology* in 1852. Six years after the appearance of *Physics and Politics* he published his *Mental Physiology*, thereby further helping to promulgate the idea that the basis of psychology must be sought in physiological investigation. Maudsley, whose *Physiology and Pathology of Mind* appeared in 1867, still further emphasised that contention, and helped to prepare the way for the modern study of insanity; and by Maudsley Bagehot was greatly influenced. The same year that Carpenter's revised book was published Spencer coined the phrase "survival of the fittest," and expounded his theory of evolution. His famous essay on "Progress" appeared in the *Westminster Review* in 1857; and twelve months later the epoch-making papers of Wallace and Darwin were first read. Spencer published his programme of investigation in 1860, and throughout the next decade his evolutionary formula was in fashion, and obviously influenced Bagehot. His *First Principles* appeared in 1861. Bain's definitive work also belongs to the fifties. *The Senses and the Intellect* came out in

1855, and *The Emotions and the Will* four years later. Almost simultaneously there appeared, in addition to *The Origin of Species*, the volume of *Essays and Reviews* which aroused such fierce ecclesiastical controversy. One of the most important essays in that volume was by Professor Baden Powell, who had already long been expounding an evolutionary theory, and had recently developed some of the implications of this in his *Order of Nature*. Meanwhile a materialist interpretation of history was being attempted by Buckle in the *History of Civilisation* (1857 and 1861). The year 1865 was especially notable. Three works then appeared, all of which contributed extensively to the formation of Bagehot's ideas, and from which he quotes at length: Tylor's *Researches into the Early History of Mankind*, Lubbock's *Prehistoric Times*, and M'Clennan's *Primitive Marriage*. All three supplied him with data for the elaboration of his thesis *autre temps autre mœurs*, which the evolutionary theory had suggested to him. Lastly must be mentioned the work of Huxley. *Man's Place in Nature* appeared in 1863, and *Elementary Physiology* in 1866. It was this latter work which gave Bagehot his ideas on the transmission of acquired characteristics.

Such was the intellectual background of Bagehot's *Physics and Politics*, which first appeared as a series of articles in the *Fortnightly Review*, beginning in November 1867, and was published in book form in 1869. It is not in any sense a book of 'research'; it is essentially a work of speculation. The central idea—the application of the doctrine of the "survival of the fittest" to the development of man and the evolution of his society—was derived from Darwin and Spencer. Hitherto the doctrine had been applied primarily in regard to the formation of biological species. Now Bagehot gave it a new application; that is why he said of his work that "it only amounts to searching out and following up an analogy." And if the central idea was borrowed so were the facts adduced in proof and illustration of it. Besides Spencer, six other writers are mainly responsible for his material: Huxley and Maudsley for his physiological ideas; Maine for his idea of early law; and Lubbock, Tylor, and M'Clennan for his ideas about custom and the nature of primitive societies.

III

Physics and Politics is a book difficult to classify. Indeed, it fits nowhere into conventional academic categories, for it is unique. The nearest approach to it is perhaps to be found in a remarkable essay written forty years earlier by Thomas Rowe Edmonds.[1] But Bagehot's work is not only the product of an older and more mature mind; it also makes use of the great development which had taken place in the biological sciences during those intervening years. Like *Practical, Moral, and Political Economy*, *Physics and Politics* is a brilliant and suggestive guess; but it is based on more firmly established data, and its limits of error are in consequence considerably narrowed. The former book quite obviously stands at the turn of an epoch between the rationalism of the eighteenth century and the positivism of the nineteenth; whereas the latter book is no less obviously within the modern period, and speaks in a language and a spirit akin to our own.

Certainly the title of the book is a misnomer, for "Physics and Politics" conveys, to the present generation at least, no idea of the scope of its subject. Professor Ernest Barker has suggested that the title should be "Psychics and Politics," and this would certainly convey a more adequate indication of its contents. But even that would not be entirely appropriate, for the psychological element in the essay is consequent upon a biological and anthropological approach to the fundamental problems of politics. It was essentially a sociological footnote to the doctrine of evolution prevailing in the sixties: a tentative peering not only outward into the remote darkness of prehistory, but also inward into the irrational and subrational forces of human nature inherited from the uncounted ages of the evolutionary process. Bagehot had an extraordinarily clear sense of the vast issues and problems raised by the "new knowledge," and it is little short of marvellous that he should have presented them so vividly in such a short compass—for his essay is only a little over fifty thousand words in length. One might almost call it a prospectus for future research work in the social sciences. To the questions he put anthropologists,

[1] See the Appendix, p. 264.

social psychologists, and biologists are still daily bringing materials for an answer; and Bagehot's successors are not to be sought in any single linear sequence, but in half a dozen different lines of research. This does not mean to imply, of course, that later workers are necessarily indebted to him, or that he alone was responsible for later developments. It simply means that his brilliant, synthetic mind achieved an *aperçu* of the implications of the evolutionary theory for the sociologist well in advance of his contemporaries, and that subsequent investigation has confirmed the reality of the problems which he envisaged. The clear statement of the issues was itself an important step in intellectual advance.

The problem for which Bagehot attempted to sketch a solution was this: Assuming the truth of the doctrine of natural selection, how are we to account for the momentous *transition* from the brute level of the struggle for existence to the human level of social organisation and co-operation? To Bagehot this *transition* problem was the essential one, and the key to all subsequent development of the human race. In reality, it was the sociological counterpart to the biological problem of the 'missing link.' In the new pentateuch which natural science was writing Bagehot essayed to provide the exodus into human society once the genesis of species was granted. This central issue naturally gave rise to certain subsidiary problems: on the thither side of organised polity was the question, What like was pre-political man? And on the hither side of established society were the questions, How is national character formed? and What are the main processes of social change? Both Darwin and Spencer some eight years previously had seen the vital importance of the issue; but Bagehot's was the first attempt to solve it, and he alone saw at which particular stage of the life-process the key to the riddle might be found. Thus did he prepare the way for Darwin's fuller statement of the question in *The Descent of Man* (1871). "No more original, brilliant, or, as far as it goes, satisfactory examination of the deeper problems of social causation has ever been offered from that day until now," wrote Professor Giddings in 1908; "it anticipated much that is most valuable in later exposition."

For his answer to the great question, How did *Homo sapiens* pass from the animal to the social level of existence? Bagehot drew upon the newly acquired knowledge already mentioned. To him it had a fourfold significance. First, by making man himself an " antiquity " it suggests the necessity of reading in man's physical structure the whole story of its past development and successive adaptations. Emphasis will thus be put, as never before, on the facts of heredity and transmission. These facts had, of course, been known previously; what recent science had done was to isolate their significance. But if the first lesson of biology is the emphasis on continuity the second lesson is the emphasis on the central position of the nervous system in that story, both as it concerns the individual and the race. Regarding the *individual*, the primary fact is that of reflex action. Bagehot here quotes Huxley in his support. He contends that the development of the individual is synonymous with the development of an integrated system of reflex actions, be those reflex actions natural—*i.e.*, arising from the structure of the spinal cord—or artificial—*i.e.*, coming *via* the brain through conscious effort. Upon these latter Bagehot places the very greatest emphasis, and thus brings us face to face with the whole of the present-day controversy concerning 'conditioned reflexes.' Following Lamarck and Huxley, he believes that conscious effort produces habit, which in its turn becomes 'fixed' as a reflex by the nervous system. Thus the body becomes " charged with stored virtue and acquired faculty." Hence the fact and possibility of education depends on this power of the nervous system to organise conscious effort into reflex acts. As regards the *race*, Bagehot merely extends the above thesis to cover the whole of time, and he cites Maudsley in his support. Life is a progressive development of the nervous system through the transformation of voluntary into automatic acts. Such transmission of acquired power takes place in accordance with the " law of increasing speciality," whereby the nervous system progressively adapts itself to the demands of its environment. Thus man becomes " but a link in the chain of organic beings." It may be noted in passing that this phrase itself is of considerable interest to the historian of ideas. Nothing illustrates more clearly the revolution in intellectual outlook than a comparison of this sentence with certain recurrent expressions to be found in Godwin's *Political Justice*. Whereas for Bagehot the reference is entirely biological, for Godwin man was but a determined unit in a physico-mathematical universe. Bagehot put the emphasis on nerve-structure and its investigation; Godwin enunciated the dogma of necessitarianism and pre-established harmony whereby human beings and their actions "through every link of the great chain of necessity are admirably harmonised and adapted to each other."[1] In these passages the attitudes of the eighteenth and the nineteenth centuries stand over against each other. In the interval had occurred the revolution in biological science.

The third lesson of the new biology is the meaning and reality of progress. This transmitted nerve element becomes "the connective tissue of civilisation," for it enables each generation to transmit to its successor qualities with which it itself did not start. Thus each age is enabled to begin with an improvement on the preceding one, "making nicer music from finer chords," however slow that process may be. Hence the fourth lesson concerns the primacy of moral causes in the developmental process. For Bagehot this is of paramount importance, and the key to his whole argument. It is the 'moral' cause of conscious effort which has physical consequences through the nerves. These consequences get conserved in the body. Thus "it is the continual effort of the beginning that creates the hoarded energy of the end," and the whole of recorded history and the formation of national character is to be interpreted in the light of this theorem. No matter how "mind" be eventually explained, the three essential facts—Effort, Conservation, Transmission—will always remain. "Our mind in some strange way acts on our nerves, and our nerves in some equally strange way store up the consequences, and somehow the result, as a rule and commonly enough, goes down to our descendants."

That assertion is the starting-point for the new sociology, inasmuch as it shows why the toil of the first generation

[1] *Political Justice* (1793 edition), p. 207. For a discussion of this side of Godwin's philosophy and its implications for social theory see *The Social and Political Ideas of Some Representative Thinkers of the Revolutionary Era*, edited by F. J. C. Hearnshaw, p. 156 *et seq.*

becomes the transmitted aptitude of the next. Moreover, it suggests a totally new approach to the problem of the origin of politics and social processes. The investigator must now undertake the difficult task—with the help of ethnology, anthropology, and the ancillary sciences—of thinking away the physical and moral accretions produced by some thousands of years of development, and of reconstructing the nature and life of man before he had built up for himself that heritage of acquired reactions and social traditions. This heritage, it must be repeated, is a double one: partly physical and partly psychological. Bagehot was one of the first to realise the importance of this fact, and not the least interesting feature of his work is his attempt to explain the relation between these two kinds of acquisition. Just recently the late Professor Arthur Thomson remarked:

> Too often one hears social evolution spoken of just as if it was a special case of mammalian evolution, which would remain illegitimate even if all mammals were beavers. . . . It seems to us that the differences between human history and organic evolution are in kind, not merely in degree. . . . And the social heritage of gains registered outside the organism altogether, as is slightly anticipated in beehive and ant-hill, becomes in man almost as important as the "germ-plasmic natural inheritance," to keep Galton's good term.[1]

This was precisely Bagehot's own point of view, as his theories concerning the "cake of custom" and the "age of discussion" make evident. Only by making allowances for this double inheritance can we get back to the starting-point, so to speak, and appraise at their true value the various stages by which man created both polity and tradition for himself; and only thus can we guard against the fallacy of reading into the remote past present-day assumptions. In particular, the new knowledge not only enables us to understand the pre-economic stage of man's development, when the principles of political economy had no meaning or relevance, but it also dispels once and for all the illusion of a Golden Age of perfection from which man has somehow fallen. So we must give up seeking "the principles of 1789" at the beginning of things, and must alter our whole attitude to the problem. Not a Fall,

[1] *Journal of Philosophical Studies*, vol. i, p. 54.

but an emergence must be sought, and an emergence hard won out of many a millennium of striving.

IV

In this process of the emergence of socialised man Bagehot sees three great stages: the stage of no-polity, the stage of fixed polity, and the stage of flexible polity; or, as he calls them, the preliminary age, the fighting age, and the age of discussion. These phases overlap, and there is no sharp demarcation between them. Moreover, they are not uniform throughout the world. Some groups have remained fixed at a remote point on the line, while in more fortunate areas progress has been continuous. During the eons of pre-history all the branches of *Homo sapiens* must have developed somewhat, otherwise there would have been no survival whatever. All men progressed from the brute level, through the stage of no-polity, into the stage of fixed polity. But there many of them have stopped. Various factors—particularly the geographical—determined the point at which interpenetration of cultures—and, with it, progress—ceased. Bagehot therefore sets himself to answer three main questions: What was the nature of pre-political man, and how did he come to form a community? What forces held man together in such a community? What social processes caused the improvement and increasing flexibility of the community, and how are they now operative? All these questions are answered in terms of the prevailing doctrine of the "survival of the fittest."

Of the very earliest pre-political man we can know nothing. But recent discoveries enable us to guess the nature of man some ten thousand years before recorded history. He must have been similar to contemporary savages in endowments, and differing from them only in his acquisitions. He was a creature of strong emotions, with no tradition, no common body of knowledge, and no foresight. His appetites regulated his life. Mortality was vast, and he could have had no respect for life. Essentially he must have been the same as Hobbes' pre-contract man. Yet during this first epoch man was undergoing a prolonged, if unconscious, education, which profoundly modified his nature—a nature plastic beyond our imagination to comprehend. That education resulted in the introduction of some measure of *coherence* into his life. The evolutionary theory compels us to assign to this stage two major processes, both of which are now entirely inscrutable: the formation of the main races of the world and the establishment of kin groups—*i.e.*, some degree of gregariousness and leadership. Each is a *datum*, found at the opening of history. "It is a great advantage . . . in the evolution theory that it enables us to remit this difficulty to a pre-existing period." Man thus comes to the threshold of the second stage with both these acquisitions, and possibly with a third—respect for omens and a sense of luck and of the propitious. This, too, would make for coherence and increase gregariousness, as the history of the next stage shows.

The second stage of social development is begun when a group custom has become established, and a custom-making power in the group capable of enforcing a common way of life. Supernatural sanction gets attached to the tribal custom from the outset, because one of the main purposes of such custom is to enforce obedience and to ensure the execution of propitious rites to prevent a "curse" descending upon the tribe. The group is, and must be, the unit, and not the individual, for there is no sense of limited liability in early religion. The tribal enforcement of conformity to these rites has survival value inasmuch as the coherence and homogeneity of the group is thereby secured. Moreover, it ensures a degree of emotional discipline otherwise lacking, and the subordination of present desire to future necessity. It is because man is a "custom-making animal" that he has become man, for custom is the only possible cohesive force of society in the ages before his reason developed. So at that stage any law was better than no law: quantity not quality counted then; for, if the inchoate creature of the preliminary age was to be tamed, obedience was before all things necessary, the "hereditary drill" which was to make of man a political animal, and give him a "legal fibre." Politics could begin only when obedience became a *datum* instead of a *quæsitum*, for it is only when the volume of tacit consent is greater than the amount of overt disagreement that there is sufficient cohesion to allow of the political process at all. That is why status must determine all things at first, and why voluntary contract must come very late in social evolution.

This idea of the " cake of custom " has important consequences for Bagehot's theories. It explains for him the origin of the backward races; it accounts for the formation of national character (as a similar theory did in Edmonds' hands); and it gives a clue to the precise application of the doctrine of the survival of the fittest to social affairs. 'Survival' will imply not the dominance of a particular physical type, but rather of a particular custom-group which has best succeeded in disciplining its members. That is why Bagehot devotes more than a fifth of his essay to the part played by war in the development of civilisation. War puts a premium on discipline, coherence, and the 'preliminary virtues' such as courage and loyalty. Hence the group most possessing these characteristics will triumph over the rest and assimilate them. And only rigid custom can develop such features. So custom has survival value in the fighting age. Moreover, every intellectual gain which a nation achieved at that period was 'invested' in war, further to augment its power. So history becomes the story of the " coalescence of competing strengths," and of the aggregate increase in the battle array of mankind, for 'coherence' goes on conquering 'incoherence' until none of the latter is left. Just as in Edmonds' theory, civilisation and fighting strength go together; and, like Edmonds, Bagehot maintains that this principle still holds good. It is not true that civilisation makes men effeminate. If the call to arms came to-day " the great cities could pour out multitudes wanting nothing but practice to make good soldiers." On this hypothesis one explanation of the 'backward races' is that they are those geographically isolated groups which have been outside the process of conquest and assimilation.

Just as the germs of the second age are to be sought in the first, so the features of the third age emerged in the second. They were, moreover, features conferring further military strength, so that once again war was the medium of the transition. The main characteristic of the third stage of development, in which we are now living, is the adaptability of society and the element of change. How did a changeable society emerge out of fixity of custom? The answer Bagehot gives is that certain chance factors introduced an element of variability into established custom. Successful groups were the successful variations. Where the capacity to admit change was lacking the group either stagnated or was conquered. But variations could be introduced into custom only by a process of " preservative addition "—*i.e.*, by maintaining the essential features and essential virtues of the previous age. Five such chance factors making both for conservative adaptation and for increased military skill are discussed. Mixture of races made eugenic experiment possible; certain " provisional institutions "—such as slavery and oligarchy—made leisure a possibility, and with it the opportunity for specialised thought conducive to originality; certain moral qualities gave extra skill in combat; a higher type of religion gave greater " confidence in the universe." But, above all, it was the acquisition of some established system of semi-free discussion which made those interstices of opinion within the group into which new ideas could be introduced. This it was which ushered in the third stage of man's evolution—the age of discussion. Bagehot is quite at a loss to suggest how it came about originally, though he adopts Maine's theory of the expansion of the family group to explain how it spread. But once the process had started obvious factors, such as commerce, colonisation, a cosmopolitan church, etc., would introduce further new ideas and produce new critical attitudes; and the habit of discussion might spread from the freer communities to the less free.

Its consequences are far-reaching. Discussion—in so far as it really is discussion and not mere oratory—effectively ensures that the community will change its basis from status to choice, from the accepted to the willed. It implies an admission of the doubtful adequacy of the established rule, and hence of its doubtful sanctity. It tends to put a premium on intelligence, as war did upon discipline and the martial virtues; and it fosters tolerance of diversity. " One of the greatest pains to human nature is the pain of a new idea," says Bagehot. Discussion gradually habituates man to this pain. Bigotry is an invariable characteristic of customary societies, and until that has been diminished political progress is impossible. So another explanation of static communities is that they are those which have failed to break the bonds of their own customs.

V

Bagehot draws some ingenious conclusions for the present and the future from his theory of discussion. He thinks discussion does, and will, modify human nature. Many of our great social problems arise from the fact that we have inherited a human nature victorious from a barbarous age. That age fostered action above all else, and man is still prone more to action than to reflection. His most conspicuous failing is his inability to stay quiet and to find out things. Science could only develop with ages of sedentary thought, and only the few are scientists. It is here, in the first instance, that discussion may possibly modify inherited characteristics. Its immediate effect is to stop action, and to foster "the plain position of inevitable doubt." It is precisely because, as Macaulay says, a campaign cannot be directed by a debating society that Bagehot favours discussion. It prevents many campaigns besides the military from being conducted, inasmuch as it ensures elaborate consideration and provides "the greatest hindrance to the inherited mistake of human nature, to the desire to act promptly." Thereby is the League of Nations provided with one of its main arguments of justification.

In another important respect, however, Bagehot looks to discussion to change mankind. He sees in it a possibility of transforming the sex instinct and diminishing its strength. That instinct is far too strong for present-day needs. During the early struggle for existence the maximum of procreation was necessary, and civilised man now inherits this excessive instinct just as he inherits an excessive impulse to action. Misery, vice, and over-population result. But even this can be modified by an extension of the principle of discussion. In support of his contention Bagehot quotes Spencer's theory to the effect that there is a constant struggle in the human organism between "individuation" and "genesis," and that as the nervous system and the brain develop they withdraw vital energy which would otherwise have been used for reproduction. So, as man continues to evolve, his powers of reproduction may be expected to decrease. Bagehot interprets this to mean that those who can be induced to lead an intellectual life will be less procreative, for the amount of energy in each individual is limited; and "nothing promotes intellect like intellectual discussion, and nothing promotes intellectual discussion so much as government by discussion." (It is interesting to observe that William Godwin at the end of his *Political Justice* put forth a not dissimilar idea. He too thought that rationality would develop at the expense of the emotions; and he even went so far as to suggest that when reason had developed completely man would become immortal.) Finally, it is claimed, government by discussion will alter human nature by strengthening the socially desirable type of character and eliminating the "strongly idiosyncratic mind, violently disposed to extremes." Then will the spirit of reserved scepticism and quickened originality be distributed throughout society.

This explanation of the main stages of social evolution, however, does not fully account for all the differences to be found between groups at the same level of development, since it ignores many psychological processes taking place within the group at the same time that the external forces are operative. One of Bagehot's most striking contributions to the thought of his day is his sketch of just these processes. They are at work throughout the whole course of human development, and are an integral part of that movement.

Bagehot had no clear theory of the unconscious mind; yet he came very near to developing one. And he fully appreciated the strength and significance of unconscious forces in shaping the social life of man. His central thought is to be found in his theorem that "the propensity of man to imitate what is before him is one of the strongest parts of his nature." This fact he used to account for much that was otherwise inexplicable in life. It was but another instance of his realisation of the non-rational forces determining human society. No attempt was made by the author to explain the genesis of this propensity; it was taken for granted, as with

Edmonds. Nor were all its implications developed into anything like a system, as was done a few years later by Tarde in his *Lois de l'imitation*. As in other matters, a few brilliant suggestions were thrown out for the reader's consideration and then left. Yet enough was said to show how far-reaching the theory might be.

Bagehot is quite clear that this capacity for imitation must not be thought of as either voluntary or conscious. " It has its seat mainly in very obscure parts of the mind, whose notions, so far from having been consciously produced, are hardly felt to exist." This " copying propensity " induces man to become more and more like his neighbours. Bagehot instances the case of literary fashions. The growth of these shows in a limited field the working of a general principle operative throughout society. Somehow, and in some unconscious way, a writer " gets a sort of start." He gives the public what it wants; and by supplying something congenial to the minds around him he sets a fashion. But it is an entirely fortuitous occurrence, a chance predominance. Nor is the man who hits upon it necessarily a great man capable of developing his accidental discovery to the full. Yet once the discovery has been made it is quickly taken up by others and amplified. Thus is the character of an 'age' established; thus does the Elizabethan differ from the Augustan age, and so forth. The whole movement from beginning to end is quite unconscious: the writer spontaneously gives the age the thought and style it demands, but no less clearly does the age make the writer by its approval and its expectation of the desired characteristics. And, as most men get to like—or think they like—what is always before them, so does the bulk of the community endorse the new conception until it becomes, in its turn, an old tradition. The principle of " use and disuse," of which biology speaks, augments the process: practice establishes the new style, and disuse causes the old one to die out.

Precisely the same processes are at work forming the national character. Chance predominance creates a model or type: probably a type which 'works' better than a previous one. The " invincible attraction " ruling all but the strongest minds does the rest and causes them to imitate what is in front of them. The bulk of men always become what they are expected to be. This is how early custom became fixed. Custom is, so to speak, but a canalisation of this imitative process. It determines beforehand the type that is to be imitated. Success in the social struggle for survival gave pragmatic vindication of the type. The movement starts from a few "strong and eager individuals," and then expands concentrically from them to include the whole community. Consequently a national character is created; in essence it is "but the successful parish character," just as the national speech is the successful dialect. It is because of this automatically operative process that such a wide diversity of group tradition is found in similar climatic and geographical areas. Bagehot allows but a small share to these forces in the growth of social patterns and traditions.

This capacity for imitation explains minor social processes too; or, rather, these other processes are but varied applications of the same principle. It accounts for continuous traditions in subordinate groups within the nation—*e.g.*, the style and attitude to be found on the staffs of periodicals. It explains the way in which "the fashion of female dress" spreads from Paris outward. It suggests a main cause not only for passing phases, but for more permanent modifications of tradition. Men are influenced by types rather than by tenets. Are we not earnest with Mr Gladstone, and less earnest with Lord Palmerston? So both in religion and in politics we may regard a great man as a great new causal factor whose influence radiates forth by the spontaneous working of the laws of imitation. Lastly, Bagehot adumbrates an outline of the psychology of opinion and belief in these terms. He was not an academic psychologist, and his view of the human mind is in places somewhat confusing. Yet he did catch a clear glimpse both of the problem of belief and of some of the factors involved—a problem on which amazingly few people have worked since his day. His main theme is not dissimilar to that of Graham Wallas in *Human Nature in Politics*—that is, the essentially irrational basis of belief in most men.

Imitation and belief are both closely related, and spring from "the obscurest parts of our nature." Just as we imitate what is around us, so we believe what our immediate neighbours believe. We all tend to yield to current infatuations. It is not so much the overt teaching of our friends and our Press: it is the circumambient *assumptions* which we cannot resist—the taken-for-granted-ness which presses upon us on all sides, so that even the greatest sage comes to imbibe the folly of his party or group. The invariable tendency is for the mind to accept as true whatever idea comes clearly before it. Unless we are on our guard the mere presentation of an idea from all sides will itself become a certificate of truth. So do men get caught by the infection of imitation "in their most inward and intellectual part—their creed." This can be illustrated from the fluctuations of belief in the money-market. There the forces of imitation can be seen plainly at work. They exert a kind of mass pressure upon the individual, involving not a little persecution, for the critical dissentient is soon put down as 'crotchety,' and becomes distrusted.

If all these sub-rational forces are operative now, at our present level of development, how much more powerful must they have been in earlier ages! Then the positive process was reinforced by a kind of negative process—the tendency to crush diversity. In an age before discussion had made man tolerant of new ideas, and when the maintenance of the tribal custom was a sheer necessity, divergence from the accepted norm would be stamped out ruthlessly. So were the national characteristics imprinted upon the group, and the great infant mortality only served to secure further conformity to the type. Only those communities progressed which had by chance preserved the little germ of adaptability, and that germ could develop only through genuine discussion. Intelligent adaptation is the key to the mystery of social evolution.

VI

"Ever since Bagehot wrote *Physics and Politics*," says Professor Ernest Barker,

> political theorists have turned social psychologists; they have approached the facts of group-life on the assumption that these facts are

> facts of group consciousness, which it is their problem to describe and explain by means of the method which a natural science uses in order to describe and explain the facts of matter. . . . His book is really the beginning of the psychological method.

This comment indicates clearly the importance of Bagehot's work for the generation that followed. He realised the implications for sociology of the theory of evolution, and raised questions which are still living issues. But he marks the beginning of the psychological approach to politics in a special sense. A psychological approach of a kind had, as is shown in the Appendix, existed since the eighteenth century; and T. R. Edmonds showed what could be made of that attitude. Bagehot's chief importance lies in the fact that he renewed that approach after a crisis in the history of thought. For the Darwinian theory had produced a great difficulty. The doctrine of natural selection was essentially an individualistic one, implying the struggle of each against all. When Darwin wrote *The Origin of Species* he had not applied the principle to human beings or human society. How, then, could society come into being and subsequently develop from such anti-social beginnings?

Bagehot attempts to solve the problem by first stating it in psychological rather than in biological terms. He projects the whole process, so to speak, on to the plane of *mind*. Development is for him the emergence of new mental characteristics. But they are characteristics which have physical consequences in a physical struggle. It is necessary to emphasise this point, because some commentators have written as though Bagehot's doctrine of the transmission of acquired characteristics was an unimportant part of his theory which might almost be separated from the rest of his teaching. But such a contention would surely destroy the unity of the argument of *Physics and Politics*. It is true that the brevity of Bagehot's book did not allow him to develop all the implications of his thesis. But to the present-day reader the argument is entirely homogeneous, and only the stricter sect of the neo-Darwinians would want to truncate it. Whereas, in fact, one can hardly classify Bagehot as a Darwinian at all, for he is much more in line with the doctrine of creative evolution than with the doctrine of natural selection. Shaw's preface to

Back to Methuselah and *Physics and Politics* both express the same fundamental attitude.

Bagehot does not attempt to explain how mind emerged in the evolutionary process; he takes it for granted. But he does state very clearly that in the struggle between the mind-body units of that process the balance was constantly being tipped in favour of mind as against the mere physical fact of bodily strength. That is why he begins his essay with a dissertation on the mind-body relationship. It is that relationship which gives mental acquisitions a physical consequence; and it is this hypothesis which enables him to state the whole problem in terms of mind. Consequently it is essential to his purpose that acquired characteristics should be transmitted. In the evolutionary struggle it is the mental traits rather than the physical which have increasing survival value. Two results, therefore, follow. On the one hand is increasing gregariousness, on the other greater control over the process itself. This control concerns not simply the mastery of external nature. The fact that it is a mental event implies control over man's responses to that nature through the growing power of self-determination of the group, and that is the meaning of the "age of discussion." By adopting such a psychological attitude Bagehot escapes the antinomies which the biological doctrine of evolution seemed to present to the social scientist, and so wrote the first chapter of the new book of social psychology. But this was achieved, it must be remembered, by interpreting evolution in Lamarckian terms (derived from Spencer's early writings) rather than in purely Darwinian terms. There is a Darwinian gloss on the essay, it is true. But it might have been essentially the same without *The Origin of Species*.

Bagehot's work was only a beginning, and much was left unexplained. In two respects in particular had an advance to be made before the brilliant suggestions he had thrown out could be developed. First, a new analysis of instinct in the light of the new biology had to be provided. It is a strange fact that Bagehot completely drops the whole of the previous teaching about instinct, which is dealt with elsewhere in this volume.[1] Where he uses the word he does so only in the old

[1] See the Appendix, p. 257.

metaphysical sense, which he rightly realises is virtually meaningless in the new biological context. Hence he is led to say that man has no instincts whatever. Perhaps some of the Behaviourists may approve of this attitude to-day, though that is not the same as saying that Bagehot's analysis of man's endowments was adequate. It was the work of Lloyd Morgan, L. T. Hobhouse, and William McDougall to pursue this line of investigation after an interval of a quarter of a century.

The second respect in which *Physics and Politics* needed supplementing was by the provision of a fuller analysis of the nature of the group mind. Bagehot had grasped some of the basic facts. He understood tradition as the common content of the minds composing the group ; and he saw in imitation and suggestion important processes for its growth and transmission. But he suggested no method for its further investigation. Nevertheless, he made a big advance on the two other writers in this field, Comte and Spencer. The former had put forward a conception of social unity which implied the interplay of all the minds constituting society, but had not pushed his analysis beyond this broad principle of interpretation. The latter had gone one step farther, and in both his sociology and his psychology had adumbrated the idea of a *correlation* between the mind of the individual and the social structure of the group. He saw that man and his social environment must be coadapted. " There is no richer thought in Spencer's sociology," says Dr M. Davies, " but he left it undeveloped." He remained content with this idea of external correspondence and of the " social type " ; and he scarcely touched upon the problem of mental processes, because he was more concerned with the investigation of structure than of function. Bagehot's suggestion was a big step forward, for he thought of mind in functional terms entirely.

Only one other investigator pursued the theme beyond this point in the Victorian age, and that was G. H. Lewes, whose *Problems of Life and Mind* (1874) deserves a far more prominent place then it usually receives in the history of social speculation. Lewes outlined a programme of investigation, and so conspicuously supplemented Bagehot. He gave both a clear definition of " the social mind " and a suggestion for its further study. Starting from the idea of mind as a reacting organ determined by its conditions, he explained the existence of common mental qualities in the members of a group: a *constant* element within the individual mind. For him, therefore, the social mind was simply the content or "sum of sentiments and ideas" existing in the minds of these individuals. The purpose of social psychology would thus be to investigate this constant content, and to understand the mutual interrelation between the individual and social mind whereby each modifies the other. This idea is, of course, only an expansion of what has been shown to be implied in Bagehot. Lewes did not develop the idea very far, however, suggestive though it was. His main interest lay elsewhere.

It is rather remarkable that the psychological interpretation of society should have gone no farther than this in the Victorian period. So far as this country was concerned, the foundations had been begun, and nothing more. C. H. Pearson's *National Life and Character* (1893), for instance, is mainly an historical retrospect and an attempt to forecast the trend of future development; but it contains very little valid psychological analysis. Specialised studies there were in abundance. Among these the work of Francis Galton is of the greatest value, and must rightly be considered as an important factor in later developments. His essay on "Gregarious and Slavish Instincts" is the first of a series of studies on mob psychology, which includes such works as Le Bon's *Psychology of the Crowd* (English translation 1897) and William Trotter's *Instincts of the Herd in Peace and War* (1916). Galton's was essentially an inductive study, being based upon data derived from South-west Africa, and is in the main line of advance from Bagehot, since it aimed at showing "that the slavish aptitudes of man are a direct consequence of his gregarious nature, which itself is a result of the conditions both of his primeval barbarism and of the forms of his subsequent civilisation."

Galton also prepared the way for later advances by his famous studies on "individual differences." He was as definitely a Darwinian as Bagehot was a Lamarckian, and his interest in both psychology and the thesis of natural selection naturally led him to apply the principles of variation and selection to the investigation of the variability of human stock and the resulting problem of individual and family diversity. His work, culminating in his plea for a science of eugenics (1904), is the most extreme statement at the end of the nineteenth century of the inheritance theory, just as Godwin's *Political Justice* was the extremest statement of the environmental hypothesis at the end of the previous century. This contrast is again indicative of the intervening revolution in biological studies.

Yet, apart from such specialised work, the subject of social psychology cannot be said to have developed far in England in the last twenty years of the Victorian era. Various reasons may be assigned for this. Partly, it may have been due to the pervasive influence of the general Spencerian sociology; partly, no doubt, to the prevalence of too intellectualistic an interpretation of emotion, which, as Graham Wallas showed in *Human Nature in Politics*, inevitably made the analysis of social processes superficial and sterile; and partly, also, to the preoccupation of academic psychology with the study of 'consciousness' rather than with 'behaviour.' But, as was observed earlier, a new and distinctive phase began at the turn of the century. Psychology in both England and America was in any case steadily expanding under the stimulus of the biological sciences, and emphasising more and more the necessary functional interpretation.[1] There were, however, particular influences coming from the Continent tending in the same direction, especially from France, and William James's *Principles of Psychology* (1890) prepared the way for them. Led by Ribot, as Professor Baldwin has remarked, this anti-intellectualistic movement "assumed the proportions of a thoroughgoing revolt." Ribot especially stressed the existence of a non-rational "affective logic" which required separate study. The work of other investigators, such as

[1] This change in outlook has recently been summarised thus: ". . . taking the evolutionary point of view [functional psychology] tried to divine at what stage in the development of the race the need for each mental process had become pressing enough to lead to the emergence of that particular process. In a general way the higher mental processes were held to meet the need for a wider and more flexible control of the environment. Thus functional psychology aimed to give psychology a place in the general field of biological science" (R. S. Woodworth, *Contemporary Schools of Psychology*, p. 47). As has been shown above, this attitude is implicit in *Physics and Politics* throughout.

Tarde,[1] Le Bon,[2] and Sighele[3] in sociology, and Charcot and Janet in psychopathology, reinforced the movement;[4] and Bergson not only contributed to its psychology but gave it a philosophy. The pragmatism of William James was but another aspect of the same tendency; and the whole 'behaviourist' trend was reinforced by the rapid development of animal psychology from the time of Thorndike's first experiments in America in 1896. Thus, by the end of the era surveyed in this volume each of the themes touched upon by Bagehot had been subject to considerable further investigation, and the possibility of social psychology as a separate and independent study had already been realised.

C. H. Driver

BOOK LIST

No history of social psychology has yet been written. The student interested in the psychological approach to political speculation will find the following books useful on particular aspects of the theme, in addition to those cited in the text.

Baldwin, J. M.: *History of Psychology*. 1913.

Barker, E.: *Political Thought in England, 1848–1914: From Herbert Spencer to the Present Day*. 1915.

Barnes, H. E.: *History and Prospects of the Social Sciences*. 1925.

Barrington, Mrs. R.: *Works and Life of Walter Bagehot*. 1915.

Bogardus, E. S.: *History of Social Thought*. 1922.

Brett, G. S.: *The Government of Man*. 1920.

—— *A History of Psychology*, vols. ii and iii. 1921.

Davies, M. M.: *Psychological Interpretation of Society*. 1909.

Giddings, F. H.: "Darwinism in the Theory of Social Evolution" (in *Popular Science Monthly*, July 1909).

Ginsberg, M.: *The Psychology of Society*. 1921.

Haddon, A. C.: *The History of Anthropology*. 1920.

Halévy, E.: *The Growth of Philosophic Radicalism*. 1928.

Lichtenberger, J. P.: *Development of Social Theory*. 1924.

Mackintosh, R.: *From Comte to Benjamin Kidd*. 1899.

[1] *Les Lois de l'imitation* (1890), *Logique sociale* (1895), and *Psychologie économique* (1902).

[2] *The Psychology of Peoples* (1898), *The Crowd* (1897), etc.

[3] *Psychologie des sectes* (1898) and *La Foule criminelle* (1901).

[4] Freud's practical work in psychoanalysis dates from 1886. The first German edition of *The Interpretation of Dreams* appeared in 1900, and *The Psychopathology of Everyday Life* in the following year. The first international congress of psychoanalysts was held in 1908—the year in which McDougall's *Introduction to Social Psychology*, E. A. Ross's *Social Psychology*, and Graham Wallas's *Human Nature in Politics* appeared.

MURCHISON, C.: *Social Psychology.* 1929.
MURPHY, G.: *A Historical Introduction to Modern Psychology.* 1928.
MURRAY, R. H.: *Studies in the English Social and Political Thinkers of the Nineteenth Century.* 1929.
RANDALL, J. H.: *The Making of the Modern Mind.* 1925.
RITCHIE, W. J.: *Darwinism and Politics.* 1895.
ROGERS, A. K.: *English and American Philosophy since 1800.* 1923.
SIDGWICK, H.: *Outlines of the History of Ethics for English Readers.* 1886.
SINGER, C.: *A Short History of Biology.* 1930.
SOROKIN, P. A.: *Contemporary Sociological Theories.* 1928.
STEPHEN, L.: *History of English Thought in the Eighteenth Century.* 1876.
THOULESS, R. H.: *Social Psychology.* 1925.
WARREN, H. C.: *A History of the Association Psychology.* 1921.

The two previous volumes in this series also contain useful material bearing upon the subject.

X

TAINE AND THE NATIONALISTS

IF it is conceded that the idea of rounding off this series of articles on great Victorian thinkers by an article on a contemporary French writer was a sound one, then the selection of Taine to fill this place needs little justification. Few would dispute the right of Taine to rank by the side of our great Victorians. He has much of their solidity and vigour, their earnestness, their hatred of dilettantism, their love of good, sturdy systems of thought, and also, although not a practising Christian himself, their subordination of literature and art to the moral point of view. A horror of all insincerity and shams pervades his work as well as his life. There are, moreover, more than mere analogies between Taine and the Victorians; there are also affinities, and very close affinities, between them. From his earliest days Taine had been brought up to a love for England [1]; he had studied its literature and its philosophy, its politics and its morals; he had been in the country several times, observed its people and their institutions, and it is to their literature that the work that is for many his masterpiece—his five-volume *History of English Literature*—is devoted. He visited Dickens and Thackeray, and was on friendly terms with Matthew Arnold, John Stuart Mill, and Herbert Spencer, with whom he corresponded frequently; while Englishmen, on their side, pleased by his brilliant and flattering generalisations on the English character, were only too ready to extend a cordial welcome to him. The links, then, that bind Taine to England are very close.

If Taine's claim to be considered as a great Victorian is a sound one his title to rank as the most representative, or at least the most influential, French thinker of the second half of the nineteenth century is even more indisputable.

[1] See F. C. Roe's *Taine et l'Angleterre* (Champion, 1923).

TAINE AND THE NATIONALISTS

There was hardly a Frenchman who came to intellectual maturity between the years 1860 and 1900 who did not undergo, to a greater or less extent, the influence of Taine's thought, whether in the fields of literature, philosophy, sociology, or politics. Even more than Renan, whose influence sometimes runs parallel with his own, he was the idol of successive generations of Frenchmen. Historians, even if they had a good deal to unlearn of his teaching, were inspired by him to base all their work on the conscientious study of documents, to accumulate methodically masses of " significant facts," and to seek carefully for the sense and the underlying laws which bind all these facts together. When Mr Guedalla said that for the last fifty years French history had been one long Taine without a turning he sacrificed less of the truth than usual to epigram. Philosophers learned from Taine to beware of vague and nebulous speculation, and to give to science the place which had formerly been given to an unsubstantial spiritualism. Novelists, whether of the naturalist school of Zola or psychologists like Bourget, owe much to Taine. Critics learned from him to find a method midway between scholastic dogmatism and airy impressionism. Politicians were taught that nothing sound or permanent can be achieved without taking into account a country's origins and its development; while to all kinds of men alike Taine offered the model of a life devoted to the disinterested search for truth. And all these lessons received additional force from the prestige of an eminently personal style, in which vast and persuasive generalisations were mingled with the imagination of a poet.

Towards the end of last century one of Taine's disciples, the Comte de Voguë, was able to say, " Most of the workers of to-day are working in the deep furrow made by Taine "; and twenty years later M. Giraud,[1] Taine's ablest biographer, echoed the truth of this. It is doubtful whether anyone would be so bold as to re-echo it to-day. Together with many of his great Victorian contemporaries Taine, or a good deal of him, has been relegated to the era of wax-fruits and antimacassars, an interesting museum-piece, which is taken off its shelf now and then to be dusted, but which ceases any

[1] V. Giraud, *Essai sur Taine* (fifth edition, Hachette, 1912).

longer to work as a vital force. He still has his admirers, a small and diminishing group well over to the Right, to whom official and university criticism, having allotted him his niche in the manuals, has now entirely handed him over. The man who refused to be recruited in his lifetime has been recruited after his death.

While the assessment of Taine's rank in his own country has been largely a question of political colour, it is fairly safe to assert that, outside the specialists, Taine is little known nowadays in England, except as the author of his *English Literature*, of his book on La Fontaine, and as the constructor of an interesting, though rather old-fashioned, literary theory —on the whole, that is, as a literary critic. His reputation as a social and political thinker is very small outside France. This is, in fact, the case with most of the French political thinkers of the nineteenth century, and it is mainly because of the narrowing effect—as Mr Soltau points out in his work on *French Political Thought in the Nineteenth Century*[1]—that the French Revolution brought about in this field. By killing local patriotism the Revolution gave birth to a nationalism which takes the form of a vast collective egoism, and this effectively precludes any independent speculation on international relations and any clear view of the position of France in the world. In such an atmosphere any political thinking there is tends to resemble mere wrangling within a family, and such wrangling has no great interest for outsiders. How far our neighbours have advanced beyond this stage is even now a matter for speculation, although one of them (M. Julien Benda[2]) has quite recently been able to assert tranquilly, not, however, without severe contradiction from some of his own countrymen, that of all European nations France is now the one whose nationalism is the least 'barbarous' of all.

The neglect of Taine's political ideas in England might again be ascribed by uncharitable people to the fact that he had none. And in a sense he had not. He admitted as much himself, and even when he was more than half-way through his great journey to discover the origins of contemporary France he had to confess that he had been able to

[1] Published by Benn, 1931.
[2] "Les Moins barbares," in *Les Nouvelles littéraires* (October 17, 1931).

find only one political principle, and that so simple that he was afraid it might appear puerile if he dared to announce it. It consisted of this one observation, "that a human society, especially a modern society, is a vast and complicated thing"! But, if he had no new and fertile views to offer on the nature of the State and of men's political relations, he had, in place of these, some strong and healthy prejudices. On these his philosophical mind and his poetical imagination worked, and, nourished on an intense devotion to his country and a profound study of his country's past, they evolved something which may not have been an original political philosophy, but which was at least a powerful diagnosis of the ills from which his country was suffering and a suggestion as to the remedies to which it should have recourse.

One might finally explain the neglect of Taine's thought in England by the fact that he never entered the political arena; not even for the briefest spell did he hold any post which was likely to throw him into the limelight and make him in the journalistic sense 'news.' In fact, he avoided publicity as far as possible, leaving his works to make his reputation, and keeping his personality in the background.

II

Taine's life, then, as one might expect, offers no exciting events. It would, indeed, be difficult to find a less promising subject for the author of a modern *biographie romancée*. He lived for the most part the quiet and retired existence of a scholar. His biographers, in recounting his life and the early formative influences of the young Taine, usually treat him to a little of his own medicine, and, taking the three factors of race, environment, and epoch, which were to form the scaffolding of his great critical apparatus, they tell us—after the event—why Taine was bound to be Taine and not somebody else. Let us keep to the few facts that are necessary to mark out his career.

Hippolyte Taine was born in April 1828 at Vouziers, in the Ardennes, not far, that is, from Germany—a fact which has been allowed to account for something of the austere, Germanic strain in his character, as well as for his love of vast generalisations and patient erudition. He was by no means of the poor peasant stock which has in later days given France so many of her great scholars and politicians, but came of a good, long-established family of *bourgeois*, who, if not rich, were at least comfortably off. His father was a lawyer at Vouziers, and there were Taines well back in the eighteenth century who had held legal or official posts. He spent his early years in an atmosphere of peace and tranquillity, of hard work mingled with intellectual pleasures. As he was a boy of delicate constitution he received his early education at home. Here he laid the foundations of a solid classical education, and after the death of his father—which happened when Taine was a boy of twelve—he was initiated into the study of English. At thirteen his guardians considered it advisable for him to continue his education at a Paris *lycée*, and in 1841 he began studying at the Collège Bourbon. He remained here, leading a life of extreme intellectual intensity, until his entry in 1848 into the École Normale. A short memoir which he wrote a few months before then (but not for publication) throws an extraordinary light on his precocious mental activity:

> Up to the age of fifteen I lived ignorant and peaceful. I had not yet thought of the future, I did not know it. I was a Christian, and I had never asked myself what this life is worth, whence I came, what I was destined to do.
>
> Reason appeared suddenly in me like a light; I began to suspect that there was something beyond what I had seen; I began to grope, as it were, in the darkness. The thing that fell first in this examination was my religious faith. One doubt called forth another; each belief carried another away with it in its fall. . . . I felt in myself sufficient honour and strength of will to live the life of an upright man even after I had rid myself of my religion. I had too high a regard for my reason to believe in any other authority [than itself]. . . . The three years which followed were peaceful; they were years of research and discovery. I thought only of extending my intelligence, increasing my knowledge, and acquiring a keener sentiment of the true and the beautiful. I studied with ardour both history and antiquity, seeking always for general truths, aspiring to a knowledge of things as a whole, to know what is man and society.

He goes on to speak of the effect which Guizot's lectures on European civilisation had on him, and says, "It was like a revelation; I set myself to discover the general laws of history, then the general laws of the art of writing." Already, then, one sees in this interesting document not only evidence of an astonishing maturity of mind, but also Taine's fervour for making generalisations and formulating hypotheses, a feature which was to become the dominating quality of all his work as well as the quality by which he judged the work of others. Later on he deplores the lack of this faculty in contemporary writers. "The Germans," he says, "make intolerable hypotheses, the French none at all, and the English do not even suspect that it is possible to make any."

The École Normale Supérieure,[1] which Taine entered in 1848, was, and of course still is, the training school for future teachers in *lycées* and for university professors, the avenue, in fact, to all the higher teaching posts in the country. It has always prided itself on being the nursery of the intellectual *élite* of France, and on having an intellectual independence which university officialdom cannot stamp out. It has not always lived up to this ideal, but at least when Taine went there it was enjoying a spell of relative freedom from official tyranny. Whether coincidence or effect, it also happened to contain among its students an unusual collection of future *littérateurs* and historians of mark—Sarcey, About, Prévost-Paradol, Weiss, Suckau, and others. Even in this brilliant company Taine soon distinguished himself for the extent of his knowledge, the breadth of his mind, and his amazing capacity for work. By common consent he was recognised not only as the finest student of his "promotion," but also as one of the finest students the school had ever had. For ordinary students the preparation for the *agrégation*, the competitive examination on the result of which depends the appointment to the better posts in *lycées*, would have been a full-time occupation. For Taine it was almost a side-line, and concurrently with it he set himself a vast programme of work, particularly in philosophy and history. His notebooks of these years are full of analyses and criticisms of Spinoza, to whom he owed more than to any other philosopher, and of Hegel; and he had already drawn up a theory of

[1] See E. Herriot's *Normale* (1932) (in the series "Nos Grandes Écoles," published by La Nouvelle Société d'Édition).

intelligence, which forms the basis of his later vast work on that subject. There was practically no branch of study which he left untouched in this great effort to achieve a synthesis of all human knowledge. In this atmosphere of liberalism, of harmonious co-operation between students and professors unhindered by the imposition of any restrictions on teaching, Taine lived a life of intellectual fullness, on which he was later able to look back with longing.

By the time Taine had finished his studies, however, and was to present himself for the *agrégation* the attitude of the authorities towards the École Normale had undergone a profound change. The Revolution of 1848 had scared the French *bourgeoisie* so badly and had given them such a horror of socialism that they were even ready to make a pact with Catholicism. The Emperor Napoleon III realised only too well that his principal support was the middle class, and that only by embracing their clericalism could he hope to retain his hold in the country.[1] Hence begins for France a period of devastating clerical domination, which makes itself felt more in the domain of education than anywhere else. The slightest tinge of unorthodoxy was closely watched for, history and philosophy were to be taught only by practising Catholics, and no attack on Catholic dogma was to be tolerated in books or Press. A rigid censorship of books for school and university libraries was to be enforced. In such an atmosphere one can foresee the kind of treatment which awaited Taine. In 1851 he presented himself for the *agrégation* in philosophy. Could there possibly be any doubt as to the success of such a student? The tributes his professors paid him are unanimous as to his extraordinary qualities. "M. Taine," said one of them, "is a distinguished pupil who will sooner or later bring honour to the school by important publications." Another said, "Irreproachable in his conduct and bearing, he will have authority over his pupils." Yet another praised his clear and supple mind, while saying that if he had any fault at all it was an excessive tendency to abstraction. His own director of studies wrote what is a singularly able character-study of him, of which the following is the most notable passage:

[1] R. H. Soltau, *French Political Thought in the Nineteenth Century.*

> The most diligent, the most distinguished pupil I have ever met at the School. Prodigious learning for his age. Ardour and keenness for knowledge of which I have never seen any example before. Mind remarkable for its rapidity of conception, sharpness, subtlety, power of thought. But understands, conceives, judges, and formulates too rapidly. Likes formulas and definitions, to which he sacrifices too often reality—without realising it, it is true, for he is of an absolute sincerity. Taine will be a distinguished professor, but moreover and especially a *savant* of the very first rank if his health allows him to continue.

Taine failed his *agrégation*. It was almost as if the university had said, "That is how we intend to treat brilliant young men who dare to think outside the bounds of orthodoxy." A fresh insult was reserved for him when he was given a minor post in the small college at Nevers. His whole soul revolted against the servility expected of him here, against the utter nullity of his colleagues and the futility of their teaching. "What is expected of a teacher," he wrote in 1852, "is absence of ideas, of passion, a machine-mind, the pedantry of the old pedagogues. The true teacher is simply a talking fossil who knows nothing of the ideas of his time."

Nevertheless, in spite of his discouragement, of his natural pessimism, which this semi-exile reinforced, he continued to work even harder than before, both at his *agrégation* and at his doctor's thesis. Although he was allowed at the second attempt to pass, he found himself once again up against the intellectual persecution of the university when he presented a thesis on the sensations. As he felt incapable of mutilating this work to bring it into line with the official philosophy, he abandoned the doctorate of philosophy and began work at the doctorate of letters, choosing as his subject "La Fontaine and his Fables," a work in which his examiners were not able to find any doctrines of which the Emperor or the Pope might be expected to disapprove. (In spite of this, Mgr Dupanloup denounced it later on in his *Avertissement à la jeunesse et aux pères de famille* (1863) as concealing the germs of a materialist and fatalist philosophy.) Although the work had not in 1853 the form in which we now know it, it may be taken as definitely beginning that series of inquiries into social psychology to which the chief of his life-work was to be devoted.

With his year's teaching at Nevers, and later at Poitiers, a stage was ended and another begun in his career. He was offered, almost insultingly for a man of his talents, a post as *professeur de sixième* in the *lycée* of Besançon, but rather than accept this servitude he obtained leave to remain without a post. He settled in Paris, and eked out by a little private coaching the small sums he was able to get from various articles and reviews, some of which were later incorporated into his *English Literature*, while others were collected into a volume published in 1858 under the title of *Essays of Criticism and History*. In addition to this he threw himself into the study of science with the same zeal that he had formerly shown for letters. He had always shown keenness for science; now it became a religion for him. He frequented assiduously the lectures of all the most famous doctors and scientists in Paris, read eagerly all the new works of science, endeavouring all the time to organise this knowledge into generalisations which would assist him in his inquiries into psychology and philosophy.

III

The history of Taine's life henceforward is mainly that of his books, of which some brief account must be given before the origin and growth of his political ideas can be traced. The enormous labour which Taine had imposed upon himself, together with the official vexations he was subjected to, had worked on a constitution by no means robust, and had so completely undermined his health that by 1854 he found himself obliged to leave Paris for a time. He went to recuperate in the Pyrenees, and from this stay he was able to extract an extremely lively and interesting guide-book, which Hachette published in 1855, and which brought him considerable renown. It has nothing at all of the Baedeker about it, but is full of picturesque and even poetic descriptions of scenery and people, interspersed with historical anecdotes and philosophical observations.

His next work, which he had begun a year or two earlier,

and which was completed in 1854 and published in 1856, was an essay on Livy, written for an academic competition. Although more remarkable as a brilliant piece of writing than as an original contribution to history, this work is not without its interest as indicating the development of Taine's thought. It represents the first stage in his search for a system on which to found all his studies of history, sociology, and criticism. Seeking chiefly a key to the explanation of genius and talent, he endeavours to work out, in the particular case of Livy, the theory of the *faculté maîtresse*, or dominating faculty, a theory not entirely his own, since Schlegel had already used it in his *Philosophy of History*. It is that all the intellectual activity of the human mind depends ultimately upon a central inner force, which is the principal motor. To study a poet, a painter, or a philosopher is simply to try and unravel, through all the series of mental operations which contribute to the unity of his work, the unity of thought which explains his general character. To know a writer means to be able to give, as it were, a definition of him, to state a formula which contains the essentials of his personality. This formula is the expression of one *faculté maîtresse* on which all the secondary ones depend, and which may be considered as the keystone of the whole intellectual, moral, and spiritual edifice of the man. Now let us see the scientific rationalisation of this principle.

In his preface Taine asks:

> Do the faculties of a man depend, like the organs of a plant, on one another? Are they measured and produced by one single law? This law being given, can one then foresee their energy and calculate in advance their good and bad effects? Can one reconstruct them as one reconstructs a fossil? Is there in us a dominating faculty, of which the uniform action is communicated differently to the different parts of our intellectual mechanism, and which impresses on our machine a necessary system of foreseen movements? I endeavour to answer yes, and by giving an example.

One sees behind this rather heavy pseudo-scientific apparatus Taine's idea: he is aiming not so much at a literary or historical study as at a philosophical thesis founded on an example. Anybody would have served just as well for the demonstration; Taine took Livy, since he was the author set by the Academy for the competition. He finds Livy's *faculté maîtresse* summed up in the formula 'historian-orator,' but it is difficult to see how much farther advanced one is when one has arrived at this definition. Apart from the fact that a writer might have several *facultés maîtresses*, each of which is dominant in turn or in combination with another, the instrument is not of sufficient precision to give any very reliable results. One might, for example, apply the formula 'historian-orator' to Macaulay equally well as to Livy; it does not help us to distinguish a writer clearly enough or to show wherein lies his particular originality. The work as a whole has, however, this importance, that it shows Taine beginning to make an application to facts of a moral order of the laws governing the relations of biological phenomena.

Taine's next work was the *Classical Philosophers of the Nineteenth Century*, which, published first in the form of articles, appeared in book form in 1857. It is in reality a bitter attack, although couched in the form of a gentle irony, but full of telling argument, on the principles on which the eclectic philosophy of the earlier part of the century had rested. The attack centres, of course, round Victor Cousin, the high priest of the eclectics, who, in Taine's eyes, was the very antithesis of a philosopher. In this work he rehabilitated Condillac's sensualism, completing and extending it, and ended by sketching out a system which applied to psychological and even metaphysical research the methods of the exact sciences. He was evidently getting his own back for the treatment he had met with at the hands of eclecticism as enshrined in the university, and also preparing the public mind to receive his own philosophic synthesis when it came. The book had an enormous success, and placed its author at once in the forefront of the literary men of the day, with only Renan as a possible rival. He was violently attacked, of course; some called him an out-and-out materialist; others a Spinozist; others made him out to be a pure positivist; and by the Catholics in general he was charged with being a corruptor of youth.

The work that began to occupy him really seriously now was his *English Literature*. Although not published until 1863, he had begun it as early as 1855. Here again it was less at a history of literature than at a demonstration of a philosophical method of inquiry that he was aiming. Criticism and history were for him only a convenient means of developing his philosophical doctrine on man and society. Although this doctrine or theory is a commonplace to students of literary history, it may perhaps be as well to outline it here, since it has its influence on the work which more definitely classes Taine as a social and political thinker. His fundamental principle, as has been seen, is that all human facts, both moral and physical, are bound up with causes and are subject to laws. It follows, therefore, that all the works of man, arts, religions, philosophies, literatures, facts of the moral, political, or social order, are just resultants of general causes, which can be determined according to a scientific method. One of these causes, as has been shown, is the possession of a *faculté maîtresse*. To this cause, which he continues to work out in his *English Literature*, are joined the famous trio *race*, *moment*, and *milieu*, whose meaning and function are explained with a persuasive clarity in his introduction to that work. Let us first examine these elements before seeing the application he made of them to the study of our literature.

" What one calls *race*," he says in this well-known introduction, " are the innate and hereditary dispositions which man brings with him when he is born, and which ordinarily are joined to marked differences in the temperament and structure of the body. They vary according to nations." So Taine takes as the starting-point for his analysis of the concept of race the *physiological* differences which exist between men. There are varieties of men just as there are varieties of bulls and horses. From this physiological diversity Taine deduces at once the existence of corresponding psychological differences. The forces which oblige a man to modify his food, his clothing, his habitat, are those which therefore modify the forms of his thought. " A different climate and situation," he says, " bring about in man different needs, consequently a different system of actions, consequently again different habits, and, as a final consequence, a different system of aptitudes and instincts." So far it is easy to recognise Montesquieu in this theory. One is reminded, too, of the applications which Mme de Staël had made of the theory in her powerful generalisations on national character in her works

On Literature and *On Germany*. Taine's originality lies in the development and application he gives to it. The factor of *race* in a people has its source, as has been seen, in the habits accumulated by its ancestors. It is the result of the incessant effort they have had to make against the hostile forces from without; in other words, it is the result of *adaptation to environment*. One sees, then, Taine endeavouring to graft Darwinism on to Montesquieu. He borrows from Darwin the three laws of struggle for life, adaptation to environment, and heredity. *Race* can be summed up, therefore, as a sort of synthesis of all the sensations and all the actions of a people, accumulated, built up, and consolidated by heredity. It would be easy enough to criticise the application in this way of biological laws to the human. Where one can at the most draw an interesting analogy Taine lays down a permanent law. He isolates the factor *race*, and yet admits that it is constantly conditioned by other features; he introduces the principle of evolution, and yet vitiates it at the very beginning by making *race* something fixed and static.

Consider next the factor of *milieu* or environment. Now, while *race* is considered as the great inner, or central, force, environment is the great outer force. What constitutes it essentially on the physical side is the climate and geographical framework, while on the moral side are the whole body of social, political, and religious institutions. This moral side is worked out particularly well by Taine in his *Origins of Contemporary France*, when he traces out the growth of the revolutionary spirit in the political atmosphere of 1793.

The third factor, the *moment*, or epoch, is, according to Taine, the result of the combined forces from within and without on an individual or a collection of individuals at a given point of their development. The reciprocal actions of *race* and *milieu* produce a sort of momentum or acquired speed, and this acquired speed exercises a pressure from the past on the future. In other words, national character and surrounding circumstances never work on a *tabula rasa*, but upon a surface on which impressions have already been made. According to whether one considers this surface at one *moment* or another so the impression made will vary and final interest will be different. So that where the other two factors are stable this one partakes of the nature of *present*. In addition to these chief factors there are minor ones, which it is impossible to examine in this article. Presented in this bald fashion, shorn of their brilliant imagery, Taine's theories no doubt lose much of their persuasive power, but at least this outline serves to indicate the scope of his method and to show how this is subordinated to the great principles which constitute his determinist philosophy.

It is clear, then, that one must not look in Taine's work for a purely critical or æsthetic account of English literature. The question he puts to himself in his introduction is this:

> Given a literature, philosophy, society, art, group of arts, what is the moral condition which produced it? What the conditions of race, epoch, circumstance, the most fitted to produce this moral condition? . . . Just as in its elements astronomy is a mechanical and physiology a chemical problem, so history is a psychological problem.

And what is the raw material from which this problem is to be worked out? Literature. When the work is rich, and one knows how to interpret it, we find in it the psychology of a soul, frequently of an age, now and then of a race. In this light a great poem, a fine novel, the confessions of a superior man, are more instructive, he thinks, than a host of historians with their histories. He would give, he says, five hundred volumes of charters and a hundred volumes of State papers for the memoirs of Cellini, the epistles of St Paul, the table-talk of Luther, or the comedies of Aristophanes. He adds—and it is worth noticing the back seat to which he relegates æsthetics:

> The more a book represents visible sentiments, the more it is a work of literature; for the proper office of literature is to take note of sentiments. The more a book represents important sentiments, the higher is its place in literature.

He tells us quite plainly, then, that in his history of English literature he is going to seek for the psychology of a people.

If Taine has chosen England in preference, for example, to ancient Greece as the matter for this study of collective national psychology, it is, as he explains, because, being yet alive and subject to direct examination, it may be better studied than a destroyed civilisation, of which we retain but the scraps. "*Subject*" to direct examination is worth noticing. That does not by any means entail the *necessity* for direct observation. The *rôle* of observation is only to afford confirmation. In this connection the well-known remark of Taine to Monod, about to depart for Italy, is worth quoting, especially in the new and livelier version of it given by M. Herriot. "Entre l'aîné et le cadet," says M. Herriot, who was told of the conversation by Monod himself, "le dialogue suivant s'engagea. 'Quelles sont, mon jeune camarade, vos idées sur l'Italie?' 'Je n'en ai point. Je vais précisément en chercher.' 'Alors vous ne verrez rien.'"[1]

Taine had, in fact, almost completed his work on English literature, and formulated his generalisations as to the English character, before he came to this country for the first time in 1860. He stayed here two months. It was quite enough for his purpose. All he had to do was to verify his generalisations. And he was extremely gratified to find that they were all correct, except on one little point. He had described English people as being rather impolite and unobliging. His first three weeks of English hospitality had shown him how far out he had been on this point. Apart from that, however, he cannot help congratulating himself on the accuracy of his formulas. "I was singularly struck," he says at the end of his fourth volume, "by the mutual confirmation afforded by observation and history; it seemed to me that the present was completing the past, and the past explaining the present."

To examine the purely literary aspect of his work would be to stray too far outside the limits of this article. It is, however, necessary to see something of the views he expresses there on England and the English, since these enter so largely into his own political conceptions.[2] Two further visits to the country, in 1862 and in 1871, at the end of which latter year he collected his observations into a volume called *Notes on England*, furnished him with more adequate, although still insufficient, detail for his generalisations, and these *Notes*,

[1] E. Herriot, *op. cit.*

[2] See F. C. Roe, *op. cit.*, and H. Sée, "Taine et la conception de l'aristocratie bienfaisante," in *Science et philosophie de l'histoire* (Alcan, 1928).

together with his own letters, provide a good picture of England as it appeared to Taine.

These years 1860 to 1870 were years of relative calm and prosperity for England, and a foreign observer could not help making flattering comparisons between this and his own country. There was a beautiful sense of tradition and continuity and of the best kind of conservatism apparent here. This country, it seemed to him, was more capable than any other in Europe of transforming itself without recasting, and of devoting itself to its future without renouncing its past. His own country, severing itself completely from its origins, had thwarted and diverted its development. And what, he asks himself, is the root of all this peaceful progress in England? The fact that in England government is the business of a class whose natural calling it is to govern. It is a spontaneous government. It is not something imported, implanted artificially; no idols suddenly raised to power by a mob of ignorant plebeians, and liable to be dethroned and replaced the next day. It is composed of gentleman landowners, watching with a fatherly solicitude over the interests of the poor. The people, in fact, recognise their natural leader in

> the influential landholder, an old county man, powerful through his connections, dependents, tenantry, interested above all else by his great possessions in the affairs of the neighbourhood, expert in the concerns which his family have managed for generations, most fitted by education to give good advice, and by his influence to lead the common enterprise to a good result.

The energy and devotion to duty of these natural leaders are really touching as seen by Taine. Would it be believed, for example, that "rich men leave London by hundreds every day to spend a day in the country; there is a meeting of the affairs of the county or of the church; they are magistrates, overseers, presidents of all kinds of societies, and this gratuitously." And their charity too!

> One has built a bridge at his own expense, another a church or a school; many establish public libraries, with warmed and lighted rooms in which the villagers find the papers, games, tea, at low charges—in a word, simple amusements which may keep them from the gin-shop. Many of them give lectures. . . . I have even seen one,

> having an enormous fortune, who on Sunday in his school taught singing to little girls!

And their kindness! "Lord Palmerston offered his park for archery meetings, and the Duke of Marlborough opens his daily to the public." What a contrast Taine sees between this aristocratic Salentum and his own mean, *bourgeois*-ridden France! Here "A firm and proud sentiment of duty, a genuine public spirit, a liberal notion of what a gentleman owes to himself, give them a moral superiority which sanctions their command." Add to all this—a contrast with all other aristocracies—the fact that they are well educated, liberal, and march in the van, and not at the tail, of public civilisation.

This is what Taine saw, or thought he saw, in England. Actually, of course, it is the roughest of generalisations from one or two visits to country mansions and from a view of the spacious parks and beautiful lawns of the "stately homes of England." Yet it is this conception of an ideal aristocracy, voluntarily devoting itself to the task of government, which forms the basis of his *Ancien Régime*. The natural corollary to such an aristocracy is, of course, a docile, respectful, and submissive people, law-abiding, and interested in preserving order, and this Taine naturally finds as well. He says:

> Two days after I arrived in London I saw advertising men walking with a placard on their backs and stomachs bearing these words: "Great usurpation! Outrage of the Lords in their vote on the Budget against the rights of the people." But then the placard added: "Fellow-countrymen, petition." Things end thus; they argue in free terms, and if the reasoning is good it will spread.

The Tainian method of generalising from one or two isolated instances is not entirely dead even now. An interesting revival of it was shown a short time ago by M. Siegfried in his analysis of Great Britain's crisis, where he was tempted to conclude, from the fact that he saw a large crowd streaming out of the Oval on a fine week-day, that England was rotten to the core with sport mania. Even M. de Grand' Combe's[1] kindly and often penetrating observations on the English are too redolent of Bristol suburbia for us to be able to accept all his compliments or all his reproaches as wholly representative.

[1] F. de Grand' Combe, *Tu viens en Angleterre* (Presses Universitaires, 1932).

If we have insisted so much, perhaps too much, on Taine's views on England it is because it was the observation and study of this country and its social system that induced Taine to observe the social phenomena of his own country with greater care. During the years 1863 to 1865 he was appointed examiner to the candidates for the military school of Saint-Cyr. It was a post which took only three months of each year, but it entailed travels in all the different parts of France. The notes he took of his observations were afterwards written up and published under the title of *Carnets de voyage*. The effect England had produced on him is evident throughout, compelling constantly comparisons to the disadvantage of his country. In these notes, more than in anything he had written so far, appears his disgust of the so-called democratic *régime* of France. To him the whole country seems to be designed in such a way as to produce nothing but mediocrities. He writes:

> The constructor of modern France seems to have said to himself, there are a certain number of good things and it is necessary that every one should have a bit; that no one should have a big bit, but that nearly all should have a tiny or moderate share.

There is no real aristocracy left in the country, he complains. Everything is split up, culture and comfort. "A society is like a big garden: you can arrange it so as to produce peaches and oranges, or carrots and cabbages. Ours is all carrots and cabbages." What prospects are there for greatness in such a place? These jumped-up *bourgeois* understand neither hospitality nor good manners. Everywhere one is hemmed in by the State, the individual is everywhere sacrificed to the State; it makes you economise, it forces you into associations you don't want, it gives you a pittance when you are invalid —it treats you always as a minor incapable of providing for your old age. Even the religion of the country is mechanical; it is a mere government machine or else a means of getting advancement. It has none of the mysticism, poetry, and fervour of English Protestantism. And yet Taine does not feel inclined to pity his country. "The more I see of France," he writes, "the more I think it has the constitution it deserves. We are just Gauls made to be herded into regiments, having as our ideals brilliant feats of devotion and deeds of chivalrous audacity."

In 1864 Taine was appointed to the chair of History of Art at the École des Beaux-Arts, a post which he held till 1870. The fact that a philosopher and a literary critic was appointed to lecture on art need not surprise anyone who is at all familiar with conditions in French universities during the last century. In any case, Taine's teaching was extremely popular and successful, although, quite naturally, psychological and social considerations came in for more treatment than æsthetics. His courses of lectures were published later in two volumes under the title of *The Philosophy of Art*. Among other works of this period were some light and amusing studies of different aspects of Parisian Society life, under the title of *Vie et opinions de Thomas Frédéric Graindorge*, two rather dull books on his travels in Italy, and finally in 1870 his great philosophic work, *Théorie de l'intelligence*. Two years earlier Taine had married and settled down in a quiet *bourgeois* way, renouncing almost entirely the brilliant Society life into which, for some years, his literary fame had procured him the entry.

IV

In 1870 came the great turning-point in his career. The Franco-Prussian War and the weaknesses it revealed in the government of France forced him to an *examen de conscience* in matters of politics which he had constantly deferred. Hitherto, in fact, he had occupied himself little with politics, except when circumstances made him feel closely any particular instances of bureaucratic imbecility. For politicians as a whole he had the greatest contempt. As early as his École Normale days he had said, when trying to dissuade his friend Prévost-Paradol from entering politics: "I would as soon be dead as become a simple machine at the service of a personal passion, of some one else's opinion, and lose my liberty, for the only liberty is in thought." When he attained his majority, and with it the right to use a vote, he abstained, saying:

I am unable to vote, for two reasons. Firstly, in order to vote I should have to know the state of France, its ideas, its manners, its opinions, its future, for the true government is one which is appropriate to the civilisation of a people; secondly, even if I knew all that is suited to France I have too little knowledge of the merit, the probity, and the opinions of the candidates to be able to choose amongst them all.

One cannot but admire Taine's thoroughness and circumspection, although a general adoption of his attitude could hardly be contemplated in a domain like politics, where reason is almost the last of man's faculties to which any appeal is made. Taine's conscientious attitude did not mean, however, that he merely wished to take refuge, in face of a difficult duty, in a culpable abstention; it merely meant that in this great and important question he was appalled at the lack of preparation of both candidates and voters.

When I look at these two troupes of fanatical beggars wallowing for all they are worth in mud I do not know whether there is any good on either side. In the midst of all the arguments I see them slinging at each other's heads I look for reasons, and I see only declamation and platitude. . . . So, leaving all these preachers of civil war, I throw myself into pure science, convinced that there is good in the present and in the future, and determined to seek for it as soon as I can, studying with that in view, diving deep into philosophy and history to arrive at the social sciences and to try and determine what is good and durable in our state of things.

For more than twenty years he had been carrying on this "deep diving" when the time came at last for him to apply its results to his country's service as he thought best. The Franco-Prussian War had come as a terrible blow to Taine, who had never hidden his German sympathies, and who had even a few months before been present at the unveiling of a statue to Hegel. The war and the horrible aftermath of the Commune in Paris were to him, as to many of the intellectuals among his contemporaries, a shattering revelation,[1] awakening him to a patriotism he had never before had occasion to show. Why, he asked himself, is my country the prey to all this strife and disaster? Why are there no great men to command respect? Why are we sunk to the level of a fourth-rate nation? It was not enough for him to know instinctively the reasons for all these things. His aim henceforward was to render service to his country by showing it the causes of

[1] See A. Bellesort, *Les Intellectuels et l'avènement de la Troisième République* (1931).

its decadence, and thereby pointing out to it the right road to progress and salvation. From this determination came the vast work to which he gave the title *The Origins of Contemporary France*, a work which occupied him until his death in 1893. The first part, *L'Ancien Régime*, appeared in 1876; the next part, *The Revolution*, consisted of three volumes, *Anarchy* (1878), *The Jacobin Conquest* (1881), and *Revolutionary Government* (1884). Of the third part, *Le Régime moderne*, one volume appeared in 1891, and the second after his death.

In this work of history and social psychology Taine endeavoured to apply the same method as for his previous works on literature and art: he collected masses of small, significant facts, grouped them together, and explained them according to the system of the three primordial forces of *race*, *moment*, and *milieu*. There is no doubt at all that Taine persuaded himself that he was thus undertaking a work of absolute objectivity and employing the scrupulously scientific method he had advocated. He says, in the preface of his first volume:

> *Ancien Régime*, *Révolution*, *Régime moderne*, I am going to try and describe all these three states with exactness. I dare affirm here that I have no other aim: a historian may be allowed to act as a naturalist; I considered my subject as I might have considered the metamorphosis of an insect. . . . Freed from all bias, one's curiosity becomes scientific and is directed entirely towards the intimate forces which lead the astounding operation.

Unfortunately, Taine was incapable of ridding himself of bias. His horror of the brutal and ignorant masses, of ignorance leading ignorance, is only too evident. Universal suffrage is a chimera which had only led to universal nullity. "Ten million ignorances," as he picturesquely puts it, "do not make up one piece of knowledge." He cannot help himself; he makes his hypotheses first, and the facts have to fit into them. Like Montesquieu, he could have said, but with even less justification, "J'ai posé les principes, et j'ai vu les cas particuliers s'y plier comme d'eux-mêmes." Not that he wilfully mutilates facts, but he selects those only which he requires to prove his thesis. Moreover, he was unfitted by his previous studies to undertake a work of historical investigation which demanded years of unremitting research at the revolutionary archives. Taine did not shirk this laborious research. He worked nobly at it for years, even at the expense of his health.[1] But, lacking any thorough initiation, he worked hastily and unmethodically. Bundles of papers which would have needed months of labour he dispatched at one sitting, once he had found the one fact he required, ignoring altogether that hundreds of other quite contrary facts might have been found in the same bundle. Although an omnivorous reader, too, he had at the same time little notion of exact and painstaking scholarship; his references are often very incomplete, faulty, and vague; his sources frequently unworthy and insufficient. As Professor Hearnshaw has recently pointed out in his valuable article on "The Science of History,"[2] there are three stages in history considered as a science: (1) collection of material; (2) criticism; (3) interpretation. Taine's error is to leap from (1) to (3) without ever stopping at (2). He accepts as equally worthy of credibility the memoirs of a valet written down ten years after the event or the jottings of a traveller. All these points and many more make Taine's work extremely unreliable as history, and no student for the *agrégation* would ever dare quote him as an authority, any more than a London M.A. candidate would think of quoting Lytton Strachey as an historical authority. So numerous and palpable were the errors of actual fact and interpretation in the *Origins* that after his death the game of Taine-baiting threatened to become quite a pastime among radical university professors, and one of them, M. Aulard,[3] composed a rather unpleasant and not altogether necessary book on the errors of Taine.

It is not entirely fair, however, to consider Taine's book simply as a piece of history. His object, as has been seen, was to undertake an investigation into his country's past to see if it afforded any means of elucidating and explaining the present, and offering it any help in the troubles it was experiencing. France was in need of a constitution which

[1] See G. Lenôtre, "Taine et le Jacobin," in *Cent ans de vie française à la Revue des deux Mondes* (Hachette, 1929).

[2] *Outlines of Modern Knowledge* (Benn, 1931).

[3] A. Aulard, *Taine, historien de la Révolution française* (1907). See also H. Sée, "Quelques remarques sur Taine, historien," in *Science et philosophie de l'histoire* (Alcan, 1928).

would guarantee it stability and duration. How could one come at the conception of such a constitution? Taine's process is his usual one of decomposing a complex object into each of its component parts and examining them separately. In the very first place a human society is composed of men, therefore it is necessary first of all to know the nature of man. By his previous psychological studies Taine is able to answer this often-asked question. His definition is that man is a carnivorous animal by nature and structure, and this primary characteristic will never be effaced. He is a ferocious and lubricious gorilla, as Taine delicately puts it; stifle this side of him, cloak it up with civilisation and culture as we may, we can never eradicate it. In moments of crisis it emerges, as, for example, during the revolutionary period, when, according to Taine, France appears to have been peopled by a whole nation of particularly sanguinary brutes. Man is, in fact, by nature mad, madness is his normal state; sanity is an exceptional state, and is achieved only for relatively short spaces of time by any individual or collectively. Hence, then, the primary necessity for disciplining his savage instincts by organisation. At bottom, therefore, a constitution is a police force.

A second point is that a constitution should be conceived not in relation to man in general (this had been the great fault of the Revolution), but in relation to a definite nation. So, after having studied man in general and what suits his nature *qua* man, it is necessary to consider the nation as a whole, and here we find how profoundly different they are one from another. Their character is shaped by climate, determined by their history, and depends in great measure on the race to which they belong. The eighteenth-century ideologues made the mistake of thinking that there was an ideal form of constitution which could be applied indiscriminately to all nations and epochs. Making abstraction of national differences, they had conceived a theoretical man who was in reality nothing but a mathematical proposition. Their model was Rousseau's *Social Contract*, a work of pure abstract reasoning, with no basis of historical or psychological study. Such an ideal, says Taine, could only apply to abstract automatons, shorn of all the peculiarities which separate one man from another. It follows, therefore, that any constitution should be relative.

Thirdly, it should be historical. That is to say, one cannot build it up without taking account of past facts or laws which condition the facts of the future. A political constitution must be elaborated slowly under the pressure of necessity. "Each generation," says Taine,

> is only the temporary guardian and depository, responsible for a precious and glorious patrimony which it has received from the preceding one, with the duty to transmit it intact to the following one. In this permanent foundation to which all Frenchmen, from the first day of France's history, have brought their offering the intention of its innumerable benefactors is in no way doubtful: they gave on condition that the foundation should remain intact, and that each successive inheritor should be merely the administrator of it. If one of these administrators, by presumption, or frivolity, or partiality, compromises any part of this precious deposit entrusted to him, he is wronging his predecessors, whose sacrifices he is frustrating, and his successors, whom he is defrauding of their hopes.

From this historical conception of a constitution there flows naturally the one fundamental rule to which every legislator is in duty bound to conform: he must not make a *tabula rasa* of the past, but must respect *tradition—i.e.*, the whole body of customs, laws, and ideas which constitutes the experience of a nation throughout the ages. Every revolution, every sudden change brought about in the *régime* established for years, runs the risk of breaking the fragile works of which a society is composed. In matters of history, says Taine, it is better to continue than to recommence. That is why, especially when the majority is ignorant, it is a useful thing that its leaders should be designated in advance by the hereditary habit men have acquired of following them, and by the special education which has prepared them for their job.

Tradition, the principle of continuity of government by heredity—that is the idea at which Taine finally arrives. This does not for him exclude progress, but progress must be slow; it can only be brought about by successive and gradual modifications, and always with the condition that these modifications should be in keeping with the country's past.

Looking at his own country, what does he see? In place

of this gradualness a violent upheaval, an overthrowing of tradition. And this upheaval was not merely the result of the fanaticism of a few terrorists. It was gradually but surely being worked out in the eighteenth century, when the classical principle of reason allied to science produced a type of mind incapable of regarding facts, capable only of elaborating ideological constructions. In the most brilliant of all his books, *L'Ancien Régime*, but also the most specious and sophistic, he works out this thesis, not suspecting that his very demonstration of the permeating of all classes by the revolutionary spirit invalidates his whole contention.

As to the application of this historical investigation to problems of the present, Taine sees, when he considers the State as it functions in his own day, two great errors: (1) that it takes no account at all of the diversity of elements which compose the nation, for it operates, he says, at the same time and over the whole land by uniform laws; it applies everywhere the same programme, manufactured beforehand as a whole; (2) it oppresses the individual by a progressive domination, which extends more and more to every domain. (He had read Spencer's *Man versus the State.*) It proceeds by imperative rules, administered by a hierarchy of obedient civil servants. "The *rôle* of the State should be limited, if it is not to encroach on the prerogative of the individual members of the nation, especially on the right of property and on the natural liberties which favour the work of the individual." To what, then, should the function of the State be limited? Simply to that of defence—of internal and external defence. And this limitation is not merely a personal desire of Taine's—at any rate, he attempts to rationalise it by an appeal to science. The limitation of the *rôle* of the State, he contends, is necessitated by the law of the division of labour. The State is no more capable than any ordinary persons of undertaking every task at once. Its competence can only increase in the domain which is proper to it, if it leaves to specialists whatever requires a different technique. Consider, for the purposes of comparison, an engine. Its whole condition is that it becomes adapted to a certain kind of work, and in proportion as it does so it becomes less and less adapted to other kinds of work. Or a cutting instrument. At the lowest stage of civilisation the savage has only one sort of tool, a pointed instrument which serves for killing and breaking and cutting and sawing. Next come the lance, the axe, the hammer, each more adapted to some particular kind of service, and less efficacious for any other, so that you would get a bad shave with a saw, and you would saw badly with a razor. So it is, too, in the social scale. Originally a society is just a flock with no distinct associations, no distinct aim, no mutual engagements. By degrees groups form, castes become established, and finally the social body is increased in scope, widened into communes and provinces; churches and hospitals are founded, corporations and companies established. Now all these different bodies are subjected to the same laws. The more they excel in one *rôle* the less well they accomplish others, and Taine quotes from his great English model Macaulay:

> An academy of painting which should also be a bank would in all probability exhibit very bad pictures and discount very bad bills. A gas company which should also be an infant-school society would, we apprehend, light the streets very badly and teach the children ill.

An analogous result cannot fail to be brought about, thinks Taine, when the State is at the same time a military chief, a tradesman, a schoolmaster, a Postmaster-General, and a railway director.

But how are these essential social services to be accomplished? Simply by the State's leaving to individuals what is not within its normal competency. This is the solution which the great psychologist, the skilled investigator of his country's past, has the *naïveté* to bring forward. These ferocious and lubricious gorillas, if left to themselves, will spontaneously form themselves into groups; they will organise workers' corporations, churches, hospitals, schools. And why does Taine think this? Because he has seen it done in England. (One remembers those touching pictures of English country gentlemen.) It would be too easy to show how utterly incomplete and impossible a system Taine's political ideas form; to show how again and again he provides the very instrument with which his own thesis can be ruined; how this pessimistic judge of human nature looks for political regeneration along lines where the most sanguine of reformers and the most ardent of patriots would hesitate to follow him.

It is not, however, in the domain of political speculation that Taine's greatness nor his influence are to be found. These are to be sought, rather, in the fact that he gave a voice and an aspiration to the growing body of French feeling, precipitated by the *débâcle*, that something was wrong with the government of the country; that years of *bourgeois* rule, with its accompaniment of a hypertrophied central organisation, an army of civil servants incapable of broad, comprehensive views, but seeking refuge in anonymous initiative and avoidance of responsibility, had brought France to the brink of ruin. Taine showed that if France was to regain the superiority which petty-minded politicians had forfeited for her it was above all necessary to sink all doctrinal divisions, to re-establish national self-confidence and pride, and to build up, on the basis of a renewed interest in her glorious past and traditions, a powerful nationalism, and so create an atmosphere in which individual greatness could work for the common good without fear of spite or jealousy.

To the rebirth of the inner consciousness of the elements of their nationality in his countrymen, and to the substitution, in place of the depression caused by the Franco-Prussian War, of a feeling of pride which helped to make "France herself again,"[1] Taine may therefore be said to have made a fundamental contribution. For him nationalism was not something to be contained within the narrow limits of a party programme, but an attitude of mind and heart, a philosophy. He would have disavowed all the sectional nationalisms, later to be compounded of a mixture of chauvinism, religion, royalism, and xenophobia, as strongly as he refused to allow himself during his lifetime to be enrolled under any political banner. When he showed in his *Ancien Régime* the rottenness of the pre-Revolution constitution and the decadence of monarchy and nobility he was almost hailed as a convert by the extreme democrats; when he began, in his succeeding books, his exposure of the revolutionary leaders cheers arose from the opposite camp. But in his *rôle* of historian-philosopher he refused to associate himself with either.

[1] E. Dimnet, *France herself again* (Chatto and Windus, 1914).

" Quand on me recrute, je proteste," he said. " A historian belongs to facts, so much the worse where they may lead him." And so, remaining aloof from parties, Taine, in the widest interest of his country, placed his talents at the service of the objective search for truth. At least, he flattered himself that he did. Unfortunately, however, the border-line between the objective and the subjective in the interpretation of history is difficult to draw, and, in the case of the Revolution, impossible. As Taine's history of the Revolution progressed, and his picture of its authors took on more and more sombre tones, he was looked to as the man who, in the face of advancing democracy, was able to restore to the natural governing classes of France their lost title-deeds. To this extent his work may be considered as the foundation of all the different forms of nationalism which exist to-day. Not that all of these would be equally willing to recognise it. When a modern nationalist is able, for example, to refer to Taine as the type of the *bonhomme système*, and to stigmatise some of his observations as models of mental debility,[1] it is evident that respect for Taine is not a necessary corollary of contempt for democracy.

Taine's influence, however, as has been said, is not to be read in modern party programmes. Where his work did bear fruit was in other spheres. In history he definitely destroyed the revolutionary legend of a vast and spontaneous uprising of pure-minded patriots; he exposed the nullity of the revolutionary leaders and the poverty of their accomplishments; and if he did not put an end to Napoleon idolatry he at least cleared the contemporary conception of the hero of a dead-weight of legendary accretion, and paved the way to a clearer view. He fostered a new interest in his country's past, and gave a stimulus and a new outlook to the study of social psychology. By his condemnation of bureaucracy and excessive centralisation, and by his insistence on the value of individual initiative and local patriotism, he infused a fresh interest into regional associations.[2] On all these points he definitely led the way to a broad nationalism, a wider and enhanced conception of patriotism.

R. A. Jones

[1] L. Daudet, *Le stupide dix-neuvième Siècle* (1922).

[2] On all these points see F. Jean-Desthieux, *Taine, son œuvre* (1923).

BOOK LIST

A. Primary Authorities

Works by Taine:

Les Origines de la France contemporaine (translated by J. Durand). 7 vols.
Histoire de la littérature anglaise (translated by H. Van Laun). 5 vols.
Notes sur l'Angleterre (translated by W. F. Rae).
Taine, sa vie et sa correspondance. 4 vols. (Vols. i and ii translated by Mrs R. L. Devonshire, vol. iii by E. Sparvel-Bailey, vol. iv not translated.)

B. Secondary Authorities

V. Giraud's *Bibliographie critique de Taine* (1902) is complete for all critical works on Taine up to that date. The following are among the more recent works:

Chevrillon, A.: *Taine, formation de sa pensée.* 1932.
Gibaudan, A.: *Les Idées sociales de Taine.* 1928.
Herriot, E.: *Sur Taine.* (A speech given at the Sorbonne, May 24, 1928.)
Rubow, P. V.: *Hippolyte Taine, étapes de son œuvre.* 1930.

APPENDIX

THE DEVELOPMENT OF A PSYCHOLOGICAL APPROACH TO POLITICS IN ENGLISH SPECULATION BEFORE 1869

[This appendix, originally planned as an introduction to Mr Driver's article on Walter Bagehot, has, because of its length and independence, been treated as a separate contribution. Its importance and interest will be speedily recognised.—EDITOR.]

FOR the purpose of such a sketch as this we may say that English speculations in social psychology fall into three main periods. The dates, of course, are merely indicative and symbolical, and are in no sense meant to denote breach of continuity.

The first period covers two centuries, say from 1651 to 1828. The publication of Hobbes' *Leviathan* marks the opening of the period. Its approximate close is indicated by the years 1828–29, when there appeared, almost simultaneously, three works of considerable importance, each representing in its own fashion the culmination of a line of speculation running throughout the previous two hundred years: Dugald Stewart's completed work on *The Philosophy of the Active and Moral Powers of Man*, which summarised the work of the Scottish school of philosophy and psychology; James Mill's *Analysis of the Phenomena of the Human Mind*, which was the final statement of the older introspective form of the association psychology; and T. R. Edmonds' *Practical, Moral, and Political Economy*, which was a remarkable anticipation of Bagehot's *Physics and Politics*, and contained a quite unique outline of a scheme of social psychology expressed in terms of the prevailing orthodox speculations derived from the eighteenth century.

The second period covers the seventy years from 1828 to 1898. During the first part of that epoch biological science was advancing rapidly in all its branches. Physiology was steadily modifying psychological speculation; Bain especially was trying to restate the old association psychology more completely in physiological terms. But, above all, the theory of evolution was rapidly being developed and applied. The year 1859 represents the turning-point of this phase. It witnessed the publication of Darwin's *Origin of Species*; Bain's *Emotions and the Will*; John Stuart Mill's *Liberty*; and in the following year came *Essays and Reviews* and Spencer's published programme of his evolutionary sociology. It was this thirty years which saw the break-up of the rationalism of the previous age—the movement away from old assumptions and the beginning of the reinterpretation of life in biological rather than in mechanical terms. The latter part of this second period, therefore, was mainly concerned with developing the implications of the evolutionary theory and the amassing of data for the purposes of such a radical reinterpretation.

So far as social psychology is concerned the year 1898 may be taken as sufficiently symbolical to mark the end of this epoch, for by then the place of psychology in the social sciences was beginning to be more adequately realised. Indicative of this is the important fact that in 1898 the Cambridge Anthropological Expedition was sent to the Torres Strait, and that it included in the party three professional psychologists: W. H. Rivers, William McDougall, and C. S. Myers. This was the first time that a psychological investigation of primitive culture had been undertaken, and it may be considered as ushering in our present age, with its own particular problems and its own efforts at restatement. This third epoch, extending from 1898 to to-day, will doubtless be associated, so far as English scholarship is concerned, with four chief names: Lloyd Morgan, marking the transition, with his works on *Comparative Psychology* (1893) and *Instinct and Habit* (1896); L. T. Hobhouse, with a complete system of sociology, but especially his *Mind in Evolution* (1901); William McDougall, with his *Introduction to Social Psychology* (1908) and *The Group Mind* (1919); and Graham Wallas, with *Human Nature in Politics* (1908), *The Great Society* (1914), and *Our Social Heritage* (1920).

There are recent indications, however, that we may be

entering upon a new period of social psychology, interpreted in terms of the 'conditioned reflex.'[1] The chief specific influences tending towards this movement (apart from the general biological trend of psychology noted at the end of the article) have so far been the American Behaviourists, especially Watson, and the work of the Russian physiologists Pavlov (1849–) and Bechterev (1857–1927), coupled with the rapid development of bio-chemistry in recent years. The purpose of this school of thought is to reinterpret in strictly mechanical terms the facts not only of physiology and of psychology as hitherto understood, but ultimately of social phenomena also. The old battle between the teleologists and mechanists has already been joined anew with vigour and with candour, as the interested student can discover for himself by a perusal of such works as McDougall's *Modern Materialism and Emergent Evolution*, Hogben's *Nature of Living Matter*, and Mr Bertrand Russell's recent book on *The Scientific Outlook*.

Fortunately, this third period, from 1898 on, may be taken to lie outside the scope of this present article. Mention has been made of it merely to indicate roughly the chronological perspective of the theme; for, after all, the development is more or less continuous throughout; and even the problems associated with the 'conditioned reflex' have their origins in the remote past. The idea of reflex action can be traced from the time of Descartes onward; and the term itself was coined just a century ago (1833) by Marshall Hall, the English physiologist.

II

The rise of a science of human nature dates from the seventeenth century. Two factors were essential for the growth of such a science, and both of these were increasingly operative in that century. One was the spread of individualism; the other was the development of the scientific outlook and method. In the second half of the century especially

[1] The 'conditioned reflex' was discovered in three laboratories almost simultaneously in 1905: by the two Russians in St Petersburg and by E. B. Twitmyer of Pennsylvania.

both influences were at work, and were influencing one another. The growth of the individualistic spirit involved new questionings on the part of the reflective: a fresh sense of the problems of human nature, its powers and possibilities. Hence the ushering in of a new period of ethical speculation. The development of natural science was no less marked. The remarkable expansion of physics, astronomy, and mathematics in particular gave rise towards the end of the century to a new scientific outlook on the universe, an outlook destined to influence social and ethical speculation of the succeeding era, just as the biological formulæ of the mid-nineteenth century came to exert influence outside the field of biological studies in which they had been formed. This new world-view, which owes most to Descartes and Newton for its construction, was conceived primarily in mathematico-physical terms. It envisaged the world as a vast mechanism, determined by mechanical forces, working according to rational laws comprehensible to the human reason. The startling success of the physical sciences stimulated the belief that human nature and social life might be explained in analogous terms. It was thought that if the forces determining man's character could be found and the processes by which his mental content was established could be determined a science of society could be constructed on a firm basis. The method to be pursued was to be the same as in physics: the analysis of the simple case to discover the universal axiom. Hartley has made the classic statement of the principle:

> The method of philosophising seems to be, to discover and establish the general laws of action, affecting the subject under consideration, from certain select, well-defined, and well-attested phenomena, and then to explain and predict the other phenomena by these laws. This is the method of analysis and synthesis recommended and followed by Sir Isaac Newton.[1]

Thus, beginning in the seventeenth century, and extending through the eighteenth into the nineteenth century, there runs a continuous line of social speculation, begotten by the new spirit, and determined by a particular kind of world-outlook. All the thinkers from Hobbes to Robert Owen are—in spite

[1] *Observations on Man*, chapter i.

of their individual differences—part of one large speculative movement. They all breathe the same intellectual atmosphere; and they are all 'determined' in their philosophies (either by open acknowledgment or by attempted modification) by a similar set of scientific assumptions. We may note four features in particular which characterise most of the speculations in this tradition. In type they are mainly *deductive* and incline to a mechanical interpretation. That is to say, on the analogy of physics they are seeking the universal 'laws' underlying the given case. Consequently, they are predominantly *rational* in their outlook, to a degree that contrasts strongly with the anti-intellectualism of recent years. Even when, as in the case of the Utilitarians, an apparently non-rational factor is introduced—*i.e.*, the pursuit of pleasure—it is assumed that conscious and rational choice will regulate the direction of the activity. In *method* they are all introspective so far as their psychology is concerned; and the conscious use of introspection *a fortiori* implies an emphasis on rationality. Lastly, the *scope* of their work is mainly concerned with the adult and the civilised. Steadily during the eighteenth century data were being brought from the remoter parts of the world concerning the primitive mind. But it was not until the nineteenth century that anything like a science of anthropology, or of comparative psychology, developed. And even then the interpretation and study of the primitive mind was for long hindered by the predominance of the old association psychology, with its rationalistic bias derived from the previous epoch. These four characteristics of eighteenth-century psychological speculation—deductive, introspective, rational, and adult—lingered long. Much remarkable work, perhaps too often minimised at the present day, was done within those limits. Yet to us the limitations are apparent. It was part of the work of the biological movement of the next age to sweep them away. Thus was an inductive approach substituted for deduction from a given hypothesis; introspection supplemented by other methods, especially the experimental, the comparative, and the genetic; rationalism, with its emphasis on the uniqueness of man, modified by a functional interpretation of mind and by a better realisation of its biological conditioning; and, lastly, the expansion of the whole area of the science to include 'mind'—or, rather, behaviour—at every level of the evolutionary advance.

As there were common features, so were there common problems to all these thinkers. Two in particular have to be stressed: the first concerned the 'intellectual' powers of mind, the second the 'active' powers. The former involved an analysis of the way in which our knowledge of the external world was built up, and consequently of how our beliefs were formed. The latter involved the problem of instincts and motives. The one gave rise to the association psychology, which is usually considered to be *par excellence* the legacy of the eighteenth to the nineteenth century; the other, less emphasised, but no less important, produced an extensive discussion of the emotional forces of mind, which held the field to a large extent down to the time of Alexander Bain. Too often is it forgotten that all through this period a controversy regarding 'instincts' raged almost as strongly as that of the last thirty years, even though the setting of the problem was different. In both cases—regarding the intellectual and the active powers—Hobbes is really the starting-point of the development. In his *Leviathan* he had put forward a doctrine of association of ideas to explain the content of mind, and a theory of the motives driving man to action. The latter was especially influential, for Hobbes painted man as essentially selfish and as animated by the merely egotistical impulse to gratify desire. The eighteenth-century speculation was to a large extent but an attempt to repudiate the doctrine of egoism, or at least to subordinate it, and to show how the 'social sense' arose. Hence came all that reflection on the 'active powers' right down to Stewart's work of 1828. The parallel with the nineteenth century is both striking and illuminating. Just as Hobbes considered man motivated by selfish desire and later thinkers tried to account for the social sense, so did the theory of natural selection posit a doctrine of struggle "in tooth and claw," and thus engender the problem, How, then, did man become human, civilised, and social? It was Bagehot who first realised the problem, and who first answered it; and in doing so he opened a new chapter in social psychology. No detailed account is here possible of either of these two lines of development, early associationism and early instinct psychology. Our only concern is to see them as operative in social speculation at the end of the first period—*i.e.*, at the opening of the Victorian era.

III

So far as the study of the ' active powers ' is concerned, the chief names are Hutcheson (1694–1746), Hume (1711–76), Adam Smith (1723–90), Reid (1710–96), and Dugald Stewart (1753–1828). How near this school approached to the early twentieth-century viewpoint regarding instinct can be indicated by a sentence from one of its minor exponents. Ferguson (1723–1816) in his *Essay on the History of Civil Society* describes " instinctive propensities " as those " which, prior to the perception of pleasure and pain, and prior to the experience of what is pernicious and useful, lead him to perform many functions which terminate in himself or have a relation with his fellow creatures." And he illustrates this remarkable definition by reference to three such " instinctive propensities " : self-preservation, racial maintenance, and gregariousness. The latter is described with especial precision.

Hutcheson really began this line of thought (though Shaftesbury realised something of the nature of the problem). He it was who first made a clear statement of the nature of instinct as a native endowment, and who first assigned to it a place in behaviour and experience separate from sensation and conscious desire. He analysed the dynamic elements of mind into six natural powers, or " senses," as he called them. These, he explained, could combine by the processes of association to form " secondary desires." Reason has a primarily directive function : to determine particular ends for the fulfilment of the non-rational impulses. Accordingly, the various forces, native and acquired, which make for social life are carefully discussed. Hume, likewise, recognised the emotional side of mental life, though his exposition was too entangled in his association psychology to develop far. He also conceived of instinct as an original impulse ; and he attributed two characteristics to it—universality and a determinate object. Like Hutcheson, he analysed emotion into two kinds : direct, arising from impulse in particular, and indirect, coming at second hand, so to speak, from the native endowments by the processes of association. Non-rational forces were regarded as the determining motives of conation, and to reason a directive function only was again assigned. But Hume went farther than Hutcheson in his full and clear analysis of the phenomena of sympathy and suggestibility, from which he derived the gregariousness of man. The formation of opinions was explained by the twin factors of suggestibility and the power of authority, and he extends these principles to account for national characteristics. " Everywhere origins of a sympathy or contagion of manners " are operative, stamping particular features on the members of particular groups. But this aspect of Hume's teaching is largely bound up with his association psychology and the consequent doctrine of the influence of environment mentioned below.

Adam Smith's main contribution to the psychology of the active powers was his analysis of the *rôle* of sympathy in society. Apart from that, he made no advance upon his predecessors. He tried to resolve the antitheses of self-love and benevolence, and of feeling and reason, by positing the spontaneous play of the native endowment of sympathy working and expanding through the imagination. Sympathy for Smith was an original fact of human nature, which was powerfully strengthened by the pleasure of its exercise. Hence, from this direct social sentiment he was able to develop an account of the growth of the social conscience without invoking the machinery of associationism. It was an important conception. Indeed, Professor G. S. Brett has gone so far as to regard Smith as the first English social psychologist. Certainly his emphasis on the genetic element of the social sense was the right one, for he clearly saw that individual sentiments were socially determined and conditioned. But he refrained from working out the consequences of this idea.

Reid introduced little that was new into the discussion, though his treatment of the subject included a comprehensive analysis of the principles suggested by his predecessors.

It was Dugald Stewart, however, who finally summed up the theories of the Scottish school, and who exercised the greatest influence. That influence was even more marked on the Continent than here. His work, says Drever, marked "the high-water mark of the purely introspective psychology." His writings may be said to sum up the eighteenth-century rational psychology, just as McDougall's *Social Psychology* summarised in 1908 the biological psychology of the previous age.

Stewart's scheme of classification is rather confusing, for, while he distinguishes the intellectual from the active powers, he subdivides the latter into "instinctive propensities" and "rational principles," and these last seem to overlap both main divisions. Nevertheless, his discussion of the irrational forces is clear enough. He regards them all as *motives.* Reason, once again, is the instrument by which their end is achieved. There are three of these "instinctive propensities": (1) *The Appetites.* These are organic, like hunger and sex; and (as with the more recent "instinct psychology") they are accompanied by feelings of uneasiness until they are fulfilled. Derivative appetites may be formed through being associated with particular pleasurable experiences. (2) *The Desires.* Five instinctive desires are enumerated: curiosity, ambition, emulation, and the desires for society and for esteem. Thus gregariousness is a natural phenomenon, and is not imposed from without, as Hobbes suggested. (3) *The Affections.* The object of these is the communication of our emotions to our fellows. From these, by an interesting development of the argument, Stewart derived the sentiment of patriotism. Space does not allow a fuller treatment of this psychology of the active powers from the seventeenth to the nineteenth centuries. Enough has been said, however, to show that, vastly important as the contribution of biology to psychology was in the Victorian era, the ground had already been prepared to a considerable extent by a clear recognition of the instinctive aspect of mind and by a realisation that human and animal behaviour had much in common.

IV

The second line of psychological speculation running side by side with the one just noted, and frequently mingling with it, and likewise passing into the Victorian era, was the association psychology. This too, as was remarked above, is traceable back to Hobbes. Locke, though hardly developing the theory, gave it a name. Berkeley, Hartley, and Hume developed it extensively, and Hartley brilliantly tried to give it a physiological basis. The Scottish school made use of the theory, though not giving it the primacy which Hartley and Hume accorded to it, but qualifying it with other considerations. Numerous lesser thinkers elaborated it, until James Mill in his *Analysis of the Phenomena of the Human Mind* (1829) gave it its completest expression to date, by a more uncompromising application than had hitherto been made of the principle of association by contiguity. The essentials of the doctrine were simple, though the question became complicated by the intrusion of another issue—viz., whether *in addition* to association some *a priori* category of the mind had to be assumed in order to explain mental phenomena (as the Scottish school maintained), or whether psychology need assume nothing beyond the *tabula rasa* at birth (as Hume asserted). This complicating issue does not concern us here; nor is it necessary to trace the variations the doctrine underwent in the course of the controversy. By all the associationists particular sensations were regarded as the psychological units. They were treated as the atoms of experience. These become combined, or associated, according to certain laws, until the whole interrelated network of the adult psyche is formed. Mind is thus, for the extreme associationists, only this system of sense impressions combined into an hierarchy of increasing abstraction. Hartley really founded the school. He it was, also, who first saw clearly the implications of the idea for what we should now call social psychology. For this idea obviously lays the emphasis on environment—*i.e.*, on the social *milieu* in the broadest sense. This was realised by radicals and reformers in this country during and long after the French Revolution, and extensive use was made of it to provide a new social philosophy. But the germ is already to be found in Hartley:

> It is of the utmost consequence to morality and religion that the affections and passions should be analysed into their simple compounding parts, by reversing the steps of the associations which concur to form them. For thus we learn how to cherish and improve good ones, and check and root out such as are mischievous and immoral . . .

and as this holds in respect of persons of all ages, so it is particularly true, and worthy of consideration, in respect of children and youth. If beings of the same nature, but whose affections and passions are, at present, in different proportions to each other, be exposed for an indefinite time to the same impressions and associations, all their particular differences will, at last, be overruled, and they will become perfectly similar, or even equal. They may also be made perfectly similar, in a finite time, by a proper adjustment of the impressions and associations.[1]

This doctrine became closely connected with the Utilitarian philosophy, as Sir Leslie Stephen and M. Élie Halévy have both clearly shown. What is less frequently realised, however, is that three quite diverse applications were made of the principle in England. It was made by different writers a main argument for anarchism, collectivism, and radicalism. Godwin in *Political Justice* (1793) converted it into an anarchistic philosophy.[2] Owen's "five fundamental facts of human nature" (largely derived from Godwin) were but an associationist basis for his collectivist creed. And James Mill's *Analysis* provided a revised psychological background for philosophical radicalism. In all three cases associationism became a doctrine of revolt, for all three groups put their emphasis on environment as the determining factor in the formation of character, and hence on education as an instrument of change. Change the environment and you change the man. It seemed a doctrine of golden promise, for it assumed approximate equality of potentialities at birth, and thus attributed primacy to nurture rather than nature. The same doctrine had spread to France through the influence of Locke and the development of it by Condillac. There it was developed to extreme lengths. Helvétius saw in it (as Godwin did here—partly through the influence of Helvétius) the key to Utopia.

If I could demonstrate that man is indeed but the product of his education I should undoubtedly have revealed a great truth to the nations. They would then know that they hold within their own hands the instrument of their greatness and their happiness, and that

[1] *Observations*, prop. xiv.

[2] See *The Social and Political Ideas of Some Representative Thinkers of the Revolutionary Era.*

> to be happy and powerful is only a matter of perfecting the science of education. . . . I feel how strongly the existing opinion that genius and virtue are pure gifts of nature is opposed to the progress of science and education, and favours laziness and neglect.[1]

It would seem that no real associationist could be a conservative!

James Mill was the counterpart of Helvétius in this country. His aim was to analyse complex emotions into their simplest elements. Influenced by the method of the physical sciences and by the atomic theory, he wanted to resolve all experience into primary "sense-atoms," determined by definite laws. Psychology was to be the science of their combination. Hence the affections, the æsthetic emotions, moral sentiment, and belief were all shown to be compound states; and, as such, all were resolved into units of pleasurable and painful sensations. The will itself was interpreted in the same way. Consequently Mill too was able to emphasise the enormous possibilities of education not only for the development of mind, but also for the formation of the emotions. This type of psychology became a sort of orthodox radicalism in the early Victorian epoch. But its limitations are obvious. As Mill's biographer Bain—the last of the English pre-evolutionary associationists—put it (in 1882): "Sensation does not cover the whole field of our primitive sensibilities; we have primary emotions also, as Fear, Love, and Anger; the attempt to resolve these into sensations and their causes is a failure."

There is one aspect of the associationist psychology which has not yet been touched on, however, yet which has had an important influence on English thought not only during the Victorian period, but even down to the present day, and that concerns the place of *habit* in intellectual and social development. It is really Hume who is responsible for this issue. Professor J. M. Baldwin, who himself developed the doctrine of habit in his *Mental Development in the Child and the Race* (1895), says of Hume's theory of habit that it is "one of the most fertile ideas of modern psychology and philosophy." [2] Indeed, it was a conception of which Bagehot made the fullest use, as is shown in the lecture on Bagehot, and it figures in

[1] *De l'Esprit*, Book III, chapter xxx. [2] *History of Psychology*.

his system as a basic assumption. Habit was thought of by Hume as supplementing the association of ideas by binding groups of impressions into "wholes," to which belief and custom became attached. This leads eventually to the empiricist theories of both knowledge and ethics, as with Mill. But it was developed further. On the one hand, the idea of individual habit was transformed (*a*) into the idea of the "inherited habit" of Spencer, by which he accounted for instinct, and (*b*) "into the 'social custom,' by which the Utilitarian moralists accounted for the practical reason." On the other hand, as Baldwin points out,

> the conception of habit has been developed enormously in a group of modern theories of the 'motor' or dynamic type: which account for the whole range of the synthetic function in terms of the consciousness of movement and activity.

The recent developments, especially in America, of the mechanistic school, of which mention was made earlier, are but an extension of this principle, and a restatement of the essential associationist hypothesis in physiological terms. For the integration-of-ideas through habit has been substituted the integration-of-conditioned-reflexes in the same way. And this restatement has become a tremendous force in Russia since the Revolution, having once more taken on a new lease of life as a doctrine of revolt and reconstruction.[1]

V

Such, then, were the two main lines of social-psychological thought operative in this country at the beginning of the

[1] Since this article was written corroboration has been given to the above suggestion as to the connection between the old association psychology and the new mechanistic school by Professor Raymond Wheeler. In his work on *The Laws of Human Nature*, published in The Contemporary Library of Psychology (Cambridge University Press), he expresses much the same theory. The following quotation (p. 27) is sufficiently indicative: "The assertion is often made that association psychology reached its climax with David Hartley, following the distinctive contributions of Locke, Berkeley, and Hume; that it declined, gradually, in the psychologies of Brown, Hamilton, and the Mills, and died with Bain, Spencer, and Lewes. On the contrary, association psychology is still very much alive, especially in educational and behaviouristic circles in the United States, and in the conditioned reflex psychology of the Russian School."

Victorian period. The results of these speculations were utilised in a great variety of ways. English political speculation between Waterloo and the collapse of the Chartist movement is shot through and through with assumptions and arguments drawn from this source, though the history of those ideas has yet to be written. But of all these writers one specially deserves mention not only as illustrative of the kind of thought such speculation produced, but also because of his own intrinsic originality and suggestiveness and his surprising anticipation of some of Bagehot's own ideas. That man is Thomas Rowe Edmonds; and his chief work was his *Practical, Moral, and Political Economy* (1828). This book is divided into four parts: the first and second deal with economic and political ideas; the third, which alone concerns us here, treats of social psychology; and the fourth is concerned with a practical programme for the application of the principles thus reached. Edmonds' debt to his predecessors is apparent; it is his working out of what others had provided which constitutes his originality.

He begins with an analysis of the human mind, on which to superimpose his later theories. Following Hutcheson, he divides the dynamic forces of mind into two parts: external sensation and internal. By 'sensation' he means what we should call instinct. Internal sensations are the primary passions, of which there are three: (1) hunger and thirst; (2) sex; (3) the instinct to pursue happiness. From these secondary passions are derived through the faculty of memory and the principle of association. These constitute the external sensations, and their function is always to gratify the primary instincts. The way in which these secondary impulses are formed is genetically traced out. It is essentially a dynamic psychology which is presented to us; "the passions are the centres about which all the sensations and the memory collect themselves." And the process is common to both animals and humans. In animals this association of end with instinct has become practically a reflex action, and "has very nearly reached perfection." This leads Edmonds to examine the nature of opinions. All opinions, he says, are secondary passions, since they are a derivative by the laws of association. So it is no good trying to change people's opinions suddenly, for they are too firmly rooted in instinct. The only way to modify them is by re-education: by getting people to understand the working of their instincts and the principles on which their associations are formed. Gregariousness, similarly, he describes as a secondary instinct. It is formed by the two primary instincts of self-love and sex being sublimated by man's "consciousness of like" (compare Giddings' theory of "consciousness of kind") and his desire for power. Knowledge expands through love of mental power, and its increase is "proportional to the increase of gregariousness or sociality." The depth of one's prejudices is in inverse ratio to the radius of one's social contacts, for 'sociality' kills prejudice. The great problem of humanity is to kill all national prejudices and to develop a social consciousness extending over the whole world.

Then he sketches a theory of evolution. "Every species of plant, and every species of animal body, are capable of improvements by means of attentive culture alone." Each improvement is transmitted from one generation to the next. What are called instincts at any given time, he says in anticipation of Spencer, are nothing more than innate faculties of the mind acquired by the animal's progenitors. Each species is continually acquiring by adaptation to environment those mental and bodily powers which are most conducive to its welfare. This process has gone on in the past, so that animals, for the most part, have already attained the limits of their particular adaptations. But man has not reached his own limit. By healthy breeding there may be no bounds to his possible improvement. The adaptations that have occurred in man, however, are of great consequence. At one stage in distant time all men may have been alike. But now, because of the process which has been in progress for centuries of conforming to different environments, great variety has been produced among different races. (This suggestion, be it noted, is an extraordinary anticipation of one of Bagehot's theses.) Thus are nations created, and "national prejudices are in some measure innate."

But in other, and even more remarkable, ways did Edmonds alight upon the essential principles of *Physics and Politics*. He discusses the manner in which national characteristics develop.

They grow in two ways. One is by the veneration of the wise by the ignorant, a development which goes on from the earliest times by imperceptible stages until a priesthood is formed, and a system of religion based on veneration is established; the other is the process of "emphasis and iteration." Edmonds has a full appreciation of the forces of suggestion and imitation. "The passion of imitation," he says, "is the earliest and commonest of passions." And he thinks that it is by the inevitable tendency of the individual to imitate other members of the group that national characteristics are chiefly developed and that better adaptation of the group to its environment is secured. This is the same theory as is found in Bagehot's explanation of the growth of a 'customary' civilisation. It leads him to emphasise the importance of history, and the necessity for analysing national customs and racial characteristics, in order to provide more adequate data for the inductive study of society. Only thus can the "mental tyranny," as he calls it, of one's own national customs be dispelled, or at least seen in perspective.

One of the most striking aspects of Edmonds' teaching concerns the part played by war in the development of society. His argument runs thus: knowledge means power, both in the case of individuals and of nations, for it gives control over the subjective and objective processes of nature. So the nation possessing most knowledge *ipso facto* has most power; therefore, he says, by a reversal of the theorem, *might is always right*, since might can be secured only by the possession of truth. This brings him to the climax of his argument: "*The law of the strongest, or war, is one of the most benevolent institutions of nature*." The logical consequence is the doctrine of the survival of the fittest, and from this Edmonds does not shrink. Once again he anticipates one of Bagehot's main theses: "Beneficent Providence has so ordained that the powerful are continually bringing the weak under their subjection, and in that way diffusing a superior culture." Not only has this process gone on in the past, raising the general standard of culture by the successive triumphs of superior cultures. It will go on in the future, and continue repeatedly. The size of nations will steadily increase in this way: Europe will become unified, and eventually a world-state formed. This will mean that a world-language—the language of the dominating culture—will be established. "The instrument which Providence uses for this purpose is power, war, or the law of the strongest." And he rounds off his theory by saying that he thinks it will be the English nation which will so come to dominate and unify the world! The rest of Edmonds' book is an attempt to apply the principles just sketched to the problems of education, crime, and political organisation.

VI

Walter Bagehot was born two years before Edmonds' book appeared. His *Physics and Politics* was published forty years later. In the interval a revolution had occurred in the biological sciences. From about 1800—as we can now see from the vantage-point of the present—the tendency of science was to draw into closer relationship the two great divisions of life as the previous age had envisaged them, Nature and Man, and to resolve the dichotomy into a unity through the hypothesis of evolution. Darwin and Wallace formulated their hypothesis in 1858. Bagehot first saw its significance in relation to man and his society in 1868. Three years after that Darwin, in the *Descent of Man*, carried the discussion a stage farther. It is not possible in this article to do more than indicate in outline the broad movements of research resulting in this scientific revolution.

So far as psychology was concerned, there were three main lines of advance, involving a steadily improving physiological approach to the science: the investigation, namely, of the problems of localisation, of neurology, and of the special senses. The first of these problems, the localisation of the functions of the brain, had scarcely been worked at in the eighteenth century. It was first brought into prominence by Gall and Spurzheim (1804), the founders of phrenology, whose work was popularised in this country by George Combe (1788–1858). It is easy enough to ridicule these men, yet in its day it had great influence (both for good and evil), and provided a needed stimulus towards physiological psychology.[1]

[1] Even scientists are now willing to admit the importance of much of the work done by these two men. Witness the following remarks by two eminent scientists: "All

G. H. Lewes declared it marked the beginning of a new era. All through the first half of the century workers on the Continent were amassing fresh data, and, in particular, one may mention the work of Legallois on the *medulla oblongata* (1811), Flourens' work on the brains of pigeons (1822–24), and Bouillaud's investigation of aphasia and brain lesions (1825). A modified form of phrenology was put forward by Carus and Huschke in 1841. Then a gap occurs in the story, and it was not until the sixties that work of any importance on cortical localisation was begun again, starting with the French surgeon Broca (1824–80).

In the investigation of neurology during this period the names of two Englishmen stand out prominently. Sir Charles Bell's epoch-making work, *A New Idea of the Anatomy of the Brain* (1811), first explained the dual character of the nervous system, and distinguished the sensory from the motor system. This was developed further by Bell himself, and by Continental scientists, particularly Magendie. The other Englishman is Marshall Hall, who investigated the nature of reflex action, and established its mechanical basis. His paper on the subject was published in 1833, and his book, *Memoirs on the Nervous System*, in 1837. This idea of mechanical reflexes was vigorously discussed and examined in the years 1840–70, and played a large part in the evolution of opinion during that period. Contemporaries, says Brett, " were for a time astonished at the prospect opened up by this conception of centres which belonged to man and yet did not live in the watchful eye of his Free Will." Once again it was the middle of the century which witnessed the opening of a new chapter, in the work of Claude Bernard, Brown-Séquard, and Leydig.

men know that of the partnership [of Gall and Spurzheim] was begot the fabric of phrenology and all the odium attaching to its study. There are fewer who know that of it was begot the doctrine of cortical localisation. . . . Probably we may say that another century will have to pass before these men receive due credit for their real additions to knowledge. . . . By a strange twist of fate it was to the researches of Gall and Spurzheim that, a century ago, neurologists owed some of the most important knowledge of the cerebellum." The same two writers go on to plead " that the phrenologists be forgiven their phrenology and admitted as the true pioneers of the doctrine of the cortical localisation of functions " (F. Wood Jones, F.R.S., and S. D. Porteus, *The Matrix of the Mind* (1929), pp. 77 *et seq.* and 208).

APPENDIX

The third line of progress, concerning the special senses, is too vast even to be outlined here. The appointment of Müller to the chair of physiology in Berlin in 1833 opened a new scientific era in Germany, and marked the beginning of a series of vastly important developments of psycho-physiology and the problems of perception. Virchow, Helmholtz, Weber, and Lotze are but four of the greatest names in a movement rich in great names, and which in every way may be considered the real prelude to modern physiological psychology. And of the vast scientific literature it produced mention can be made only of Lotze's work on *Medical Psychology*, which not only made important contributions to the main trend of the movement, but was productive of further researches in the domain of medicine and surgery.

It was Alexander Bain more than any other man who was the channel through which this new teaching came to England, and modern social psychology can trace its direct filiations to him. He had specially mastered the German physiological findings, and he attempted a thoroughly empirical statement of association in terms of those results. He was the first Englishman, it has justly been said, to put forward physiological explanations capable of being taken seriously, and admitting experimental physiology as essential. The conception of the reflex arc and of instincts was fundamental to his psychology. He was throughout "thinking in terms of inborn reaction tendencies which undergo modification through experience." Moreover, it was Bain more than any other English writer of the nineteenth century who 'popularised' psychology, in the sense of making his contemporaries realise something of its full significance. As Murphy has lately pointed out, Bain was the "first to write a comprehensive treatise having psychology as its sole purpose." And his lucid style and vivid concrete illustrations secured him a wide public. But, though he was more concerned with the mechanism of instinct than any previous writer here, yet it must be remembered that he wrote his chief works before the publication of Darwin's *Origin of Species*; and, although he lived long after that, and did not found the journal *Mind* until 1876, yet he never restated his doctrine in the light of the evolutionary theory. Nevertheless, he remains in a special sense the father (or perhaps the grandfather) of modern English psychology in all its bearings.

The theory of evolution by natural selection was given to the world by Darwin and Wallace in 1858, and *The Origin of Species* was published in the following year. Some indication has been given already of the way in which preparation had been made in particular studies for the reception of the doctrine. And the story has often been told of the other great movements contributing to the formation of an evolutionary outlook. Philosophy, biology, and geology were all tending to converge upon a 'developmental' scheme. Philosophically, the idea of development, and of an unfolding, is very ancient, and traceable almost to the beginnings of human speculation. In the eighteenth century it was being applied in many directions. The French materialists made full use of it along one line. It steadily became more prominent in German philosophy from Leibnitz, through Lessing, Kant, and Schelling, to Hegel, with whom it becomes a system. As applied to man, and to the progressive upward movement from the barbaric to the civilised, Vico laid the foundations of the theory, and Condorcet, Herder, and Comte made of it a gospel of human progress. Biologically, the idea begins with Harvey's theory of epigenesis in the seventeenth century, and was developed along several lines down to Buffon, Erasmus, Darwin, and Lamarck. Even the particular idea of natural selection was suggested by William Wells forty-five years before the Darwin-Wallace paper. Von Baer propounded the theory that embryonic development was always from the homogeneous to the heterogeneous. Spencer seized upon this idea and made of it an obsession, incorporating it into a doctrine of organic evolution, and combining it with the Lamarckian doctrine of the transmission of acquired characteristics. This was seventeen years before Bagehot's book (1852). And in the realm of the inorganic sciences Laplace in astronomy and Lyell in geology had given a further application to the idea of a vast development over æons of time. *The Origin of Species* but marks the climax of many lines of development. It is as much a symbol and a focus as it is an originating force. Indeed, there are not wanting thinkers in our own day (such as Mr Bernard Shaw in his preface to

Back to Methuselah) who maintain that this book served only to give a distortion to the doctrine of evolution by stressing one factor alone in development—namely, " circumstantial selection."[1]

C. H. Driver

[1] Bagehot, although greatly influenced by Darwin, certainly cannot be criticised on these grounds, as the article on him attempts to show.